CULT

HEROES

NOTTINGHAM FOREST

CULT HEROES

NOTTINGHAM FOREST

David McVay

This edition first published by Pitch Publishing 2012

Pitch Publishing
A2 Yeoman Gate
Yeoman Way
Durrington
BN13 3QZ
www.pitchpublishing.co.uk

A CIP catalogue record is available for this book
from the British Library

ISBN 978-1-9080516-5-3

Typesetting and origination by Pitch Publishing.

Printed in Great Britain by TJ International.

Contents

Acknowledgements

With grateful thanks from the author to:

Frank Clark
Alan Hill
David Stapleton
Bob Fairhall
Carolyn Maginnis
Fraser Nicholson
Joe Fish
Neil Footitt
Danny Kirkman
Danny Taylor
Danny Mouncer

For Paul. During his formative years, Henry Newton was always his big hero. You were always mine, bro.

To my gorgeous Debby and the gruesome twosome, Tom and Jess. Love always.

In memory of John Brindley – we were the egg men, koo koo katchoo…and great balls of fire Billy.

Introduction

IT WAS NOT THE usual suspects that attracted us to the City Ground. Not the prospect of fluent football being played at the highest pinnacle of the domestic game. Not the twinkle-toed inside-forward Colin Addison, the effortless pass master John Barnwell or the supremely athletic and reliable centre-half Bobby McKinlay. Nor was it the imposing pipe-smoking centre-forward Frank Wignall or his partner in crime on the left wing Alan Hinton, possibly one of the finest crossers of a football of his generation. Not even Henry Newton. No, a perverse personification of muscle and grace was the man we went to see in that Forest side of 1964 vintage.

Joe Wilson inspired our first visit to see Nottingham Forest: me and my grandad that is. Joe Who? to a new generation of Forest fans perhaps and even some of those who were regulars at the time might echo that sentiment. But in August 1964 Joe Wilson was the reason that Bill McVay took me on the 61a bus from Clifton Estate to climb the steps that led to the splintered, weather-worn benches of the old wooden East Stand at the City Ground. It was sunny, I think, but then all opening Saturdays of any football season since time began have been noted for being unseasonably scorching. The view then behind the East Stand embraced meadow land, Lady Bay and the meandering course of the River Trent as it made its way downstream towards the sluice gates at Holme Pierrepoint and beyond to Hazelford Lock, Gunthorpe Bridge and Newark.

Not that Birmingham City had a chance to survey the panorama that Saturday afternoon, although defending a 3-1 lead with less than 20 minutes remaining, it appeared that some of their players found their thoughts drifting further afield to a win bonus and a night on the town. In flighty, flirty and fun-filled Small Heath perchance? Hinton – whose stock would plummet dramatically in later years with Forest fans before rising, deliciously enough, with Derby County – Addison and Barnwell were all instrumental in retrieving the deficit and overturning it to secure a 4-3 victory out of the jaws of almost certain defeat.

So exhilarating and so euphoric was the experience that my grandad felt it incumbent to return. With me.

There was another reason. Joe Wilson.

So exhilarating and so euphoric was the experience that my grandad had forgotten the object of his enterprise in originally purchasing the two bus and football tickets: to let Joe Wilson know he was there.

Joe, like me and my grandad, was Workington-born and migrated south from the depressed and largely redundancy-blighted county of Cumberland in the same year, 1961. It was not only the home calling and a chance to reacquaint himself with a native of the Lakes that appealed to grandad. Apparently, Joe Wilson had lived several roads away from our own home in Salterbeck and communities being somewhat more welcoming and less fragmented in those days, it was inevitable that he would instantly recognise a friendly accent whose dialect still baffled local Nottingham traders, but had sheepdogs running obediently to heel from miles around the neighbourhood.

The next opportunity to offer Joe Wilson some Cumberland pearls of wisdom arrived on 5 September. Forest at home to West Bromwich Albion; as they say, another 90 minutes of your life you'll never get back. After the drama of the previous match it was destined to be a 0-0 draw and no matter what rose-tinted spectacles through which you observed, this First Division game was as dire as anything the Premiership could conjure up today.

Even Addison eased into the spirit of things. Awarded a dubious penalty with time running out, he shanked his spot-kick so wide and high into the Bridgford End that I'm sure the clock at the back of the terracing stopped momentarily for fear of its second hand being dismembered by the errant Addison's aim. Yet, while the clock was ticking normally, the seconds turning into minutes and the minutes dissolving, well into another minute of desperate tedium, there was one incident that made that September afternoon remarkable and worthwhile to this nine-year-old fledgling football fan.

Shortly after kick-off, the ritual passing of youngsters down to the front of the terracing had taken place, over heads, round the side or underneath legs depending on age and size.

My grandad's tactics had been shrewder, more calculated this time. The elevated reaches of the East Stand had been far too isolated to make meaningful contact with anyone except supporters or passing bargees on the Trent. This time, we headed for the main stand, the one that would be incinerated within a few more years, and stood close to the players' tunnel. As the half-time whistle went, in a novel role reversal of sorts, Bill McVay launched himself towards the front barriers as the teams trooped off for a cuppa.

"Joe lad, owsit ga'rn." The Cumberland accent is lost in translation and years, but grandad, with his regulation tweed hat and St Julien tobacco roll-up hanging from one side of his mouth, seemed to get his message across.

Did Joe Wilson look up? Well yes. Was there a flicker of recognition? Who knows? But maybe he heard the dulcet tones of a familiar lilt among the boos from disaffected home fans among the 28,334 crowd (not sporting an anorak in those days or inclined to train spotting, I didn't count them, it was Ken Smales' marvellous reference and history book about Forest that filled in the gaps).

It was sufficient for Bill McVay. His mission had been accomplished. Joe Wilson suffered a groin injury several weeks later and never played for Forest again, moving on to Wolverhampton Wanderers. Being an astute and philanthropic man, environmentally conscious ahead of his time, my grandad probably realised that the volatile cocktail of a Cumberland accent and the lament of a Black Country dialect, colliding head-to-head at Molineux in similarly loquacious fashion, could tip the planet off its axis and obliterate the natural order. To save mankind, a selfless gesture to humanity I suppose, Bill McVay did not pursue Joe Wilson to the edge of darkness at Wolverhampton.

Strangely enough, my path with Joe Wilson would entwine one more time, far less threateningly to civilisation, by which time Man's first footprints on the moon were imminent. In between, I had returned to the City Ground regularly. Tottenham Hotspur would register their usual win on Boxing Day, but I missed Jimmy Greaves, absent with what was euphemistically called a tummy bug or bad cold. Hot dogs from the Trent End as Joe Baker weaved his magic against Burnley in March 1967; a 1-0 home defeat by Liverpool on a balmy September evening the following season. Jumping on and off the back of moving buses and their open platform entrances, enough to induce nervous twitches in the modern health and safety zealots. My brother Paul seeing a declining Best, Law and Charlton still get the better of the Garibaldi Reds; March, 1969. You could set your life and formative years by it sometimes.

And then came Notts County, just over a fortnight later. Nerdy ahead of their time like my grandad was green ahead of his (apart from his drinking Home Ales best bitter, fuelling smokey corners of political debate in his local pub and allowing our boxer dog to fart and crap indiscriminately on the Farnborough Road playing fields), Notts County offered refuge from the sexy, glitzy Forest that had emerged on the south bank of the river during the 1960s. Fronted on the Trent by three buildings that masqueraded as rowing clubs, but were in fact women-magnets and pulling dens of iniquity for teenagers ridden with angst and Led Zeppelin, Forest represented everything that was young, vibrant and psychedelic that befitted the so-called swinging decade. Notts County, on the other hand, represented your parents. Black and white, drab, impervious to change and immovable in opinion. In short, Forest were as cool as Woodstock. Notts County as naff as the Black and White Minstrels.

Which is why, shamefully, I admit to heading for Meadow Lane to see Workington on 16 April 1969 for a meaningless Fourth Division fixture. But why?

The freedom to wander around the County Road stand without hindrance perhaps was one attraction. To listen to those long-forgotten and long-lost Cumberland strains, all 30-40 travelling fans who had made the journey down on that balmy spring evening.

Then again, there was another irresistible attraction. Joe Wilson. Now back at his native Workington, the old limbs were not as malleable, the vision not quite so perceptive, but the tackling, eliciting screams from the unfortunate County winger reminiscent of those poor cows being slaughtered across the road at the Cattle Market abattoir, remained as brutal as ever. There was no crowd to push aside to see Joe Wilson at close quarters that night. And in truth, there was not the slightest sign of recognition when I shouted his name from behind the goal in front of the old County Road stand.

It would be many years until I returned to Meadow Lane. As an aspiring professional footballer on trial at a club that Jimmy Sirrel had elevated from being re-election certainties to enjoying parity with Nottingham Forest. The year was 1973, Forest had been relegated and, until Brian Clough arrived, Notts County could claim a brief but glorious ascendancy on Trentside. Permit that solitary moment of gloating.

The hardest task when asked to write about the cult heroes of Nottingham Forest is not who to include, but who to leave out. Question players and fans alike about their hero, and the list is diverse. Naturally so.

For me, some are less difficult to omit than others. I have watched, grown up with, heard tell of and played against some who are rightly celebrated in this book. One, though, will not have a dedicated chapter in this book. He helped introduce me to football, an irrevocable bond that has endured through thick and thin until today. He also inspired a bond with a grandfather that I can recall through an undulating life and the haziness of time with a clarity, and a poignant yearning, that comes with advancing years.

That was Joe Wilson: my Nottingham Forest Cult Hero. The rest, as my old boss Jimmy Sirrel used to say, is just opinion.

David McVay

The Garibaldi Reds – an allegorical tale?

The Garibaldi Reds sobriquet came about when the club was formed in 1865. The year before its inception, Italian revolutionary general Giuseppe Garibaldi had stirred emotions and courted crowds during a short visit to England highlighted by a parade in London. It also inspired the original Forest committee, which met in a pub on North Sherwood Street called the Clinton Arms. Members insisted that the Forest shirts should replicate the blood-red scarlet uniform worn by Garibaldi's followers in fighting for the eventual unification of Italy, which had been achieved in 1861. Garibaldi was associated with swift, daring tactics and noble aspirations, hence the desire to copy. A century later, the Clinton Arms was associated with seedy strippers, busty topless barmaids whose nipples lodged in flat pints of Shipstone's ale and scarred for life many an under-age adolescent who sneaked furtively through its doors. The old Clinton eventually was liberated to serve as a bar for Trent Polytechnic students and latterly attendees of the risibly named Trent 'University'. The downward spiral continues unabated in North Sherwood Street and on the south bank…for now.

Arthur Dexter

1923-1937: 274 games, 0 goals

WHEN ARTHUR DEXTER left home for his first day at work as an aspiring professional footballer in 1926, the cautionary words of his father still echoed in his ears as he reached the City Ground. "He told me never to gamble. 'If they ask you to play cards, tell them you don't know how to. They won't ask again'," Dexter recalled. "He also told me not to drink beer. That wasn't too difficult. I never did have the taste for it."

(When he was 88, in 1993, I interviewed a charmingly ageless Dexter about his life and times in Nottingham and with Forest. He died in his 90s after a long and happy retirement on the south coast in Worthing some years later).

Hardly the ethics of your typical footballer then, particularly if your name is Collymore, Baxter or Bowles. But if he was the antithesis of the calibre of some of those later Forest legends (Stan Bowles: liked a bit of a flutter; Peter Hindley: liked a bit of a tipple; Jim Baxter: overdosed on both), Dexter's tale reflects a relative period of innocence and stability, not only in the game of football, but in a world recovering from the horrors of the Great War.

Dexter had been just 16 when he set off on that undulating journey into manhood, an apprentice goalkeeper whose horizons were limited by the skyline around his native Basford, framed by back-to-back terraced housing, Shipstone's grandiose Red Star brewery and the vast buildings that stored grain and cotton in an intensive industrial Nottingham suburb.

It was 1921 and Dexter was attempting to escape the humdrum routine of shift work at Forman's Printers, an offshoot of the T. Bailey Forman clan, who were one of the largest local employers with investment in newspapers and print works. Despite his signing on the groundstaff for Forest, his employers, Forman's, were not amused at the shenanigans of their own young apprentice printer. "Suffice it to say they were not best pleased. I had joined them earlier in the year and they made me serve out of my time."

There was fleeting fame for Dexter during the ensuing years before he returned to the City Ground as a professional to establish himself in the goalkeeper's jersey that in those days came replete with standard polo-neck, an armour plating thickness to deter predatory centre-forwards and an insulation efficiency that made it essential equipment for budding polar explorers, as well as the most popular and enduring pre-Second World War Forest player.

IN 1921 FOREST WERE actually a side going places – attractive to the aspiring, dreaming young footballer – soon to be crowned Second Division champions for the 1921/22 season. Having climbed to the top of the table in November, they remained in the ascendancy as crowds between 15,000 and 20,000 gathered at the ground of what were then the poor relations of Nottingham football, anticipating a return to the First Division after a decade's and world war's absence.

In fact the last time Forest had stood on the threshold of promotion to the top flight of English football, celebrated striker Enoch West had scored 14 goals in 33 games as the Reds had romped to the title in 1907. The following season the former Hucknall Constitutional player obliged with 26 in 35 games, including four goals in one game against Sunderland. Forest ended up ninth, with the great inside-forward Grenville Morris, the club's record goalscorer with a tally of 217 from 460 matches, chipping in with, for him, a miserly seven goals. The pair were the great heroes of the day, and fine candidates for their own inclusion in this book, but ultimately they merit an honourable mention.

West's move to Manchester United in 1910 was a catalyst for Forest's decline and, also, ironically the player's. The man nicknamed 'Knocker' became embroiled in an unsavoury scandal surrounding a 2-0 win over Liverpool, an end of season result that was crucial in United escaping relegation. Allegations of attempting to bribe the Merseysiders to throw the match were proven and, although West protested his innocence all the way to the Court of Appeal, the testimony of colleagues was as damning as Liverpool's slipshod performance and he was banned from the game *sine die*. Poor old Knocker never returned to Old Trafford and was still pleading his case when he died in 1965, aged 79, the same year as his ban was quashed when the Football League declared a general amnesty. It was also the same year that England internationals Tony Kay and Peter Swan were imprisoned as the high profile culprits of the infamous 1960s match-fixing scandal. Both those men admitted their guilt; but did West really deserve the sentence (the longest in Football League history) that blighted his career and ruined his life?

Whatever the truth, West will always be revered and recalled with great fondness by Forest diehards everywhere. Why? Among his many prolific hauls, a hat-trick on 21 April 1909 demands attention. Alf Spouncer and Billy Hooper also scored three apiece in a 12-0 victory as Forest recorded the first of two wins in their last two matches that would confirm First Division survival. That the opposition happened to be Leicester Fosse, East Midlands arch rivals to compare with Derby County, is a legacy of unmitigated love for Forest fans. Leicester players claimed they were still suffering from the inebriated effects of dallying too long at a colleague's wedding reception two days earlier: a limp effort in the Paul Gascoigne book of excuses, perhaps, but good reason to toast a famous victory in the red corner of the region ever since nevertheless. That it also remains Forest's record league victory (realistically a triumph that will never be eclipsed) is further reason to pay homage to West.

BY THE TIME Dexter had joined the club on a full-time contract, it seemed only bribery would work, at least on the opposition, to inspire a decent run of results. A dismal period perennially avoiding relegation from the Second Division became the order of the day during the mid-1920s, punctuated by the occasional glint of silverware with a decent FA Cup run.

How different it had been when young Dexter wended his way to the City Ground with Forest blazing a trail towards the First Division.

He took heed of his father's parting words on his first day at the club, but admitted to having developed a certain weakness. "I did rather like sherry or the odd whisky," he said. Could Jim Baxter be heard describing his own liquid longing so conservatively? "I also drank a port and lemon after a meal when we stayed away before matches. That was a popular drink with the players." You can almost hear Slim Jim's casket revolving.

Initially, opportunity knocked for 18-year-old apprentice Dexter on 1 September 1923, when regular goalkeeper Sam Hardy was injured. Hardy himself was something of a legend in the game then, having been the most famous netminder in the country at the turn of the century, with Queen Victoria still on the throne, and subsequently prolonging his fame for more than two decades. Hardy set the precedent of prodigious England international goalkeepers that emanated from Chesterfield, emulated later by Gordon Banks. Despite his advancing years when he signed for Forest on 27 August 1921 (Hardy had celebrated his 38th birthday the day before), his presence tightened up a fragile defence and formed the bedrock for their Second Division championship season as only 24 goals were conceded in 32 matches. Two years previously, at the end of the war, Hardy had helped Forest to secure the Victory Shield as a guest goalkeeper, a sort of unofficial championship that united various regional sections in a final that brought Forest a 1-0 win against Everton over two legs.

Hardy would retire after a 1-1 draw with Newcastle United in October 1924. Whether through injury or old age, who knows, but like the splendid veteran he was, his timing was perfect, exiting stage left during the season that Forest were relegated to leave the young pretender on the throne. "Hardy was a former England captain, so I never expected to get my chance so early, but he was getting on a bit then," recalled Arthur. "Apparently he had a touch of lumbago, so they drafted me for the game against Everton."

At the City Ground that Saturday afternoon, Hardy's pain in the back allowed nearly 18,000 to see Dexter keep that item of bedroom linen most cherished by goalkeepers, but despised by George Best imitators – the proverbial clean sheet – in a 1-0 win over the Merseysiders. He added a second at home to Tottenham Hotspur in November, deputising for the lumbago-laden Hardy once more. These sturdy introductions were surely worlds apart from his previous appearances for, in chronological order, Bulwell St Albans, Vernon Athletic and Stapleford Brookhill. But then that was it. For the best part of four years!

"I just couldn't get the time off work to play for the reserves and keep my fitness levels up and improve my game. They used to turn out on Thursday afternoons when I was working on the shop floor at Forman's. The only games I could really make were the ones away to the likes of Rotherham United or Sheffield Wednesday. It wasn't too far along the Hucknall Road to the Victoria Station, up and over Mansfield Road past the Goose Fair site, so I could pack up work and dash to the station to meet the players on the platform."

Despite the hardship or unpredictability of the regime, Dexter never regretted being forced to serve his apprenticeship. "When I reached 21, I finally signed for Forest full time and I left Forman's on good terms with the offer of a job whenever I wanted to return [he did just that when his career ended]."

IMAGINE THE FRUGALITY that football agents would endure (great joy) had they been forced to eke ten or 20 per cent out of the £2 10s (£2.50) weekly wage that Dexter earned as a young professional in 1926. And there were precious few win bonuses in Dexter's early wage packets as his efforts to establish a first team position were floundering on a formidable figure: one Leonard Langford.

Given the modern trend for nanny state and health and safety zealots and the potential for obesity or coronary failure amongst English No.1s of the early 20th century, or an epidemic of the more common mad-goalkeeper disease, surely a ban on lard and dripping sandwiches as enjoyed by custodians such as Chelsea's William 'Fatty' Foulke would have been merited. Albert Iremonger over the Trent at Notts County was simply huge without being flabby, but Langford, although not strictly overweight, had the frame of a heavyweight boxer and the brawn of Nottingham's old bare-fisted brawler William 'Bendigo' Thompson; which was just as well because a clause in his contract gave him time off to indulge himself in that other sport – perhaps not of his preference, but one in which he had been blessed with ample muscle and bravery to compete.

As a pugilist, Langford's boxing career was not the most distinguished, yet his four years at Forest yielded 144 games, 98 of those consecutive ones over two and a quarter seasons. "I got my chance when Len got injured and he never really got a smell after that," Dexter recalled with a glint in his eyes. "We didn't really get much over 20,000 at the City Ground for most games and we weren't the richest club by any means. But we always had packed houses when we travelled to Sunderland, Sheffield or London. I played against some of the greats, at their peak, and it was a privilege, truly. Dixie Dean, Alex James and Hughie Gallacher. They were fantastic players and could put themselves about a bit too."

In the environmentally friendly, human and animal rights-conscious Britain of today, Parliament no doubt would have debated long and hard about the preservation of the endangered species that was goalkeepers. Up until 1957, when Aston Villa's Peter McParland kyboshed Ray Wood in the Manchester United penalty area during an FA Cup final, goalkeepers were stalked and hunted by packs of well-nourished centre-forwards, whose prey was primarily large and immobile and clad in a furry jersey. Fox hunting may well be banned in the current climate, but the laws of the game that disallow physical contact whatsoever, apart from when a goal is scored among consenting adults, conveniently have disposed of the ritualistic slaughter of innocents, which regularly saw the likes of Dean, Lofthouse and Lawton flatten opposing custodians into the mud.

Remarkably, though, while other goalkeepers weighed in at over 13 stones as a bare minimum, Dexter was 11 stones wet through. His physique contrasted bizarrely with the imposing Iremonger across the River Trent at Meadow Lane. Imagine an identity parade with Hugh Grant in baggy pants and ill-fitting jersey stood alongside Peter Crouch with muscle definition. Scary. "I was a bit slight, it has to be said," laughed Dexter. "The other lads had plenty of beef, but then they needed it in those days. You'd always get a good battering for your troubles. It was legal to kick the ball out of a keeper's hands and players could obstruct you at corners all the time. The games always came fast and furious over the festive holidays, I remember over the Christmas period we could play three or four times, in quick succession. Christmases at home were few and far between."

On mudheaps or frozen and rutted pitches with treacherous 18-yard boxes, goalkeeping scarcely could be described as an exact science. These days, the surfaces are as unblemished as the kit keepers wear. Gloves, boots and garish shirts are more fashion accessories, or a sponsor's demand, rather than essential tools of the trade. But some similarities remain with their predecessors, who wore, predominantly, green.

"We'd train from ten till noon and then the rest of the day was our own," Dexter recalled. "Some things never change. We had some rogues and rascals then. An Irishman by the name of Morgan [Gerry from Linfield Athletic] was well known around town. Nothing as bad as a Gazza, though, I can tell you. But in general I studied after training instead of waltzing around town and going to the snooker halls. I was very fond of accountancy and eventually passed an RSA exam."

Despite that commendably conscientious approach, earning £8 a week in the winter, £6 in the summer, £2 for a win and £1 for a draw, even accounting for inflation in the 21st century, this does not sound like the level of income on which David James or Paul Robinson could sustain their respective fashion and meat pie obsessions does it?

And goalkeeping coaches? Behave!

"There was no special training for us," Dexter explained. "What could we do? It was mainly a lot of shooting in at us, kicking and running, especially down the River Trent during pre-season. That was the worst part of it, but I suppose that would not change over the years.

"There was a regular golf day, usually at Wollaton Park, and we were always there as a squad for the whole day. We went by rail, in style and if there was an overnight stay, we were treated well [two port and lemons after dinner as opposed to the two lap dancers nowadays maybe?]

"When we got back to Nottingham after an away game, most of the young lads, who were staying in digs, went to the Victoria Halls dancing rooms on Wollaton Street or the Palais de Danse.

Myself, I liked the old style music hall acts. I was partial to the theatre and used to get tickets for the Empire, just across from Forman Street. A marvellous old place with lots of variety acts."

MODESTLY, DEXTER FORGOT to mention to me that, as he matured to be the resident keeper at Forest, he failed by the merest whisker to win an England cap on several occasions. In those days, a committee of selectors sat around a table to pick the side and more than once he lost out by just one vote from the gin and tonics in blazers brigade, whose successors have extended that tradition of incompetence with an astonishingly seamless continuity until the present day.

For all that, Dexter enjoyed some marvellous years and games, which saw his star shoot into the ascendancy as Forest's pre-eminent early cult hero. In his breakthrough season, a stirring FA Cup escapade included a 2-0 replay defeat of Derby County, after extra time, at the City Ground – always a good start with Forest supporters. It was all the more pleasing a victory as it was also a lucrative one, with Forest banking the best part of £3,000 in receipts paid by a crowd of 35,635.

Over 52,000 turned up at Bramall Lane for the quarter-final tie with Sheffield United. Sadly, 'Dexterous' Dexter, as a contemporary local cartoonist had by now dubbed him, suffered a blow to his hand early on. No longer so dexterous, he soldiered on in pain, but the Tykes triumphed 3-0.

Two seasons later, in October 1929, Johnny Dent joined Forest from Huddersfield Town for a fee of £1,500. The opening of his Forest chapter elicited an instant rapport with the crowd and a wealth of goals for the centre-forward. With a name like that, he should have been wearing winkle pickers and leading a radical Teddy boy group called the Mashers three decades later instead of wearing hobnail football boots and leading a line of pipe-smoking conformist footballers. At any rate, Dent made his debut on a Thursday afternoon (3 October) in a 1-1 draw at Bradford Park Avenue, then scored his first goal for the club in another 1-1 draw with Spurs at White Hart Lane two days later. His third, of 122 in 206 appearances, arrived at Boothferry Crescent in a 2-1 win over Hull City and coincided with Dexter's restoration to the first team, the start of a fruitful relationship between first and last line of defence.

Dent scored ten times in as many games, including an FA Cup third round treble against Rotherham United. Dexter for his part saved a twice-taken penalty in a 1-1 draw at Barnsley on Boxing Day. The day before, Christmas Day, Dent had claimed one in a 4-0 demolition of the same side at the City Ground, his sixth strike in six games. Dent, though, would be absent as Forest progressed once more to the quarter-finals of the Cup, beating First Division Sunderland, known as the 'Team of all the Talents' for their transfer policy of buying an array of the best, and most expensive players about, after a replay in the previous round. English champions-elect Sheffield Wednesday, on the cusp of a second successive title, awaited in a tie which enthralled the city. Around 2.15 that Saturday afternoon, 1 March 1930, Arkwright Street was almost deserted. A few stragglers in blue and white scarves with Owls rosettes wandered disconsolately outside the City Ground, mingling with equally despairing men clad in red and white struggling to get into the packed ground.

Inside the locked gates, a record attendance of 44,166 supporters were about to fixate on a pulsating Cup tie of the finest tradition as the mighty Wednesday strolled into a two-goal lead within 17 minutes. The crowd, sprinkled naturally enough with those odious free-loaders we have come to regard as politicians and their good ladies these days, but known then as civic dignitaries that included the esteemed Lord Mayor and Sheriff of Nottingham jostling to get in on the act, may have scented blood about to be let before a massacre as well as the horse manure drifting across from the VIP block.

While there remains no known antidote for the stench of the latter, at least the former was erased as two of Forest's less heralded individuals, William Dickinson, who had scored both in the 2-2 draw at Roker Park, and Joseph Loftus, who claimed one against Sunderland in the 3-1 replay success, retrieved the deficit, the goal by Loftus acclaimed as a screamer of a rising right-foot shot that would have graced any Wembley final.

"The noise was the thing on the day," recalled Dexter. "I'd played in front of big crowds before, but never with such volume. When we equalised in the second half I thought the whole ground was going to give way. An incredible experience."

For the second time in three seasons, the trip to the Steel City proved to be Forest's FA Cup nemesis. Dexter remained fully fit on this occasion, but Wednesday's superior skills prevailed in a 3-1 win. To compound the sixth round elimination, Forest were fined £50 for turning up late at Hillsborough!

A TRIP TO HOLLAND, a portent perhaps because that became a regular excursion, along with Majorca, for Brian Clough and his fledgling professionals to attend the annual Blauw Wit Easter youth tournament, ensued the following season. Forest had been chosen as England's ambassadors for the game against a Netherlands national XI at Sparta Rotterdam's ground. Dent, almost inevitably, Dickinson and Harold Smith registered a goal each as Forest won 3-1. If it was uncharted territory for the Reds, the spirit of adventure, and discovery, was not lost on Dexter. "It was the first time I'd come across a football without a lace. In the end I kept it and took it back to England with me."

Throughout a thoroughly ordinary passage of Forest's history, Dexter was able to boast that he had watched from the opposite end of the field as Tom Peacock scored on his debut against Oldham Athletic on 9 September 1933. By any standards, it was a dramatic introduction for the gangling centre-forward, a grammar school product from Derbyshire who furthered his education and ambition to be a teacher by studying at the University of Nottingham (the proper one opposite Highfields and the Nottingham Tennis Centre). His impact was to be even more impressive, however.

Peacock bagged four in a 6-1 drubbing of Port Vale in December; next season, he scored 21 goals, including two doubles in March which helped secure 5-0 wins over Oldham Athletic and Burnley, while Johnny Dent scored hat-tricks in both games. For good measure Peacock bagged two more on three separate occasions before the season ended, one against Manchester United when he shared his benefit match with three other players.

It was the following season, though, that Peacock's name was etched indelibly into Forest record books. On 9 November 1934, he scored four against Barnsley in a 6-0 win; two weeks later, at the same City Ground, hapless Port Vale were on the receiving end of another Peacock quartet, this time in a 9-2 humiliation that eclipsed their pathetic effort of two seasons ago. Then on Boxing Day, at home to Doncaster Rovers, Peacock claimed another four in a 6-2 triumph. "Quite remarkable," as David Coleman might have put it had he been around to comment.

In just nine games, Peacock had been the architect of a four goal salvo on three separate occasions. In between, he nabbed one in a 4-1 victory over Tottenham Hotspur for good measure. But for those exploits where would Forest have finished other than the lowly 19th to which they succumbed at season's end?

Peacock's hat-trick against Fulham in September 1937 was in many ways his swansong. A cartilage injury that required surgery, far more complicated, painful and damaging than the techniques of today, virtually ended his career. His exhilarating pace was curtailed and, as every centre-forward knows, losing a yard also loses the element of surprise they hold over defenders. Peacock served in the RAF during the war, where he occasionally turned out as a guest for Chelsea and later returned to teaching. His prolific goalscoring remains a source of envy and inspiration to those who aspire to emulate him, a source of pride to fans.

AS WAS DEXTER'S contribution in that Forest team. The official record shows that he joined the club in 1923 and stayed for 14 years, playing 274 times until his final game in 1937. Of course, between September 1923 and November 1927 he turned out only twice, his devotion to duty being divided between the City Ground and Forman's Printers.

Dexter may not have had the physical presence of a Langford or the legendary status of a Hardy between the sticks, but his cult status, if that could be applied in any form of pre-Second World War vernacular, are his Basford roots and an unyielding loyalty to his hometown club, the very basic nurturing of local talent so absent in the modern game of quick fixes, Johnny Foreigners and Johnny Rotten agents. Shamefully so.

His final decade at the club may have been notorious for the Great Depression, but at the City Ground, it was more grey skies and showery intervals with occasional sunny spells. "They were great days at Forest. It was a terrific club even though we weren't in the First Division. We might not have had the best team in the country, but we had the best playing surface, that's for sure! There were some terrific times, great Cup runs and some marvellous players. I would not have missed it for the world."

He returned only a few times to the City Ground during his lifetime, but Forest always made a fuss of him on his rare trips north of Brighton in the 1990s, as he was then the oldest surviving Forest player. "I may not have gone back much, but I still had one thing in common with the fans. I hated to see Forest lose," he said on his last visit to his old stomping ground.

Comedians and thespians always cite timing as crucial to their art and Dexter, like his enduring predecessor Sam Hardy, had it in abundance. He took his final bow at White Hart Lane in March 1937 in a 2-1 defeat. Employment back in the printing trade and Forman's beckoned, a job that would take him to Liverpool, Dublin and London before retirement in Rustington, near Brighton, where the sound of the sea is a melodic backdrop on a summer's day or winter's night.

The week after Dexter's finale Percy Ashton stepped up to take over between the sticks in a 6-1 defeat of the woeful Welshmen of Swansea City. Ashton had deputised earlier that year in January when Dexter was taken ill on the train shunting the side to Coventry City. A 1-1 draw at home to Blackpool ensued, but then fate took a turn for the worse for poor Ashton. Blackburn Rovers away on 10 April 1937 is a date that rankles with Forest fans. At least it should, because inside every *Rothmans Yearbook* or statistical document about Forest, it is normally there in black and white. Blackburn Rovers 9, Nottingham Forest 1 (record defeat). That Forest's solitary effort was a Blackburn own goal, obligingly turned in by captain Bob Pryde, only adds to the misery in that the home team actually scored ten on the day!

Somewhere in the distance later on that season, some thought that they heard Arthur Dexter whistling. "A-ho, a-ho, it's off to work I go…" as he gambolled along Mansfield Road to Forman's. Rejoicing, perhaps, in a narrow but historic escape from infamy.

Billy Walker

1939-1961: 650 games, 272 wins

GEOFF THOMAS WORE the look of a condemned man as he trudged back to the visiting dressing room for a half-time brew at Kenilworth Road. Even today, hanging by the neck seems a preferable alternative to an afternoon spent in Luton High Street, but in February 1952 the Forest full-back's trepidation involved more than just the unpleasant environs in which he had been thrust that Saturday. Bill Whare, the regular right-back, was absent from the side that had travelled to play the Hatters. Normally used to operating on the left side of defence, Thomas had tried manfully, but failed abysmally to deal with the threat of the Luton left-winger. It scarcely mattered that the pitch resembled a bog. Oh well, Luton on one of its better days perhaps.

There was another sticky problem for Thomas and Forest at the interval. They were 3-0 down. The outside-left had scored two and made the other. Rocket science and the Ministry of Defence were not needed to pinpoint the weakest chink in their armoury.

If Thomas's body remained in an unrelenting twirl from the events of the previous 45 minutes as he walked down the players' tunnel, his head swiftly followed suit: in a spin.

Opening the dressing room door, he saw Billy Walker sitting in his place beneath the peg where his smart suit was hanging and gleaming black shoes poked out from the bench. Walker, a benign, almost avuncular, figure, was sipping a cup of hot tea. Two sugars and plenty of milk. Thomas, though, knew his half-time cuppa would be anything but sweet and warm. Walker's selective positioning revealed his target instantly. If Billy was sitting in your place, your number was up. "I'm in for a rollocking," Thomas whispered beneath his breath, hoping for some sympathy from downhearted colleagues.

Unfortunately for him Tommy Capel, a veteran of football battles and the jungle war in Burma, was the closest ally to hear his murmurings. "I should bloody well think so. That bloody outside-left has run you ragged, scored two and all three are down to him."

So much for team spirit!

What followed was a trademark Walker pep talk. "Where do you usually stand at kick-off, Geoff? Well, wherever that is, I want you to go and stand as near to their left-winger as you can. Every time he gets the ball, I want you to be there. And I don't care if you get the ball or not. Is that clear?"

Thomas understood only too well. As the bemused left-winger blanched at the Forest full-back's stalking tactics during the second half, Capel piped up a word of encouragement to his opponent. "Don't worry, son. He's been told to follow you no matter what. So I'd be careful when you go to the toilet because he'll be right behind you."

The strategy worked. With the supply lines to the winger drying up and the recipient himself fearful of accepting any sort of pass that might compromise his legs, Luton went to pieces and Forest rallied magnificently to steal an unlikely, Walker-inspired point in a thrilling 3-3 draw.

If the story seems to relate a tale of a blinkered tactician whose priority was to stifle and intimidate, it's a false impression. More it highlights the diversity and flexibility of the man who, just as Brian Clough would be named Forest's greatest manager by some distance, would be nominated as the second best by an equal distance of several furlongs.

AS A PLAYER, Billy Walker graced the inside-forward role with aplomb for Aston Villa, with whom he secured an FA Cup winners' medal in the 1920 final, beating Huddersfield Town at Stamford Bridge. Just four months earlier, despite the insistence of his footballing father, George, who was a well-known former Wolves forward, that he should get a trade and become apprenticed to a local engineering firm, Billy had made his debut and scored twice against then non-league QPR at Villa Park in the third round of the competition. A centre-forward by nature, he developed into an inside-forward whose shrewd passing game, both long and short, became his stock in trade. That, and an uncanny knack of hanging in the air and making contact with crucial headers when all around seemed to be floundering. His ability makes him still the holder of the Villa career goalscoring record with 244 goals in 531 appearances.

That progression brought him the captaincy of Villa and England, representing his country 18 times, scoring nine goals over a 13-year international career, which saw him win his last cap aged 35 as he skippered his country to a famous 4-3 victory over the Austrian 'Wunderteam' at Stamford Bridge in 1932. He even turned his hand to goalkeeping on one famous occasion. In 1925 Fred Fox of Millwall won his one and only cap against France in Paris. With England leading 3-1 and already a man down thanks to an injury after half an hour to centre-forward Vivian Gibbins, Fox injured himself in vainly trying to stop French right-winger Jules Dewaquez netting to make the score 3-2. Walker volunteered to go in goal and performed heroics, along with the remaining nine outfield players as England hung on for a hard-fought victory.

Following retirement from playing in November 1933, Walker then set off on an initially successful managerial path with Sheffield Wednesday, steering the Owls to their first Wembley FA Cup final victory, beating West Bromwich Albion 4-2 in 1935. It was a feat he would repeat at Forest 24 years later to join an elite group of managers who have lifted the trophy with two different clubs, which, in fact numbers only himself and the legendary Huddersfield and Arsenal supremo Herbert Chapman.

That FA Cup triumph, however, was Walker's Sheffield zenith. Three years later he resigned in a fit of pique after a turbulent boardroom meeting when fingers were pointed, especially at Walker, following the Hillsborough club's relegation and decline.

Grammar school education had imbued sufficient common sense and confidence in Walker to realise that his chance would come again, although a call by non-league Chelmsford City was perhaps not necessarily what he wanted to hear. Even so, he answered it, although his departure from that club was also acrimonious. Still, his study of the continental game and the magnificent Austrian national side of the time, against whom he had himself played so splendidly at Stamford Bridge, kept him ahead of others in the game. Even so, when Forest offered him the job in May 1939, a whiff of desperation lingered about the appointment of someone perceived as yesterday's man, whose chance of success had already gone. This despite the fact he was only 41 years old.

If Walker's healing powers had been spent, Forest would soon find out. His urgent task was to avoid relegation from the Second Division, a fate that his predecessor Harry Wightman had managed in dramatic circumstances the previous season. Forest had travelled to Barnsley on the final day of the season knowing that the losers would be relegated along with Stockport County. On an afternoon of goalkeeper howlers at Oakwell, when a million Woodbines blighted South Yorkshire's carbon footprint for eternity, Forest drew 2-2 thanks to a controversial late equaliser that owed as much to Dave 'Boy' Martin's sumo wrestling skills as his predatory acumen.

Barnsley were down by 0.002 of a goal.

To avoid a repeat, Walker was appointed in March, but promptly saw his new charges beaten 3-2 by Blackburn Rovers at Ewood Park. Still, nine games remained and four wins and two draws did the trick, although astonishingly Forest travelled to Norwich City on the final day of the season once again playing the team who would survive if they failed in their mission. This time defeat was acceptable, however, since Norwich had to win by four clear goals to prevent relegation. A 1-0 home win was a result for Forest and Norwich were relegated.

FOOTBALL AND ITS relevant issues became fittingly inconsequential matters when war was declared on Germany by Prime Minister Neville Chamberlain on 3 September 1939. It was a period of time that would shape, ruin, destroy or enrich people's lives, but without dwelling on the morals of the conflict, for the miniscule particle that was Forest during those cataclysmic years, the club prospered as Walker established a youth policy that saw his Colts team provide a steady flow of players that would enhance and extend the club's potential for expansion.

It was around this time that Bob Fairhall began a love affair with Forest that has endured seven decades. An aspiring professional in 1945, Fairhall admits he was not good enough to be a Forest player, settling instead to sign for Mansfield Town. Through a lifelong association from committee member to benefactor, he is now academy director under the Nigel Doughty regime, but recalls his early days watching Forest under Walker with a smile and gratitude.

On 22 December 1945, Fairhall attended his first Forest match, a wartime fixture against Arsenal at the City Ground. Forest won 3-2. Four years later, Bob suffered along with the other Forest faithful as their side were relegated to the Third Division South, but significantly the board retained their faith in Walker to succeed in the long haul. If it was a gamble, it was one that paid off handsomely.

"It was the year that Notts County signed Tommy Lawton and he struck up a magnificent partnership with Jackie Sewell at Meadow Lane," says Fairhall, born at Balderton near Newark and who as a young man accepted a wage cut from his regular job to play for Mansfield. He stayed for 18 months without making the grade and eventually ended up with Macclesfield in the old Cheshire League, a hotbed of talent in the 1950s. "I couldn't get to many games then, but the first thing I always asked was 'How did Forest get on?' Then, when I started work again, I became a spectator at the City Ground on a frequent basis. The relegation was a blessing in disguise, although at the time no-one knew that."

Forest eventually regained their Second Division status a year after the Notts County Tommy Lawton-Jackie Sewell-inspired side had been elevated from that same section in 1950. "Walker was a master at getting older players in," Fairhall recalls. "Doug Lishman [from Arsenal] and Eddie Baily [from Port Vale]. Sadly today you can't get that sort of player at that level because of the money situation. They've had that much they wouldn't come down to Forest to play for £4,000 a week. But in the 1950s, your old internationals came for the standard wage, and not just at Forest. It added so much to clubs lower down. Walker had already built a fine side that took them back up to the Second. Tommy Capel had a magic left foot. Even with the old leather ball from outside the box, Tommy could find the top corner, like a rocket.

"It was that year they got promotion [1951] and you had five forwards in them days, and if you look at the league records, every one, every forward got double figures. I mean the team scored 110 goals and every forward got at least ten goals. When you look at some of the pitches and the playing surfaces now, you know, they are billiard tables. I tell you what, they wouldn't play on some of those pitches we used to play on. In the old Third Division South they were ploughed fields. I mean, by the time you came to January, the only grass was tufts at the corner flags, and everywhere else was worn out, and mud heaps, I mean there was no drainage as such."

Given such treacherous and uncooperative conditions, it is a wonder that Walker persisted with his passion for playing the ball on terra firma or more terra musheda and soggia.

"He always signed footballers who could play," insists Fairhall. "I remember he bought George Wilkins from Bradford Park Avenue, the father of Ray Wilkins. My dad and brothers used to say to me that he was so old that he couldn't even straighten his leg, but he was a great ball player that would look up, send a ball 30 yards and find the man to the inch.

"We'd catch the bus from Newark in those days to watch midweek matches. There were no floodlights and I'd skive off college at 2pm because kick-offs were usually 4.30pm. We were playing Chesterfield at the City Ground once, the season we got relegated. The old Milburn brothers, who were related to the Charltons, were playing for Chesterfield. There was George and Stan. George was a centre-half and Stan a left-back and I think they were nephew and uncle. I shall never forget that game, even though we lost 3-1."

Walker's chain-smoking habits might explain why Jeff Whitefoot, when he first considered signing in 1956, decided against it, finding the manager a difficult man to understand. Whitefoot's eventual, but belated, arrival two years later perhaps is an indicator not only of Walker's persistence, but of a more ruthless streak to prevail, an essential if sometimes distasteful trait in the world of sport. The side he had moulded to regain Second Division status was fading away; Wally Ardron had gone. Tommy Capel and Colin Collindridge, the other leading players, departed in 1954. It was, still is, the nature of the beast that is football that there is little sentiment once the athlete or workhorse has served its purpose. In the same year, 1954, Ken Dodd made his professional debut at Nottingham's Empire Theatre. As the Knotty-Ash tickling machine was being driven past the Market Square by taxi to his venue, he asked the cabbie what was the name of the extraordinarily ornate green-domed building all lit up for impending festive celebrations.

"That's the Council House," replied the driver.

"Really. Can you put my name down for one like that?"

Capel, staunchly supportive of Walker, also reveals property deals that confirm his manager's astute business acumen. "We had great respect for him because he was an international in his own right and had won the FA Cup as a player and manager. He scored a lot of goals with his head and he used to tell me how he'd hover above the rest while he scored. Hooky was a brilliant tactician as well. [Hooky was the army nickname Capel used for anyone called Walker, just as Chalky was to White]. He always said he never really watched us in the first half, just the opposition because it was in the second half that games were won and lost. And for the most part he was right.

"I remember when we used to get on the coach to the West Midlands, playing Birmingham or even Walsall, he'd tell the coach driver to drive by Villa Park. He'd point out row after row of houses that he said he'd bought. His dad had told him to invest in property when he was at the Villa and he maintained then that he was worth thousands. There was no doubt he was as shrewd in business as he was in football dealings. He cut deals with Redmayne and Todd's for boots for the players and then, years later, I ran into him and he was telling me about a deal he did with a house near Ruddington, on Clifton Lane. It was just after the war and this house was more a mansion, its own massive grounds, tennis courts, nine bedrooms or more, the lot. It had been empty for a couple of years, but the asking price was £30,000, which in the late 1940s was one hell of a lot of money.

"Eventually, he found out who was selling the house and then discovered that Clifton Estate was going to be built in its backyard, or near enough. He'd made inquiries with the land registry. So he went back to the owner and said to him, 'I'll offer you £20,000 and every month you refuse, I'll drop the price by £1,000.' After four months the owner finally got back to him and sold it for £16,000. 'How on earth did you know?' he asked Walker. But that was the way he was. Very clued up and a good businessman.

"He applied that to football as well. His motto was 'If you are winning, don't alter anything.' During one season, he worked out that we kept losing home games, but winning away. He worked out that it was all too easy for us coming in to the City Ground and that we were too comfortable just coming in, stripping off our clothes and getting changed. When we went away on the coach, we gelled better, so we started staying away for home games. Coincidentally, Cloughie used to do the same with his first team squad at Derby County, when he took them away to the Midland Hotel the night before games. It worked for Derby and Walker made it work for us.

"He introduced golfing days on a Tuesday, a 9am start in Radcliffe-on-Trent, lunch in the club house, then an afternoon round. It was a brilliant day out. And he used to get the wives involved, taking us all for a day out to Skegness. He loved Skeggy and would often give us a call at the last moment to go, or when we were playing away at Norwich on the east coast, we'd always stay overnight at Skeggy."

It's an uncanny comparison to Clough, whose desire to involve wives and girlfriends was a pioneering motivational scheme. He too was obsessed with a tourist resort that boasted sea and sand – there the similarity ends. Skegness had fish and chips and brown ale, Cala Millor had slightly more refined cuisine, if nowadays the clientele is identical.

AS WALKER DISMANTLED the title-winning side of 1951, Jack Burkitt, Stewart Imlach and Johnny Quigley emerged as their successors. They required guidance, though, and in signing Doug Lishman and Eddie Baily, Walker demonstrated a masterclass in the transfer market.

Lishman scored 16 goals in 27 matches before retiring at the end of his first and last season for Forest, the promotion campaign of 1957, including a hat-trick at Bramall Lane that secured a 4-0 win over Sheffield United on 27 April, an Easter double and more importantly, promotion to the First Division.

Baily's contribution was at first more sedate. A former England inside-forward and part of the famous Spurs 'push and run' title-winning team of 1951, he gradually found his pace and range and established himself among the Forest all-time maestros in terms of passing the ball. He stayed for another season in the First Division, most memorably an emotional return to White Hart Lane where Forest triumphed 4-3 in a classic that presented Quigley, aged 22, with a debut goal as eager youth began to knock on the door of an anxious older generation.

Even so, Baily was chaired shoulder-high off the pitch by both teams after a controlled and influential performance from the middle of the park, the former Spur granted a thoroughly merited standing ovation at the final whistle.

And the chances of something similar happening now?

CHARLIE THOMSON, KNOWN universally as Chic, was another old stager who joined the club and assisted it during this upwardly mobile period. The Scottish goalkeeper, who had won the league title with Chelsea in 1955, was accustomed to the bright lights and thespian celebrity of the King's Road, so he found Forest slightly stodgy, not to say stingy, by way of contrast.

As the tall, lithe and agile goalkeeper stood head and shoulders above his colleagues on the platform of the city's Victoria Station in 1957, Chic pondered why the first team had not been given their train tickets. This was his first trip back to the capital, ironically for the game that Baily was afforded his wonderful reception.

Having won a championship medal with Chelsea two years previously, he had grown accustomed to first class travel, first class theatre tickets, in fact first class in most departments. "I couldn't believe it when Bill Whare [the Forest full-back] told me that we had to wait for the tickets to be bought, then handed out," recalls Thomson. "By the time we got on the train, we were walking down the corridors asking people: 'Excuse me, is that seat taken?' and so it went on until we were all seated. But we were scattered all over the place, which didn't do much for team morale on the day. To make matters worse, when we came back, we went through the first class dining compartment and saw the Rotherham United squad, who had been playing in London as well, sat down and eating. They were Second Division, and near the bottom, and here we were, a First Division side, having to make do. It was just the way Forest were then. They had come up from the Third Division South and were run by a committee who thought they were still there."

Of all the games that vindicated Walker's achievement, notwithstanding the pinnacle of the 1959 FA Cup final victory, the contest between his newly promoted Forest and Manchester United's marauding Busby Babes at the City Ground on 12 October 1957, stands the test of time. Bob Fairhall was there, too. "I always came down with my brothers and bought a ticket in what was known as the Popular Side. That made way for the East Stand and the United match marked its opening. There could not have been a more fitting debut, either."

Just one defeat in their opening nine matches, including a 7-0 thrashing of Burnley at the City Ground, had thrust Forest into the role of pacesetters at the top of the table. So it was no surprise that a then club record crowd of 47,804 clamoured to catch a first glimpse of the Babes, tragically their first and last with their fated February date with catastrophe at Munich just a few months away. There was also the opportunity to gauge progress against the defending league champions. If it was a benchmark Forest fans were seeking, they certainly found it that day – encouragingly the home team was not that far short of the standard, either. Except for one player – and what a player. His name was Duncan Edwards.

"The atmosphere, well, it was something else, they were passing the kids over the wall and they sat on the grass inside the wall," Fairhall recalls. Forest had slipped to third despite that Baily-inspired 4-3 away win at White Hart Lane, but with a game in hand on the top two, Wolverhampton Wanderers and West Bromwich Albion. However, the two-point cushion they enjoyed over United would be eroded by quarter-to-five that Saturday afternoon thanks to as one-sided a 2-1 victory as you can imagine. "I can remember one pundit said this game should have been filmed and every school kid should be made to watch it," remembers Fairhall. "Forest started well, but in the second half, they were really overrun by United. That man Duncan Edwards took over the middle of the field; such a brilliant player. We didn't realise that after what happened in February 1958 eight of those lads, Edwards as well, would never be coming back to the City Ground."

Fairhall still has a match report that he sent to Walker, which was mounted and hung in his office. It appeared under the nom de plume Old International, otherwise Don Davies, the respected *Manchester Guardian* journalist.

"A case of flawless manners of players, officials and spectators gave to a routine league match the flavour of an idyll…Since the club colours clashed, United danced out in their Tennysonian strip

– 'clothed in white samite, mystic, wonderful' – white stockings and all. It lent an air of ballet to the scene...Forest poured out in blood-red shirts and with that high-stepping action so beloved of modern footballers, as of lusty gamecocks spoiling for a fight. Rarely, if ever, has expectation of a football treat been more thoroughly roused; rarely, if ever, has it been so quickly and completely satisfied."

And on it flowed, perhaps not in a style favoured by the current sports editor of the *Daily Mail*, but at least the *Sun*, *Daily Star* and *Daily Sport* could have turned that 'white stockings' reference into a photo-shoot opportunity for Page 3 Tracey. But this writer was of the old school. Davies once wrote of the immensely gifted John Charles that he was "as powerful as Hercules, as authoritative as Caesar".

Despite his Manchester bias, Davies' objective view of events illuminated the pages and was a testament to Walker's team and the values he had instilled in it.

"Consider United's opening goal...coming so soon as it did within four minutes of the kick-off, it might have knocked the heart out of its victims completely, but herein lies the merit of the splendid Forest players...they played on with added fervour all through as though they were able to wipe the impact from their consciousness...if they had not squandered scoring chances as freely as they made them, they might have added to the memory of a glorious day the satisfaction of a glorious victory. One could detect the four cornerstones of Forest's recent successes... [Jack] Burkitt and [Bill] Morley, the veteran schemer and strategist Baily and that bundle of fiery endeavour and with a keen football brain and long, raking stride... Imlach. [Remember, all four were either Walker discoveries or his astute signings]. He has a strongly marked gift for intelligent roaming, in pursuance of which he once crept up behind Blanchflower [Jackie, the United centre-half] unawares and gave the Irish international the shock of his life by suddenly thrusting a grinning face over his shoulder while he nodded a long, high centre form Quigley unerringly home... what will be acknowledged without dispute is that this was a great exhibition of football, in which skill was the final, and only, arbiter, and where the splendour of the performance was enriched by the grace of sportsmanlike behaviour."

Clearly here was a man passionate about the game of football and on that October afternoon when the piercing sunshine contrasted with the raw nip of winter at the City Ground, Davies basked as one sated to ecstatic levels.

On 6 February the following year, Davies was one of eight journalists, including Frank Swift, the former Manchester City and England goalkeeper and best mate of Tommy Lawton, who perished at Munich. In all, 23 of the 44 passengers and crew died and it would be Forest, at an emotion-charged Old Trafford in a league match on 22 February, who would provide one of the first steps to rehabilitation following the crash as United began the long, painful grieving process.

FOREST WOULD FINISH tenth that season, but it was the following one, 1958/59, for which Walker will always be feted by Forest supporters.

Jeff Whitefoot (at the second time of asking, this time from Grimsby Town), Joe McDonald (from Sunderland) and Roy Dwight (from Fulham) were added to the squad and Forest, although destined for the sanctuary of mid-table, had created a Cup-winning side of inestimable grace and guile. Allied with a huge dollop of luck granted on an ice-bound and rutted Tooting and Mitcham pitch in the third round, it was an irresistible force that lifted the FA Cup in May 1959.

Somewhere along the Wembley way playing the Walker Way, via a replay against the Tooting amateurs, it is impossible not to imagine someone inscribing 'Forest' on the Cup.

A semi-final win thanks to Quigley's solitary goal of the tie at Hillsborough, home of the club Walker managed as Cup winners in 1935, over Aston Villa, with whom he won the famous old trophy as a player in 1920, might have indicated that the omens were favourable. Not even Dwight's fractured leg, that reduced Forest to ten men, could halt kismet's progress. People call it fate; others mock the very idea. However, more than most other winners, before or after, it does appear that their name was written on the silverware from the off that season.

The triumph brought to an end a pivotal decade for the club that had begun in the Third Division South. Under the Walker regime, they were now FA Cup winners and one of the esteemed members of the top flight.

"Billy Walker played such a huge part," Fairhall says. "I don't think people realise. Yes, he took them down, but not only did he get them back, he started building. Billy didn't like saying it, but they could have had five or six that day at Wembley because they were absolutely cruising until that accident [Dwight being carried off]."

Only a fool would argue that Clough was anything but Forest's greatest leader, yet there were parallels in Walker – he was that good, and that loved. "He was a bit like Mr Clough in a lot of ways," Fairhall says, retaining the 'Mr' as a mark of the respect in which he still holds the former manager. "Billy Gray was an outside-right, but he converted him into an inside-left and indeed later in life Billy became a left-back, but his partnership with Stewart Imlach was absolutely remarkable.

"One of the last games I played in amateur football was in the Notts Alliance and Tommy Wilson was an outside-right playing for Cinderhill. Billy converted him into a centre-forward and had Roy Dwight on the wing. Both of them could play in either's position, so they could interchange. Add Johnny Quigley and the great Bobby McKinlay, and it was a great little side. Make no mistake. And how Jack Burkitt didn't get any England caps no-one is sure. Ronnie Clayton at Blackburn seemed to get the nod, but Jack was deceptively quick and read the game brilliantly. I remember talking to Roy Dwight once about how he used to put extra padding down the inside of his leg because of Jeff Whitefoot. He used to tell me that no matter if Jeff hit a pass from four yards or 40 yards, it came at the same pace and he had to bring it down. It was bruising the inside of his right leg, so he'd put some padding there to protect it. I've asked Jeff about it, but he only laughs!"

It was no laughing matter, though, as Forest succumbed to the malaise that often afflicted FA Cup winners back then. Today the FA Cup final is no more than a minor showpiece, perhaps even an inconvenience, a financial inconsequence to the millions offered by satellite television and the Premiership/Premier League/however Sky decide to brand it next. In the 1950s and most of the ensuing three decades, however, it was *the* most important day in the football calendar and a long, lasting and cherished fame was guaranteed if you succeeded in it. Fortune did not necessarily arrive by virtue of kicking a spherical object accurately over 20 yards then, although strangely enough tapping it ten yards to an opponent on a regular basis does these days.

Forest, perhaps, adopted the latter tactics in 1960, narrowly avoiding relegation, as in the following year. Contagious strategy, perhaps, as the world narrowly avoided relegation to atomic dust and Armageddon in 1961 as the Soviet Union and the United States met head-to-head at the Bay of Pigs in Cuba. The decline was equalled by Walker's diminishing health. By the end of the season he had gone, to be replaced by Andy Beattie, a former Scotland international and renowned for discovering Denis Law at Huddersfield. Walker was appointed to the Forest committee as reward for unflinchingly loyal service that crossed four decades. In 1963, he fell victim to a stroke and he died in November 1964, aged 67. His legacy, though, was hugely significant. In some respects, he shaped the Forest teams of Carey and Clough that have been acclaimed among the best. "We were never a hoofing side. It was the 'Walker Way' to feet," Bob Fairhall assesses Walker's contribution. "Go through all the managers and they always played that brand of football, and we were noted for it. Like West Ham, whenever you got Forest against West Ham, you were going to see a football game; and it was true. My brothers, who were older than me, used to tell me if I wanted to see goals, go to Notts County. But if I wanted to see football, then go to Forest."

That might sound like a sly dig at the dour, black and white Magpies and a gloating approval of the more colourful Garibaldi Reds, but, in fact, Fairhall is merely reflecting the prodigious goalscoring talents that Sewell and Lawton introduced to Meadow Lane and the template for County sides to come; a big lad up the front occasionally partnered by a sidekick with equally polished finishing skills. As it happened, the County stable of No.9s, while never coming close to Lawton's legendary status, records an impressive list nonetheless: Jeff Astle, Tony Hateley and Les Bradd all etched their names indelibly in the club record books. Bradd, later to work for Forest in their commercial department, remains County's highest goalscorer.

Even though the Lawton-Sewell alliance secured promotion back to Division Two a year ahead of Forest, in 1950, Walker remained true to his principles. He wanted to create a Forest team that could play and pass along the floor, as his Villa side that claimed the FA Cup in 1920 had done. It truly was the 'Walker Way' and of all his splendid legacies, it is the one that Forest fans have embraced the most while subsequent managers have observed the technique that complemented one of the best and most level playing surfaces in the country, laid with Cumberland turf.

Johnny Carey's nearly men of 1967 adhered to its principles as did all of the Clough-Taylor teams that the pairing sent out to represent Forest. In a way, it's as much a burden as the club's European achievements. Forest supporters expect their football to be more purist than push and run. More guile than grit. More fluid than fancy. Under Walker they were weaned on it. Under Carey and Clough, they gorged on it. What's that about feast and famine?

Wally Ardron

1949-1955: 191 games, 124 goals

HORACE GAGER WAS a durable centre-half, respected Nottingham Forest captain and defender, who, from all contemporaneous reports, should have been honoured by England for his consistency and defensive ability. Each day, the east London-born stopper would enter the City Ground dressing room with a graceful, almost aloof, manner and begin the formalities of undressing as a prelude to donning the moth-eaten, mud-encrusted attire that passed for training kit.

Often, in moments of solitude and quiet reflection, he would decline to train with the rest of the 'boys' and perform a solo circuit that comprised six or seven brisk laps and a few more jogging at a leisurely pace. In all, he completed a dozen. Job done, Gager would retire to wash in the communal bath, fully populated with his colleagues or not, towel himself down and dress to return to normal life outside the cloistered confines of the Forest first team changing room. "He was a great player, but one of the most miserable blokes I ever knew in football," recalls contemporary Tommy Capel.

Part of Gager's final ritual before departing the dressing room was to don his Trilby hat that was hanging from a hook above his allotted place. It should noted that a hat was a fashion accessory for mature men then rather than an oaf's crown that it has become for dunce druggie pop stars.

If Gager's methodical precision annoyed Capel and some of the younger element in the Forest camp, it irritated the hell out of Tommy Ardron. So much so that the former railway fireman from Yorkshire had a plan to disrupt Gager's routine. "I'll cure him of that," he told his team-mates. So the following day, once Gager had again disappeared out of the dressing room and onto the running track to conduct his running in splendid isolation, Ardron leaped into action. He'd arrived at training with a bag of six-inch nails and a hammer and promptly drove one in to the offending – at least to him and several others – Trilby, connecting it securely to the side of the wooden hook stand.

Gager returned, towelled and began dressing before the inevitable happened. Strangely there was a full house in the senior dressing room that morning, looking sheepishly at one another and trying not to laugh. "Eventually Horace tried to put his hat on, but, of course, the thing was stuck rigid to the wood," Capel says, smiling at the memory. "He pulled it so hard that eventually he ripped the rim off it and it was ruined. He was furious and turned around to ask who had done it."

Ardron owned up straight away. A south Yorkshire lad who had worked in heavy duty industry, he didn't like what he perceived Gager stood for, a distant, almost middle-class demeanour that looked down on his ilk. That might have been grossly unfair on Gager, but in the rarefied atmosphere of a football dressing room, Ardron sniffed confrontation. As a former lightweight boxer of some repute and someone who sparred with Bruce Woodcock, his mate on the railways and a British Empire heavyweight champion boxer who once defeated Freddie Mills, a man who would go on to become world lightheavyweight champion in his heyday, he also sniffed blood.

Gager, gentleman player that he was, calmed the situation with a diplomacy learned from his responsibility as captain and laughed off the episode. It would not be the last time that the feisty Ardron would try to tempt fate and Gager into fisticuffs, but then the captain knew that any untoward or boisterous behaviour off the field was more than tempered by his prodigious goalscoring feats on it.

MENTION OF ARDRON should be enough to have most Forest supporters of a certain age drooling. Then again, that might just be the certain age unable to contain the morning cup of tea through the dentures and dodgy respiratory system, so younger fans, and by that

I mean those born post-1950, may not know of his repute. Had he been playing now, Wally Ardron would have induced the younger generation to that toe-curling bowing ceremony that is normally reserved for royalty, cringing enough though that is when you see the likes of Elton John scraping the floor to be dubbed by HMQ.

In simple terms, Ardron was a working class lad who scored goals at a prodigious rate. His 36 in the exhilarating promotion season from the Third Division South in 1950/51 remains a club record that illustrious successors ranging from Joe Baker, Ian Storey-Moore and Duncan McKenzie to Nigel Clough and Stan Collymore have conspicuously failed to equal, never mind eclipse.

As well as his roots and his rare talent in front of the white posts, he also had another invaluable side that endeared him to fans and friends alike. Whisper it quietly in the dressing room of today, but Ardron was also a bit of a character. In short he was in possession of something virtually extinct in the modern game – a personality.

In deepest winter, he'd run out onto the pitch with his sleeves, already short in the fashion, rolled up to his shoulders, displaying a muscular, angular frame that dipped in and out of the penalty area with such potency. Now and again, decisions might go against him. Paid or not, referees have always been prone to the odd blunder as Rob Styles can testify. Instead of demonising the poor old official, though, Ardron would run back to his position, making a beeline for the man in black and ruffling the referee's hair in a manner somewhere in between tolerance, fondness and downright ferocity.

His ultimate riposte, though, lay in his goals and a rapacious desire to score them, fuelled by rapier-like reactions and the instinctive bravery of a ring fighter, bobbing and weaving, taking the knocks but always coming back for more. In 182 league games he scored 123 goals for Forest, a remarkable effort only surpassed by Grenville Morris's 199, although it took the old maestro 423 games around the turn of the century to amass them. Ardron's strike rate over such an extended period has not come close to being surpassed in the club's history, but then the rumbustious striker was primed in the art from the age of 11. Playing for Swinton Bridge Boys, he laid claimed to nine out of ten goals in a 10-1 win and thus his appetite was well and truly whetted.

Initially he played for Denaby United in the Midland League in the early 1930s, but then joined Rotherham as a part-timer, working a gruelling shift as a fireman on the railways. During the Second World War he worked at the local colliery and steel works while representing Sheffield Wednesday as a guest forward in a war-time cup semi-final before returning to his railway occupation when hostilities ceased in 1945.

He became the railway company's champion for 'putting the weight', a contest that required workers to manhandle a solid steel heavy ball with some dexterity and then throw it. Imagine if you will a rock-hard Wayne Rooney, impervious to metatarsal breaks, rather than a waif-like Michael Owen, and you'll be about halfway to the toughness that Ardron personified.

Clearly not afraid of hard labour, graft and getting his hands dirty, the largely unseen and undervalued, but essential, virtues of every successful leader of the line, Ardron scored 230 goals for Rotherham in nine years as a part-timer, many of those not valued officially because of the war. He had already established a club record of 40 goals in one season for the Millers, one that would be beaten by his successor Jack Shaw in the same year that Ardron was creating his new and thus far unyielding record at the City Ground.

No less than 17 other clubs were showing an interest in him when he became available, despite the fact that he had remained a part-timer with Rotherham as his goalscoring exploits unfolded. Ardron was just three months shy of his 31st birthday when Billy Walker travelled to the Crown Inn at Bawtry to cement the deal in June 1949. The location, a few miles east of the A1, was a busy interchange for football folk travelling to and from Nottingham and the north and north east. Years later, it was the venue, for example, where Forest officials travelled on covert missions with brown paper envelopes of cash; happy money to keep Terry Curran in clover and payment in lieu of signing the Doncaster Rovers winger at the end of that 1974/75 season.

There were no such shenanigans on this occasion. Walker, whose side had just been relegated to the Third Division South, had £10,000 in his transfer kitty, the fee he had received recently from Southampton for inside-left Jack Edwards. For a thirty-something forward, whose proven pedigree was only at the same level in the northern section, it was something of a risk.

"Before I sign, do you know how old I am?" Ardron recalled of that meeting with Walker.

"Yes I do. But we want you to do a job for us at Forest, score us some goals and get us back in the Second Division," Walker replied.

"I told him that a team gets promotion, but I knew what he meant," continued Ardron when we met. "Nottingham was near enough to Rotherham, Forest were a good club and I liked the place."

Although Ardron's tally was 25 in his first season, Forest had to settle for fourth position. The next campaign, though, was a whirlwind, with goals lashed in from all quarters of the pitch, although Ardron's party piece was to arrive just in the nick of time to convert crosses from right-winger Freddie Scott.

"The funny thing was Wally was always best coming in with crosses from the right," team-mate Tommy Capel recalls. "It sounds daft, but he wasn't very good with the right side of his head or flicking balls on. He'd dash in and crash, in it went. Over half of his goals came from that tactic. It was his movement and Scotty's perfect crossing that did the trick. Some players are like that. If you watched Tommy Lawton at County, he always met the ball full on with his head, very few were flicked. Then again, when he headed it, the ball went harder and faster than most players could kick it!"

CROWDS FLUCTUATED AT the City Ground, although there was one dramatic peak the day before Bonfire Night in 1950 when Millwall were beaten 2-0 at home in front of the season's best 33,472. Arkwright Street and its pub on every corner that defeated nine out of ten blind optimists who took up the challenge of the Arkwright Street Run, a pint of Home Ales or Shipstone's in every corner house up and down the thoroughfare, must have been bulging that dank Saturday afternoon of November 4.

Tales of the players cycling to games or catching the bus to Midland Station and the Queen's Hotel at the top of Arkwright Street and walking among streams of supporters were common. The Second World War had bonded people like never before and that togetherness extended, if not beyond the rigid class system that divided the nation between rich and poor, then among the working classes who had stood shoulder to shoulder for what had seemed an eternity, never knowing if the cigarette they were smoking or a sharp intake of breath as another Luftwaffe bomber dropped its incendiary bombs would be their last.

In people like Ardron, working class to the core, the man on the Trent End could identify a kindred spirit who had been blessed with a talent to entertain in the sporting theatre. He did not disappoint. Jack Burkitt, the cultured left-half whose proudest moment would arrive when he lifted the FA Cup for Forest in 1959, remembered Ardron's impact. "He could shoot with both feet, but his real strength was in the air," the Forest captain recalled in an interview some years before his death in 2003. "He'd cut his head on the old ball – you'd do that because it was heavy and had proper lacing – but just played on. His forehead would be a right mess with cuts and grazes and gashes, but it wouldn't bother him. If things got really bad, he'd play with a sort of skull cap he'd made from plastic. But he'd always play."

During his Rotherham days, Ardron's special skull cap came in handy after he received 16 stitches in a particularly bad head wound, but being a true pro, or more accurately part-time pro, but one fearless from his pugilist days, he defied doctor's orders and turned out against Gateshead. Tommy Callender, the redoubtable Geordie centre-half marking him that day, shouted across. "What's up then, Wally?"

"Best keep out of the way this afternoon," replied Ardron with the straightest of faces. "It's ringworm…and it's catching."

Typically, Ardron scored a couple that day – both with his head. As Tommy Lawton, possibly the finest header of a football there has been, used to say in his charmingly understated self-deprecating way: "Where there's no sense, there's no feeling!"

In many ways, Ardron seemed impervious to injury. "At one time he fractured his collarbone, but still went out for the next game," Burkitt said. "If the manager asked him to play, he couldn't say 'no'. That rolling his shirt sleeves up when it was cold was a way of showing how strong he was. He frightened defenders to death. They knew he wouldn't back out of anything. He was always fair, though. And he couldn't half hit a ball. I remember at Brighton once and we liked to pass it around, build from the back in those days, Wally wasn't that far inside their half with his back to goal. There was nothing on and I was in a bit of space and so I shouted for it. He just took a couple of strides, swung his boot, put it in the net and came up to me and said: 'Sorry, Jack, but that's where it wanted to go. It did as well.'"

Apart from his goals, Ardron's shrewd judgement also influenced Forest's early restoration of their Second Division status. When Walker eventually secured his centre-forward, the manager asked his opinion on the league he had just departed, the Third Division North. Being on the cusp of the north-south divide, Forest were entitled to argue a case of dropping into either section following their relegation in 1949. Ardron's advice was thus: "If you are going in the northern league, you can expect a bit of hammer. But if you're looking to play a bit of football, then it's the southerners you want." The first definition of southern softies that eventually would lead to Clyde Best in woolly gloves at West Ham and Keith Weller in tights at Leicester when the temperature dropped to boiling point? Who knows.

But if Walker had been in any doubt before, Ardron's assessment would have vindicated his unflinching belief in the ball along the floor and the passing game. By the sort of ironic twist that sport frequently reveals, Forest returned to their previous status in 1951 with a record haul of 110 goals and 70 points. In the northern section, Rotherham United were also runaway champions, with a meagre 103 goals, but with one more point than southern 'softies' Forest.

Calling Ardron anything vaguely as demeaning as that would have been sheer folly. Those sparring days with Bruce Woodcock honed physical and mental strength. Remember Woodcock, a big mate who was a railway colleague in the heavy plant works, was the first post-war British heavyweight champion and held both the British and Empire crowns from 1945 to 1950. He lost just four of his 39 fights in an age when good boxers were plentiful and plenty tough. That in his later years he kept a pub called The Tumbler, in Edlington near Doncaster, reflects how even those who achieved the pinnacle of sporting greatness had to settle for the life less glamorous in their dotage.

Tommy Capel recalls Ardron as a player who could handle himself, but also a character who tried to enliven what could be a stolid dressing room. "I suppose there was myself, Colin [Collindridge] and Wally," Capel says. "Some people called us the three trouble makers, but I like to think we were the joy makers. When we'd go away by train to games, Wally was always up front of us all and wanted to get up on the footplate with the engine driver and his fireman."

In the days before diesel and electric trains, those of the steam idyll recalled through rose-tinted spectacles in Ealing studio's *The Titfield Thunderbolt*, Ardron would hop aboard the front engine of the locomotive with the words: "This is how yer do it lads," and start shovelling the coal to fire the engine.

Then there was the excessive taunting of Gager, the inscrutable captain and centre-half as Capel explains. "We were playing Norwich over Christmas and travelled over to East Anglia on Christmas Day for the Boxing Day game. It was snowing like hell and we didn't get to the hotel until late. Hooky [manager Walker] sorted us out some sandwiches around 11.30pm, but for the whole journey Horace had sat at the back of the bus on his own doing crosswords. As we got off the coach, Wally waited for the captain at this revolving door and planted his foot in it, just to stop him short. He was laughing like a Cheshire cat, but Horace didn't see the joke as he stood stranded outside the hotel.

"Anyway, as we ate the sandwiches later, in a big room with a huge blazing fire, Horace eventually joined us, even though he seldom talked to the lads. Wally had these stink bombs, horrible things they were, and he dropped a couple on the fire. One by one, the lads started to leave the room. The smell was bloody vile, a right pooh. He just wanted to get a reaction from Horace, you see."

Despite turning his nose up at what was clearly a childish prank, Gager eventually could take no more, arose from his comfy seat and demanded to know who was responsible, glaring intently at 'Tot' Leverton, one of the younger lads in the squad.

Quick as a flash, chest almost bursting with pride, Ardron owned up and confessed. "It wer me."

"Well, that's all right Wally, I can see it was only a joke."

If he wanted to rile the captain, his ruse had once again failed.

But Ardron would not be denied his moment of confrontation at the end of that, his first season with Forest. In May 1950 the club embarked on a short tour of the Low Countries, Holland and Belgium, and then on to West Germany. It was there they played against Gottingen 05, and drew 2-2 with the West German Third Division side. Ardron, needless to say, almost scored one of the Forest goals, but it was more his target practice on the unfortunate Teutonic net-minder that captured the mood and caught the imagination of thousands of Allied soldiers still stationed in what was occupied territory.

Hans, for we shall call him that, and a not very careless one at that moment, was bouncing the ball around his 18-yard box as Ardron stalked the area like a paparazzo waiting to snap its prey. In those days the German No.1 was perfectly entitled to his ball-bouncing eccentricities. The Harlem Globetrotters gleaned their finely tuned dribbling skills and knowledge of zonal possession from English goalkeepers. Once, a colonial spat in the Belgian Congo had begun and ended with 5,000 casualties in the same time span that it took Gil Merrick, the Birmingham net-minder, to catch a ball, dally awhile and launch it upfield. Now the Germanic ball-bouncer was trying Ardron's patience. The Forest man gave Hans a meaningful glare.

"Are you going to kick that ball?" he asked without a hint of humour. The German kept grinning, failing to understand the language or detect the underlying menace in Ardron's demeanour. One more bounce broke the camel's back and Ardron flattened the goalie and planted the ball in the back of the net. Cue cheers from all around the ground, well the British forces anyway. The referee, though, and not least poor old Hans, were not amused.

"But referee, back in England, the goal would have stood." Ardron argued a lost cause after the effort was disallowed. The following day, local newspaper blasted out their headlines. Ardron the Bullock, they boomed. Maybe, like the contretemps with the Gottingen goalie, something was lost in translation. Either way, Ardron sat out the remainder of the tour; a victim of diplomatic niceties deemed necessary with Europe still recovering from a devastating conflict which had ended a mere five years previously.

ARDRON'S FOREST LEGACY, though, was far more than a rampaging bull at a gate, a practical joker and railway fireman who could punch his weight with the best of them.

He scored a hat-trick on five occasions for the club and enlisted in the elite regiment of those who have scored four, the winning total in a 4-1 home win over Hull City on Boxing Day 1952. One of those trebles was against Gillingham at Easter in the title-winning season; a motorcycle escort then guided the team coach back to the station where, with seconds to spare before departure, they boarded the London-bound train to their overnight HQ before the following day's game at Southend United.

Forest lost 3-2 at the Essex club, and with Norwich City in hot pursuit of that solitary promotion place, nerves could have been forgiven for setting in, but successive home wins against Bournemouth and Swindon Town settled things and Ardron eclipsed the previous Forest goalscoring record against the Robins, his 32nd of the season creating a fresh benchmark.

A cartilage injury severely disrupted Ardron's Forest career in 1953, but as the *Evening News* reported in September of that year, he did pop in to surprise team-mates after three weeks' rehabilitation in Newcastle.

"Aa've coom back lads," he announced to the dressing room in his distinctive Yorkshire tones. He said he 'felt champion' and revealed that his wife had expected him back home on Monday night, but he had made a beeline for the City Ground and his dinner had been put in the oven and 'dried up'. You can only imagine Posh and Becks having the same casual arrangement and culinary habits.

ARDRON CONTINUED TO score goals for Forest, but not in the same prodigious fashion. After all, what could top that 1951 season when it pelted down with goals? "To get goals, you have to put your head in when the boots are flying," he once reflected when asked about why he scored so many, rebuking modern forwards [this was in 1972] for not being brave enough. Whatever the truth of that, no-one would argue with Ardron's bravery. He was a piece of granite with a jewel in the centre that reflected a shining, piercing character in pursuit of goals and fun.

One of his sons, Keith, played against Henry Newton in the Nottingham Schoolboys sides of the 1950s. He had trials with Forest, but ended up with Rawmarsh, of the Yorkshire League, a tad homesick. His illustrious father was coach to the Rawmarsh team. Later both Keith and his brother Barry played alongside one another for Clifton Rovers, another team coached by Wally, who had become physiotherapist at Doncaster Rovers after retiring from football through injury, before scouting for Allan Ashman, the Carlisle United manager.

Illness dogged Ardron's latter years. In 1972 he underwent an operation for a duodenal ulcer. Six years later, aged 59, he died. Only a few paragraphs in the *Nottingham Evening Post* recorded his passing.

The words of Jack Burkitt, one of Forest's finest defenders of all time, perhaps provide a more fitting epitaph. "Wally might not have had the finesse of Tommy Lawton, but it's still quite a compliment that he is compared to him when the pair were both playing in Nottingham at the same time."

Tommy Capel

1949-1954: 162 games, 72 goals

THE VOICE AT the other end of the telephone was fragmented, fittingly so. Desperately fitting. In the modern vernacular, Tommy Capel was in pieces.

On the day I asked him to be part of this anthology of Nottingham Forest players, his beloved wife Vera had died. Married for 59 years, she had lost a short and imbalanced fight against cancer, that most pernicious of predators. The scheduled world cruise they had planned to celebrate their diamond wedding anniversary in February 2008 had already been cancelled.

"We met just after the war at Belle Vue in Manchester," Capel explains a few weeks after he had said farewell to the love of his life. Although the tears had by now subsided, the framed colour photograph on the living room sideboard portrays a couple in happier, younger days.

Next to it stands another, a carefree and attractive 30-something woman captured with a beaming smile at what looks like a festive occasion. Tommy Capel's daughter Christine passed away when she was 40, in 1990, suffering from hepatitis that swiftly developed into cancer of the liver. A month after a camping trip to Switzerland, the most prominent figure among youth organisations in Bingham was dead. Does life get this intentionally cruel on purpose? Or is the random selection purely down to luck, bad or good? The sombre and cold analytical light of day only confirms Bill Shankly's observation about life and death and football as the utter tosh it was, a reflection that doubtless the old Liverpool manager strenuously would deny for all his whimsy.

During our interviews, Tommy Capel didn't dwell on fate's misfortunes. A proud Lancastrian with a smashing sense of humour and self-effacing perception of his own status, the former Forest inside-left lives as he played his football, with creative incision and frequently looking forward. Now and again a lapse to the past pertinent to the post-war generation of footballers whose return from the horrors of war did not always coincide with a return to normality is allowed.

"Belle Vue was the speedway track and I followed it with my mate. The ticket allowed you into the dance hall afterwards on a Saturday night. So we went in and I was watching from the balcony down at the ballroom below. I think it was Joe Loss and his orchestra playing that night. My mate pointed out his cousin Vera and after the dance we were introduced. We just clicked. Three months later, we got married."

That was during his last season as a professional at Manchester City, the club that had taken him on as an aspiring 17-year-old spotted playing for Goslings, the equivalent of the City A team.

A few weeks later, England declared war on Germany and the expectations of a generation suddenly shifted dramatically. Aged 19, Capel was called up to serve king and country two years after signing for City. He tried to join the Air Force, but found there were no vacancies and ended up in the Navy, attached to the Royal Naval Air Service, in other words one of the elite band of Marines.

Unlike many pro players there was no easy ride for Capel despite his footballer status. Years later his path with Tommy Lawton would be intertwined in the heat of unforgettable Trentside derbies, but their war experiences could not have been more disparate. The great man Lawton was in fact 19 when war broke out, a prodigious teenage talent whose 34 goals in 38 games had spearheaded Everton's title-winning campaign the previous season. Throughout the ensuing years, he was ordered to remain in England and continue his 'war job', i.e. playing football in charity games and internationals to raise funds and morale for the troops. Much as he was maligned in some quarters for this easy, comfy option, it was not of Lawton's choosing. Neither was Capel's theatre of operations – so vivid in contrast to Lawton's war. The fledgling Manchester City professional was sent for training in Deal, Kent, then South Wales practising barge landings before being shipped from Liverpool off to India, where hostilities would take him to Ceylon (now Sri Lanka), Japan and Burma.

"I ended up in the jungle, on the River Irrawaddy, trying to ferret out the Japs from either side of its banks. It was thick jungle undergrowth on either side. It was tough at times."

The understatement betrays his veteran roots. Like so many of his ilk and holders of the Burma Star for fighting in that region, he seldom talks about his experiences. Mention of the Irrawaddy is a byword for the courage and fortitude that was necessary to sustain, let alone survive, if lucky, a significant conflict in the hostile environment.

The truth was that the battle of attrition was as much against a determined, fanatical Japanese enemy as it was against the mud, malaria and monsoon weather that took the lives of so many Allied servicemen.

"There were 120 of us in our battalion, mostly young lads like myself. I did get dysentery once, spent three days on the toilet," he laughs, forgetting to mention the hand-to-hand fighting that weeded out the resistance, or the clearing of jungle scrub to transform into makeshift runways for incoming Dakota planes laden with supplies or troops.

THE WORD 'CULT' certainly was knocking around in the 1940s, its connotations quite different then, but had it borne any resemblance to the definition it embraces today, Tommy Capel by any criteria would have been known as a cult hero; a working class lad reared in the cobblestoned streets of Fallowfield, a Marine embroiled in jungle warfare in the Far East, who returned to Maine Road where his football career had been interrupted before it had scarcely begun some seven years earlier.

Capel did not require the shallow sycophancy and exhibitionism of players who kiss the club badge on their shirt after scoring a goal. Nor did he wallow in his patriotism or loyalty with incessant public declarations and bleatings of gushing pride. He just got on with the job, quietly, unobtrusively and without recourse to vacuous ingratiation or adulation. Impossible to imagine today or even relate to, after seven years away from home Capel was ordered, in keeping with his contemporaries, to go back to his previous pre-war occupation. Professional footballer.

Even at 85 years of age, celebrated on 27 June 2007, Capel's gait is good, a firm handshake and body revealing the physique of a pedigree sportsman, a teetotaller who never smoked. Still tall and lean, he says he lost around a stone during Vera's rapid decline. Even a few pounds heavier, he could cut a striking figure at any of the golf courses he still hacks around to good effect in Nottinghamshire, notably Fiskerton near Newark on the River Trent. That natural fitness helped restore him to the Manchester City side that won the Second Division title in 1947, the first official league season following the war. He was restricted to nine appearances then and with City chasing a natural left-winger, his days at Maine Road were numbered.

Billy Linacre, a young Chesterfield lad, who had matured as a player at Saltergate while Capel evolved from callow youth to man in Burma, was seen by new City boss Jock Thomson as the lad to ignite their First Division season. Bobby Brocklebank, the Chesterfield manager, was allowed two players in exchange. He chose Capel, who would be united with his younger brother Fred, also a Goslings graduate, at Saltergate, and right-half Peter Robinson. Tommy's path to Nottingham Forest was already taking shape, albeit in a tortuous fashion.

When, in January 1949, Brocklebank applied for and secured the vacancy at First Division Birmingham City left by the departure of Harry Storer, Capel was soon on the move again, despite scoring 27 goals in 62 games for Chesterfield in two Second Division seasons. The circumstances were unusual, however. "Me and Vera were on our holidays in Blackpool taking a stroll along the promenade. Then this taxi pulls up alongside us and it's Bobby Brocklebank. 'I've been looking all over for you Tommy. The lady at the digs said you'd be out for a walk. I said when I got a job in the First Division, I'd take you with me. How do you fancy it?' We had a quick chat and then I dived in the back of the taxi and signed there and then with the forms on the seat. Birmingham had agreed a fee with Chesterfield for £11,000, which was a fair bit of money then [the record transfer fee stood at £20,500 for Len Shackleton's move from Newcastle to Sunderland].

They sorted me and Vera out a house and we moved over to the West Midlands the following week."

The acquisition of Bobby Brennan, the Northern Ireland inside-right who joined the St Andrew's squad a month after Capel, was to prove the expeditious catalyst for Capel's west-east transfer across the Midlands. "We just didn't gel together, don't know why, but Birmingham had paid more for him and because he was an international the manager told me that it was me who had to go. Fair enough, I thought."

Birmingham's loss, Forest's gain? Without a shadow of a doubt, even if Forest had to pay a club record £14,000 for his unorthodox talents. Billy Walker persuaded Capel (£15 a week, £12 in the reserves and £13 in the summer) to drop two divisions to make a 5 November debut without fireworks, a routine 2-0 home win over Crystal Palace thanks to two goals from former Raith Rovers inside-forward John Love.

Yet by the end of the season, Birmingham had been relegated and within a couple of years it would be Forest stalking the Bluenoses in the Second Division as both clubs narrowly failed to make the top two promotion cut, Birmingham agonisingly missing out on goal average to Cardiff City.

The dwindling but devotedly enthusiastic number of Forest supporters who can actually claim to have seen Capel perform will recall his fluid, almost languid style that belied a killer pass, cunning skills and the one asset that England expects but rarely delivers – a cultured left foot. Stories of its mercurial qualities are the stuff of myth and legend among City Ground peers. Capel says he has visited most of Europe through football and treasured family holidays with Vera and Christine. Had he stopped off at Lourdes with a few Garibaldi Reds on vacation, the casualty rate might have been high in the rush to touch his left peg for its ability to cure and heal.

It was a quirk of kismet and more traditional and proven healing procedures that shaped and moulded that famous left foot. "It was when I was at school in Fallowfield. The teacher, Mr Evans, had moved me up from the seven-year-olds to the under-11s, saying I was a bit too good for the younger lot despite my age. We used to live at one end of what was called Platt Lane. It was a road about a mile long. At one end was the school, the other our house. There used to be these steam tractors that ran up and down them, the sort you see at fairs with solid wheels and that. We'd play football at the school. Then, if we couldn't be bothered to walk home, remember we kept our boots and studs on and didn't fancy ruining them on the cobbles, we'd wait for one of these tractors to come along and hang on the back. Dodging a lift we used to call it, about four of us. At the end of Platt Lane, we'd let go and jump off and the driver didn't know a thing about it.

"There were also trams running up and down the road as well and unfortunately one day as I was waiting to jump onto the tractor, I got my studs caught in the tramlines. Couldn't move my right foot this way or the other. Then – bump – the tractor's wheel ran right over the top of it. I was sent to hospital straight away in agony and stayed there for four or five weeks. I missed school for a couple of months, too, and when I went back, I had no feeling in that foot. I still struggle with it to this day.

"I used to play right-wing for the school team, and Mr Evans told me that I was too good to forget about football, that I should start thinking about it seriously. So every night, straight after school, he'd stay behind with me on the playing field and help me practise. 'Now go on and develop that left foot,' he'd tell me. He put a carpet slipper on the bad foot and a football boot on the other and just passed the ball to me and watched me sharpen my skills. They do say that if you lose the power in one limb or eye or whatever, it goes into the other one. And I think that's right."

Agony for Capel at the time, ecstasy for Forest fans who had been starved of success, as well as eggs, fresh meat and just about anything else that rationing prohibited, for over a decade.

Capel, though, aided and abetted by a solid Forest side, was about to change all that, a reversal of fortunes that gathered an irresistible pace during the 1950s that would culminate in that wonderful day out at Wembley in May 1959. In fact, following two successive defeats, Capel's signing inspired a four-game winning sequence; right-winger Freddie Scott scored two at Bournemouth, then Capel claimed both goals, his first for the club, in a 2-0 home win against Bristol Rovers.

The red half of the West Country city turned up the following week in the FA Cup first round. Forest, through a Gordon Kaile goal, moved into the second round in front of the 15,567 fans who saw a substandard match between a couple of Third Division (South) opponents.

Arkwright Street, the main drag from Midland Station to the City Ground, must have been especially bugling that Saturday afternoon of 26 November. Unthinkable nowadays, but Notts County were also at home in the FA Cup, against London League amateurs Tilbury. Unthinkable now as well, but the Magpies attracted a crowd almost double that of Forest, with 28,584 turning up at Meadow Lane, many of them making the short stroll from their Meadows' homes to see County in a stroll too, a 4-0 win easing them through to the second round.

There was a reason, of course. The County No.9 and captain, Tommy Lawton. "He was a cut above," the other Tommy across the Trent recalls. "It's funny because there didn't seem to be the great derby rivalry that I knew in Manchester between City and United. In fact after training we used to meet up at Tom's café, at the top end of Meadow Lane. There would be about ten of the County lads and the same from our lot. Lawton never came. He was a great player and he got his perks all right. His car was free and he'd been promised a job with a typewriter firm to supplement his income [in fact the company Sterling Seimig, owned by a County director, went bankrupt and Lawton never did get the job he was promised when he'd signed for a British record fee of £20,000 in 1947]. One of their lads told me how he'd done an interview with a magazine about golf and the reporter had given him a dozen Dunlop 65s, the best golf balls around at the time and costing five shillings each [25p], a lot of money back then. The reporter told him to hand them out to the lads because he knew they all played golf, as we did. Word got back, though, that the County lads did get a Dunlop 65 golf ball apiece – at a cost of five bob each! He'd sold them on to his own players."

Whatever Capel's opinion of Lawton's fiscal enterprise and philanthropy, and in Nottingham there is a wide division of opinion on the subject, his admiration for the England centre-forward's prowess is undiminished by years. His first confrontation came a week after those FA Cup ties north and south of the Trent when the first Nottingham derby since February 1935 saw 37,903 attend the City Ground. Despite fond tales of there being only one bobby to man the inflated crowds of the post-war era, in fact 90 officers and two mounted policemen were on duty that day. Result: overtime pay was up, but not one arrest and good-natured banter was exchanged between both banks of fans. Anyone there that day will recall perhaps the most famous goal from any Trentside derby, a magic Lawton moment that won the game and maintained County's ascendancy in the city and their advantage at the top of the Third Division (South) – five points ahead of second-placed Forest before the game – that was never relinquished during their promotion season.

"I can still see the goal today," says Capel. "I was standing just outside the penalty area in the left-half position and I saw Lawton coming from the edge of the box. Broomey [Frank Broome, the County right-winger] had sent over a great corner and Lawton just met it on the full; a brilliant, unstoppable header that beat Geoff Thomas and Harry Walker [the right-back and goalkeeper respectively] who were on the line. Lawton was a real superstar."

In fact Broome tapped in a second from Lawton's low centre. Forest's most expensive player Capel pulled one back late on, but County deservedly held on for a 2-1 win. That balance of power was confirmed when County completed the double in April with Lawton once more their nemesis in a 2-0 win. He scored one and Jackie Sewell, Lawton's equally prolific forward partner, the other in front of nearly 46,000 at Meadow Lane. Forest's gates had declined to just above 12,000 as a consequence of that earlier December defeat and, while there was a late surge through the turnstiles as Forest rallied in vain, County's command performances overshadowed what had been an encouraging fourth-place finish for Walker's team.

AND YET SOMETHING was stirring at the City Ground. Just as surely as Lawton and Sewell held sway in 1950, the following year it was to be Capel and the irrepressible Wally Ardron who would galvanise Forest to be champions and eclipse, in terms of scoring feats, County's dynamic duo. Those two and Barnsley-born left-winger Colin Collindridge. Capel calls the trio the "trouble makers. No, more joy makers" – a teasing triumvirate and either description could apply in terms of tantalising opponents and colleagues both on and off the pitch.

There was a pleasing balance to the side that was about to begin the climb back to the peak of domestic football. Horace Gager, a gargantuan centre-half from Luton Town, was the very essence of that period's typical No.5, seemingly hewn from granite with a nerveless exterior and rugged demeanour that was essential in an era when centre-forwards resembled and sometimes performed like the last man standing in Ron Taylor's boxing booth on the last Saturday night of Nottingham's Goose Fair. A young Jack Burkitt was emerging with a confidence that should have brought, like Gager, more England recognition. 'Tot' Leverton, later to defect to Notts County, was another versatile addition at inside-forward. There was also Freddie Scott on the right side of that swashbuckling attack that would plunder 110 goals on the way to the Division Three title. A vital cog in the works as Capel explains. "One of the things I had was this sort of Beckham-type pass, switching the play from left to right. I could hit the ball with my left foot over to Scotty who was running at pace and he'd take the ball in his stride, breezing past the full-back. He then had this knack of getting a cross over first time and more often than not Wally would be on the end of it. He'd know what the plan was and he'd be running at pace as well into the box and getting the drop on the defender."

Capel estimates that at least half of Ardron's record tally of 36 goals came from that source; others claim that 27 of them came from that rich supply vein. Whatever the truth, they were among 110 goals scored that season as Forest and Ardron toppled records aplenty amid a succession of high-scoring victories such as the 7-0 thrashing of Aldershot, the 6-1 win at Crystal Palace and 5-0 triumph at Exeter.

If one game exemplified that free-flowing movement and shared responsibility for goalscoring it was perhaps the 9-2 home defeat of Gillingham on 18 November 1950. Ardron scored a hat-trick and Johnson a couple, but Capel eclipsed them both by scoring four and taking home the match ball. "I've still got it, not signed of course. We didn't bother with anything like that in those days. Besides, you couldn't have written your name on those old leather balls, let alone seen it."

Capel's season's tally was 24, including one scored in an FA Cup second round defeat by Rotherham United at Millmoor. Collindridge's contribution was 18, including two in the 6-1 first round drubbing of Torquay, a feat equalled by Tommy Johnson who could count a hat-trick in that same Cup tie amongst his final total. Even Scott, busy creating chances for Ardron, hit double figures.

True, Lawton had scored 31 in 37 in County's successful championship the previous year, but Forest's 70 points, never surpassed in the southern section, was 12 points – the equivalent of six wins then – better than the Magpies had achieved. Rather like Wilson, Keppel and Betty, the celebrated Egyptian mimics and sand dancers of music hall fame, Ardron, Capel and Colly entranced audiences and led their detractors a merry dance. Simple arithmetic confirms that the trio accounted for 75 of those 110 league goals. Capel and Ardron claimed 59 of them. In context, the nearest any combination of Forest forwards has come to emulating that phenomenal achievement was Pierre van Hooijdonk, the striking Dutchman in every sense of the phrase, and Kevin Campbell during the 1997/98 Division One championship-winning season. Van man's league total was 29 (he also claimed three against Doncaster Rovers in a two-legged League Cup tie, another against Walsall in the same competition and one in a 4-1 FA Cup reverse away to Charlton Athletic). All Campbell's goals directed Forest back to the Premiership, equalling Capel's league total of 23. Even so, that's seven short of the record and besides, Capel's role was not quite in the same outwardly attacking mode as Campbell's foil to van Hooijdonk.

After that, the 1967 season, when Forest finished runners-up to Manchester United in the First Division and were losing FA Cup semi-finalists to Tottenham Hotspur, conjures up perhaps one of the club's most famous double acts in Ian Storey-Moore and Joe Baker, not dissimilar to Capel and Ardron in that Storey-Moore was a fleet-of-foot player, drifting in and out of events from the left side. Still, Storey-Moore (21 in the league, four in that glorious FA Cup run) and Baker (16 league; three in the Cup), were well adrift of their predecessors, even accounting for Baker's season being curtailed by injury after the FA Cup quarter-final win over Everton in April 1967.

Aside from goals, Capel boasted a compelling trick that warmed the hearts of Forest fans throughout his stay. This was his famous 'bicycle trick', a left-foot shimmy, better known to the modern fan as a device used by Chris Waddle, that Capel says he learned from a player during his Maine Road days. "I saw this guy do it once and thought 'I'll have a go at this'. I'd never seen anything like it. I used to cock my leg up if a player was at the side of me and stop. He'd stop as well and in one movement I'd move the ball forward and be gone, giving myself about four yards on the marker, who thought I was going to play a back heel."

Using his trick, in an era of few fancy flicks, Capel earned the tag of being the artist and entertainer amongst the Forest ranks and a loyal fan club of admirers.

In securing promotion the Capel and Ardron partnership had produced a prodigious effort that almost inevitably could not be sustained at the higher level. Three seasons knocking at the proverbial door were to prove fruitless for Forest. In Capel's fifth year with the club, he would be turning 32 in the summer of 1954, while his great pal Collindridge was nearer 34. He could sense the tide turning in Nottingham's football hierarchy, but knew it was time to move on also. "You knew Forest would move out of County's shadow because we had a much better youth set-up, there were good lads coming through like Bobby McKinlay and Jack Burkitt. County's team were much older and it was breaking up whereas we stayed together and consolidated after promotion. That was important and the manager [Billy Walker] knew that."

It was nevertheless an awkward departure – for both himself and Collindridge. "A chap who had a business in Beeston used to come and watch us training nearly every day. I think he wanted me to be on the board. Anyways, one day he stopped in the car park and asked me if I wanted to work for him in the afternoons. He had a huge provisions warehouse near the station in Beeston. There were no Tescos or big supermarkets in those days, so he employed travellers to go around the Midlands region with an order book and establish a collection round. I agreed and talked it over with Billy Walker; he was all right about it too. So I trained in the morning and went out in the company car he provided in the afternoons. Within about six months I'd built up a decent few clients. Most of them knew me and, while I was happy to talk football, I'd ask them how many tins of peas or corned beef they wanted to order off me!"

It was an ideal transitional period for a player needing to find his way in the big wide world post-football, especially with a five-year benefit of £750 due that summer. Not for the first time in Forest's history, or any other club for that matter, the delicate matter of finances caused a somewhat fractious reaction. Attendances had been good and Forest had finished fourth in Division Two in 1954 and Capel even scored in what transpired to be his final game for the club, a 3-1 win away to Oldham Athletic. Billy Walker was adamant, however, that the club could not afford to pay him and Collindridge, also owed £750 for his five-year benefit, the £1,500 to which the two players were entitled contractually.

"In the end, Coventry City came in for both me and Colin, so the club had no excuse not to pay us. But they tagged it on the end of our final wage packet, so part of the money got taxed at 19s 6d in the pound [97.5p]. Some benefit! Still, I came out with around £450, which was a good amount of money and I put a deposit down on a new house being built on Aspley Lane."

It was perhaps fitting that the left-wing partnership should depart in tandem, moving on unbowed and unbroken to Highfield Road in 1954. The pair left behind audiences they had delighted with precocious touches of flair and a left-sided legacy and love of that area of the pitch and its performers in particular that would be extended through Stewart Imlach, Ian Storey-Moore and John Robertson. "Apart from that pass to Scotty, me and Colly had this thing, I suppose you'd call it the wall pass. I'd stand up side of him and, as he lifted his leg to pass it inside, I'd lift mine to confuse the defender. Off he went sprinting to the corner flag and I'd just flick it with the outside of my left foot, bending it for him to run on to. Then he'd whip it in for one of our lads to get a touch on it. Mind you sometimes it didn't work. Sometimes, he'd get to the byline and get a cross in and the next thing he'd look around and see the ball nearly in the back of the Forest net!

"'Well, how did that happen then, Tommy?'

"'Well, I think you must be bloody colour blind, Colly.'

"'Why's that then?'

"'Because you've got past your man and slipped it to that bloody player in red. You gave him possession.'

"'Well, how did that happen?'

"'Colly we're playing in white today, our lad!' I used to remind him when we changed strips. [Teams would then only change when kits clashed, rather than automatically when playing away from home.] 'If you're going to dip into the near post today, Colly, look out for white. All right?'"

Perhaps neither player grew accustomed to the Sky Blue at Coventry. Their stay was brief, Capel going on to play for Halifax Town and then score almost at will for part-timers Heanor Town in his latter years, winning the old Midland League title at the first attempt under the stewardship of Kevin Rawson. Nottingham, though, remained a more permanent fixture in Capel's life. He lost his job at Beeston when the owner died and a new broom swept him away, but he found similar work as a travelling salesman for Burton's, that wonderful emporium of fresh food, fresh fish, freshly ground coffee and a whole host of aromas to entice the senses that dominated the shopping stalls beneath the Council House dome until its demise in the 1980s.

Vera continued to work at the London Brick Company offices off Bridlesmith Gate as Capel relentlessly worked on reducing his mortgage and handicap in the game of golf to which he was introduced at Forest. Later he would work for Trent Concrete and as a furniture maker in Colwick before retiring, aged 65, in 1987.

"I look back at Forest and they were the best days of my football career. That's part of the reason why we never considered moving back to Manchester. We'd been away too long, besides our friends there had got on with their lives. Me and Vera had left when we were so young and just married and we really liked Nottingham. The youngster had just been born here and people were very kind to us here and we made some good friends."

JUST AS LAWTON'S derby header is the stuff of legend, so Capel has a goal to cherish with an equally spectacular and explosive finish. Sadly, though, unlike Lawton's bomb of a header, it is not in the record books.

"When you were knocked out of the FA Cup in the early rounds the club always arranged a friendly because if you were not playing on an FA Cup weekend, there was no revenue coming in. So we had Bolton Wanderers down at the City Ground one Saturday afternoon. Nat Lofthouse and Malcolm Barrass, the England centre-forward and centre-half, were playing for them. There was a decent crowd in that day because of that attraction and with about 20 minutes to go we were 3-2 down. I think it was Bill Whare who played a ball down the line to Freddie Scott and as he did, I looked up and saw their goalkeeper on the penalty spot. I shouted to Scotty: 'Hey Fred, pull it square' and he rolled the ball just inside the centre circle where I was standing. I just hit if first time with my left foot and it went – ping – fifty yards. The goalkeeper turned his head this way as it went past him and hit his left-hand post then that way when it went across the line and hit the other one and then hit the back of the net. And you know the ball never went above about six inches from the ground. It was one of those leather balls that you struggled to get off the floor depending on the weather. I had a decent left foot that could hit a ball then. Well, it was brilliant; the crowd went into bloody uproar. It's the first time I've walked five yards back over the halfway line to restart the match having scored a goal.

"On the Monday, Billy Walker and the lads came out to measure it. It turned out to be 57 yards all in. They made a big wooden plaque to mark the occasion, one of the longest-range goals ever scored by a Forest player. It was in the trophy room beneath the main stand, but it went up in smoke when it got burned down [at home to Leeds United in 1968]. It was my finest goal ever, though."

Coffin-dodging Forest fans may recall Capel with a glint in their eye, but Tommy still retains his Manchester accent and a card that is the privilege of all ex-Manchester City players who belong to that association and entitles him to free entry to any games upon displaying it at the turnstiles. Forest, seemingly, do not have a similar fondness or fraternity for former players who helped to make the club what it is today.

In the interim, the imagery of bicycle tricks and a cultured left foot that graced with guile the beautiful game and occasionally blasted through it like a blunderbuss will have to suffice for Tommy Capel and his many admirers.

Jeff Whitefoot
1958-1967: 285 games, 7 goals

THE ROAD FROM Cleethorpes had been a long and winding one. Most routes to the east coast are fiddly and congested at the best of times; both today and in the summer of 1958, the dawdle factor was apparent. Mercifully there was one thing in Jeff Whitefoot's favour that flaming June day. He was heading west. Not exactly the uncharted Indjun-infested Wild West that settlers had to tame a few centuries ago in America, but nevertheless he was seeking something of a new life for himself and his wife Ellen and their fledgling family.

The three-hour trek came to a conclusion and journey's end in West Bridgford for the Busby Babe, who had joined Nottingham Forest just a few weeks earlier. It was an inauspicious first step, however. Rolling up like the Clampetts, the eccentric family from *The Beverly Hillbillies*, with the furniture van in tow, Whitefoot discovered the keys to his new kingdom were not there. "We'd been told the keys would be there with someone to greet us, but there was nobody. First day at the club and we were locked out of the house," Whitefoot says with a smile on his face. Contemporaries in the Forest side he was to join so auspiciously, vouch for a club that had moved up to the First Division a little too rapidly for its own good, the remnants of its Third Division roots evident in the manner of its operation.

There were mixed feelings for Whitefoot that day. After all, he had grown up among the elite of Old Trafford – in the team known to the world as the Busby Babes – and remains to this day the youngest player to make a debut for Manchester United, aged 16 years and 105 days when United played Portsmouth on 15 April 1950. On the other hand, Forest had offered an escape route from Grimsby Town, where he had languished for the previous two seasons since somewhat curiously opting for the Second Division backwater when departing United.

"In the end we had to send for the club secretary, Dennis Marshall, who came around with the right set of keys. It wasn't the greatest of first days, but believe me, Nell [his wife Ellen's pet name] was just delighted to get out of Cleethorpes!"

If it was not the most encouraging of fresh starts, once the teething problems were over, Whitefoot's arrival transpired to be an outstandingly inspired choice.

JOHN BRINDLEY BECAME a member of the Forest ground staff in 1964, during the latter stages of Whitefoot's Forest career, but remembers a half-back with casual grace and two impeccable feet. "I don't think I ever saw a bloke pass the ball with both his left and right foot so well," Brindley recalled a few weeks before his death on Easter Friday, 2007, aged 60. "He was a veteran by the time I joined, but I'd seen him play quite a lot before then. Jeff had class, you could see the Manchester United grooming in him. He was one of those players who seemed to have oceans of room and all the time in the world on the ball. But anyone who's played the game at any level knows how little time you get to dwell on the ball. It can be like a battlefield in the middle of the park so you know quality when you see it."

The word battle is apposite in Brindley's case. He was a solid, rugged full-back whose dedication on the pitch was matched by a flamboyance and colourful character off it, attributes that endeared him to fans on both sides of the Trent when he became one of the few players to make a successful transition from the south bank to the north. His place in Forest folklore may not equal that of Whitefoot or some of the illustrious names in this book, but he did make one significant contribution to City Ground history, scoring the fastest goal by a substitute when he touched in Alan Hinton's raking cross less than 20 seconds after coming off the bench in a 3-1 home win over Southampton. That was on 1 April 1967; his first and last competitive goal in Nottingham.

Whitefoot's place in Forest folklore is more spectacular, as is the team's passage into the sport's record books. At the time of writing, only he, Chic Thomson, the goalkeeper, and Billy Gray, the right-winger converted to inside-forward to devastatingly good effect by Billy Walker, remain alive from the 11 men that were reduced by one come Roy Dwight's injury, and thus became the first and, unless the rules alter dramatically, last side to win the FA Cup with a mere ten players.

Actually Whitefoot's impact in the Forest annals could have been far greater. Two years earlier he'd been in talks with manager Walker about a move to Forest when he was in the act of leaving Old Trafford, but they faltered over finances and a lack of communication. "He was a very funny chap," Whitefoot says. "I remember coming to the Forest to have talks, but I couldn't get a straight answer out of him. He seemed to cough and splutter a lot when I asked him key questions, so I thought this wasn't for me."

Thus he opted for the rigours of the east coast sea air and a two-year stay in Cleethorpes.

LIKE MANY OF HIS generation, Whitefoot learned to use both feet by sheer hard work, an ethic instilled in him by his headmaster when he was selected to play for Stockport in the English Schools Shield. He had joined the United ground staff in 1949, one of the first Busby Babes preceding the golden but doomed generation that was decimated on a snow-ravaged runway in Munich nine years later. His early football style was dictated by Jimmy Murphy, Matt Busby's indispensable right-hand man, whose motivational skills were legendary in the game. As an exemplar, Wilf McGuinness, just a few months older than Whitefoot when he was handed his debut aged 17 in 1955 and now an accomplished after-dinner speaker, tells the story of how one Friday night he was whisked away to the Norbreck Castle Hotel on Blackpool's promenade, a favourite refuge for United before home games and for team-bonding breaks. The following day, Wolverhampton Wanderers, the reigning champions and the other luxury liner of domestic football at the time, possibly even sleeker in cruise control than United, were the visitors to Old Trafford. "I'd left a note on the kitchen table saying 'Gone to Blackpool, picked in first team'," recalls McGuinness. "The next day I'm in the dressing room sitting in the corner as quiet as a mouse. Then Jimmy comes over to me and sees me a bag of nerves.

"'How have you got into the first team, Wilf?'

"'By listening to you, Jimmy.'

"'Well listen to me today. I hate black and gold.'

"'I hate black and gold as well Jimmy, so don't worry.'

"'Yes, but the player you're playing against is Peter Broadbent and he's an England international. And you know what, he's out to take the bonus out of your pocket, so you won't be able to go home tonight and treat your mother and father.'

"'Oh, give us that flaming ball, Jimmy.'"

Suitably wound up, McGuiness strode onto the Old Trafford pitch where Broadbent, hearing the rumour of a teenage debutant and recognising the youthful appearance that must be him, walked over quietly and patted him on the back.

"All the best today son."

"Sod off you thieving bastard!" came the McGuiness retort, almost frothing at the mouth.

United won 4-3, but Broadbent, the gentleman footballer that he was, still shook hands with McGuinness after the final whistle.

FUNNILY ENOUGH, IT WAS the Old Gold that also witnessed Whitefoot's debut in the red of Forest; a game as inauspicious as his attempts to move into his house a few weeks earlier. This time, Bobby Mason rattled in a hat-trick at Molineux as the home side won comprehensively. No disgrace, really, since that was the opening gambit in a title-winning campaign for the Black Country club, rounding off the decade with their third championship pennant of the 1950s.

Further irony and further despondency for the new recruit landed on Forest's doorstep during the next game, when Manchester United inspired a 44,971 crowd that bulged around the four corners of the City Ground on a hot August midweek evening. The game ended up 3-0 to United and Billy Walker may have mused about the nature of his summer reinforcements. Along with Whitefoot, Roy Dwight, a Billy Whizz winger from Fulham, and Joe McDonald, a full-back who bucked the trend of the day that required as essential priority for his ilk the ability to deposit wingers in the main stand, preferably Block B, Row Z for convenience, tempted from Sunderland as cover for the 30-something Geoff Thomas, had been signed to improve the squad. So far in 1958/59, the 97,627 who had seen Forest concede eight and score one – Dwight at Molineux – were probably less than convinced.

Whitefoot, though, was not regretting his choice. And neither was his wife Nell.

"I had some great times at Manchester United, but my chances of getting in the first team were being reduced all the time. These days, players would get their agents on the phone to start ringing around for them, but I just kept going in to see Matt Busby to see what the situation was. The club had been good to me since I was a lad and we were all on the same money, me, Jackie Blanchflower, Mark Jones, one of the few who had a car, a Ford. Matt kept telling me: 'Give it 18 months and we'll see.' By then Eddie Colman was beginning to emerge and that was when they decided they could let me go.

"After I had not seen eye to eye with Billy Walker, Grimsby suddenly came in for me out of the blue. I'd known their manager Allenby Chilton at Old Trafford, he was in the 1948 FA Cup-winning side. I drove down there with Nell and I remember her telling me when we arrived at Blundell Park, driving along Cleethorpes main road to get there, whatever I did: 'Please don't sign for Grimsby.'

"I don't know what possessed me, but I came out of the office and I'd agreed to sign. Nell was almost in tears. She calls it now my brainstormer. And we'd only been married six weeks!"

The newly-ish weds eventually moved in to Cleethorpes in January, one of several months of the year when the East Lincolnshire coastal resort is best avoided. Not that the locals weren't welcoming, their club house in Scafell Road was impressive and the cod and chips, well, legendary in fish and chip shop circles. But the club itself was wallowing around aimlessly like a gleam of hunted herring or a shoal of freshly netted haddock in a Grimsby trawler's hold. The mood was infectious.

"The training was terrible and nobody seemed to be too bothered and after a while I wasn't either," recalls Whitefoot. "I put on a stone in weight and my game just deteriorated. I think they named a trawler after me, but I'm not sure whether that was a compliment or not."

The combination of the fat-fryer in the local chip oil and the relatively sedate lifestyle on the East Coast, certainly in comparison to Manchester, led Whitefoot to seek a move. Urgently.

"I was knocking on the manager's door just about every day for a while, but he kept telling me there was no chance of me going. The chairman then was an FA councillor so he knew all the ins and outs of the legality of the situation. In the end, I made it as awkward as possible and they agreed, reluctantly, to let me go. Clubs had the upper hand then, no freedom of contract or anything like that. I got a telegram from Billy Walker telling me he wanted to talk. This time, my situation was totally different. I was desperate to get away from Grimsby. I met him in Nottingham and he told me that the club would pay £165 removals costs to help me settle and that Grimsby should pay the other half. Then, he said: 'Any trouble, any problems, see George.'

"'George who?'

"'George. He's got the newsagent's shop on Central Avenue. He'll sort you out.'

"It was all a bit strange, but I needed the move. That shop, incidentally, is where Brian Clough's son has his newsagent's now.

"I went back to see Chilton and he told me, no way were Grimsby going to pay £165. 'You'll get nothing out of me,' he said. They made it so difficult for me, but that's how clubs behaved then and that was even though I'd known Chilton at United. But when I look back it was absolutely the right move. In footballing terms, Forest were my salvation."

FROM CLEETHORPES TO West Bridgford may not sound the most romantic journey ever undertaken, but the Whitefoots' lives were transformed by the move. Nottingham entering the 1960s was in keeping with a society unsure about its future with the threat of Cold War implosion, a nuclear-powered sword of Damocles dangling over civilisation and, worse, George the fixer newsagent on Central Avenue.

Fortunately the Black Boy was still the social gathering point for young and old before an evening out on the town and the County Hotel and its Shire Bar, adjacent to the Theatre Royal, offered a touch of the quaintness associated with the departing decade. The George Hotel, at the top of Hockley and George Street, met the requirements for more refined sorts, which remarkably enough included professional footballers in its elitist ranks back then. Famous for one esteemed overnight guest the previous century, one Charles Dickens, writer, it was to embrace the age of celebrity, as did the 1960s, when Elizabeth Taylor and Richard Burton (married during that particular week) rested awhile there in between cocktails and performances at the local theatre; doubtless, in no special order, feasting, feuding or, er, fornicating.

The Palais de Danse still held its Wednesday afternoon tea dances, a rapidly vanishing etiquette of a more genteel era being engulfed by the modern trend, although the Plaisance Club, opposite the Embankment and Meadows across the River Trent, was a trenchant symbol that things were not quite as innocent and soft-centred as they may have seemed. Once a sporting pavilion donated by Jesse Boot, the wealthy philanthropist who founded Boots the Chemist and donated the land and many of the buildings upon which the University of Nottingham now stands, the clapperboard colonial style building eventually became known as the Yacht Club until the early 1950s. Under new ownership, it became a jazz club bordering on the sleazy, if not quite seedy side, that attracted late night revellers, after-hours drinkers, a few dodgy experimental spliffs or tablets and PC Plod in equal measure.

Drugs and alcohol did not surface on the average footballer's radar in 1958; there were no George Bests, Paul Mersons or Stan Collymores. The Forest side of that vintage were not angels by any means, as Whitefoot confirms, but in general the social scene was far more restrained rather than restricted or prohibitive. Away from the social niceties, Whitefoot perhaps thought the omens were against him when Portsmouth, against whom he had made that record-breaking debut for Manchester United, were next up at the City Ground. He need not have fretted. Scarcely 24,000 bothered to turn up following the Manchester United defeat, but reliable Roy Dwight was again on target. So were Johnny Quigley and Tommy Wilson, scoring two each in a 5-0 drubbing that was to set a precedent in what was to be a season of vastly undulating fortunes.

A few days later, the return with Manchester United and 51,880 at Old Trafford saw Forest deservedly snatch a point in a 1-1 draw. Wilson, the North East lad recruited from Cinderhill Colliery Welfare, scored, as Joe McDonald was effective and impressive on his

Forest debut. "The thing about Joe was that he liked to pass the ball to feet, which was unusual for full-backs of the day," recalls Whitefoot. "He'd rather get it down and try to play football whereas most others just wanted to get rid of it, hoof it down the pitch and let the forwards and half-backs scrap it out there. Joe was the exception to the rule, but that didn't mean that Bill Whare was any worse. He was just the old-fashioned style of full-back; hit anything that was in front of you."

And if that included the ball as well as the winger, well that was considered a bonus. The vagaries of that early First Division form book reveal a 4-0 thrashing of West Ham United, then a 4-1 reverse at Stamford Bridge in late September. A young Jimmy Greaves scored two for Chelsea that day, his first goals against Forest. Even Denis Law devotees may concede that Greaves was the finest goalscorer of his or any British generation. Forest folk might also concur. By the end of his increasingly alcohol-fuelled career, Greaves had scored another 27, the highest strike rate against the Forest by any player. And that included some infamously mysterious stomach bugs, which history subsequently would reveal as blinding hangovers. On three occasions, he had the audacity to score four goals – and, the cruellest blow of all maybe – he punished that incongruous Terry Hennessey error in the Hillsborough semi-final with Tottenham in 1967, which cost Forest a place at Wembley.

If the 1958/59 league form steadied, it was far from consistent, though sufficiently solid that relegation was never mooted. The same could have been said of the FA Cup during Forest's well-documented entrance and, almost, humbling exit in the third round at Tooting and Mitcham United. A frozen, rutted pitch undoubtedly narrowed the gap twixt Isthmian League amateurs and First Division pros, yet the Sandy Lane environs, brimming to the rafters with 14,000 fans, was to be the home side's undoing. Two-nil up, a terrible bounce resulted in an own goal of farcical proportions from a routine back pass, then another unpredictable movement off a frozen divot elicited a dubious handball decision and a penalty from which Billy Gray gratefully restored parity with a quarter of an hour remaining. The job was completed with a 3-0 victory in the replay.

Whitefoot's goal against Grimsby in the next round, his first for the club, was a moment to savour – not least for it being against the side he had escaped from so recently. He scored his second and last of the season a week later, also at the City Ground, in the 3-0 league victory over Bolton Wanderers.

ABOVE ALL, 1959 was an exciting time to be a Forest fan. The side was playing a brand of football ahead of its time, an eclectic mix of young and old, fearless and downright dangerous, whizzing the ball around with a varying degree of success. When it worked, it was magical. When it went pear-shaped, it could be mayhem. But always entertaining. Remarkable given the input of management.

"I think the team largely took care of itself," Whitefoot maintains. "It was similar to Manchester United in that Tommy Graham [assistant to Billy Walker] took most of the training as did Jimmy Murphy [Busby's assistant at Old Trafford]. He'd get us to run out of the tunnel during the week, jog a few laps and a few sprints on Tuesday and Friday mornings. It wasn't a case of tactics or team talks. The thing about that Forest team is that it just all gelled in the one season."

A season which, of course, culminated in one of Nottingham's most joyous and celebrated sporting occasions on 2 May 1959; the FA Cup final at Wembley Stadium, *Abide with Me* and the traditional and fitting finale to a football season. Birmingham City (at the third time of asking), Bolton Wanderers and Aston Villa, through Johnny Quigley's opportunist effort in the semis, three finalists from the previous three years, had all been removed en route. That left as final opponents Luton Town, conquerors of giant-slayers Third Division Norwich City at the semi-final stage. Which left no Manchester United or Wolverhampton Wanderers to entice viewers. And which left the nation hanging by a boiling kettle, manual lawnmower or rapidly drying paint on a garden fence as an alternative to the FA Cup final. Boring. Even the BBC intermission breaks, the potter's wheel and the cuddly playful kittens discovering the delights of a cotton ball of *Mrs Dale's Diary*, would be preferable and more engrossing. Surely.

Fortunately, sport has always been a pastime full of surprises: the first exchange of banners between opposing captains at a Wembley Cup final, Jack Burkitt and Syd Owen doing the honours and a team of twirling keep-fit fanatical women from Coventry before kick-off; the Queen and the Duke of Edinburgh as well as Field Marshal Montgomery among the dignitaries. More jolting even than the royal presence and an impromptu Swamp Dance performance (River

Dancers everywhere owe a debt to those plucky lassies) was the football at its finest that uniquely cohesive Nottingham Forest team unleashed on an unsuspecting audience – 100,000 in the Empire Stadium and viewers at home, and a bewildered Luton Town.

With Stewart Imlach imperious on the left and Roy Dwight darting on the right, Forest were 2-0 up within half an hour. It was Imlach's cross that created Dwight's opener, Billy Gray's delicately floated centre that invited Tommy Wilson to head a second. Then, a shade after 30 minutes, Dwight was off, an innocuous challenge by Luton full-back Brendan McNally fracturing a bone in his right leg. Dave Pacey pegged one back for Town as ten-man Forest flagged in the heat of the second half, but after 61 years, Forest had secured the FA Cup for a second, and thus far, last time.

The champagne came late, but once the bubbly had been glugged, the players dashed to the hospital bed from where Dwight had watched those nail-shredding closing minutes of the final. It had been a group effort from day one. This was truly a team that would not be divided.

In a marvellously euphoric state, the people of Nottingham paid tribute the following day. Nearly a quarter of a million of them lined the route from the City Ground, along the Embankment and onwards to the Council House's civic reception. It was a spontaneous moment in time – of its time. "The whole experience, the Cup run, the final, the procession, it was incredible," Whitefoot says. "That team played some fantastic football, I mean really fantastic. To feet, all the time, quick and sharp. There was no stopping us on the day. Remember that, after the semi-final, we hardly won a league game [three in 13 in fact, including a 5-1 defeat at Luton Town].

"It was an amazing year, my first for the club. Simply amazing. There was a great camaraderie, not because we socialised together really. We all went out now and again, but others, like Jack Burkitt, kept themselves to themselves. Nothing wrong with that at all. There were lads who liked a drink, liked a bet and liked the ladies. Some more than others, but nothing has changed there in football. But that day at Wembley, I honestly believe we would have gone on to score five or six – maybe more. Might have broken the Cup final record. You could sense it, the way we were playing. Roy's injury put an end to that. The final whistle was just a blessed relief. We were all absolutely on our knees by then. Totally cream-crackered."

WHITEFOOT IS IN AN enviable position of being able to gauge the transition from the gentleman footballers of the 1950s to the new breed of rebellious, fractious players that suddenly became rather well off overnight when the maximum wage was abolished in 1961. "It didn't really affect me or many others at Forest, I can tell you. The most I ever earned was about £40 a week and never more than £4 for a win bonus. I remember when I was doing my National Service in the Air Force with United I was on £6 a week with a bit of expenses. But then I suppose our mortgage was £9 a month when I was playing for Forest, so money didn't really bother you too much. There was always enough. I was a veteran when the likes of Ian Storey-Moore and Henry Newton were coming into the first team. It's hard to compare our team with theirs. We had no star players, but we played some incredible football."

In the age of relative innocence, with modest investment from purely domestic sources, more often than not localised ones at that, most clubs endured the famine and the feast as a matter of course. The world was not ready for media and dot.com tycoons from the colonies, as the Soviet Union was not prepared to embrace capitalist oligarchs – just yet at any rate. Satellites were generally called Sputnik or Telstar and had a negligible effect on sports broadcasting or even television drama, which appeared to be happily sating its audience with *Dr Finlay's Casebook* and *Z-Cars*.

How choice and diversity have diluted the market into celebrity claptrap or vapid vanity, the equivalent of the pound shop live in your front room with an ubiquitous regal ghost just waiting to materialise at the drop of a budget or feature from the schedule. 'Tunnel vision' as it's known in programme-planning circles.

Forest's plight was virtually inevitable since the team that secured the FA Cup was an ageing one and among football's many unforgiving and fickle traits, its lack of sentimentality is perhaps one of its cruellest.

Right-back Bill Whare retired in November 1959 and, within a season or just over, fellow Wembley heroes Chic Thomson (Rugby Town), Stewart Imlach (Derby County) and goalscorer Roy Dwight (Gravesend and Northfleet), as well as Tommy Wilson (Walsall), who headed the crucial second, had all moved on. In 1961 as Jack Burkitt also retired, Joe McDonald joined Wisbech Town. The manager, too, departed, after another below-par league season followed the Cup-winning one; Billy Walker citing ill health as one of the reasons for his leaving after 21 years in charge.

Whitefoot, however, remained to his retirement in 1967 when, in keeping with a fine tradition, he became a publican, owning, amongst other well-frequented beer stops, the Three Horseshoes at the south Notts village of East Leake. During those latter years, he witnessed Forest's initial foray into European competition, participating in the Inter Cities Fairs Cup in 1961. They might have wished that the invitation had gone missing in the post after losing the first leg 2-0 to Spanish maestros Valencia in Spain in September. Next month, coinciding with the arrival of the annual Goose Fair on the first Thursday in October and perhaps as a mark of respect, the City Ground resembled a coconut shy as Valencia clobbered Forest 5-1, a result which featured an immaculate Nunez hat-trick and two from Machado Waldo, described by *Evening Post* reporter and later sports editor Harry Richards as a 'Brazilian bombshell'.

No matter how good the execution that night, few goals are recalled with such fondness and incredulity as Dick 'Flip' Le Flem's weaving solo that helped beat championship challengers Burnley at the start of December 1962. "Sheer brilliance," Whitefoot recalls of what is largely considered to be among Forest's finest finishes, alongside Storey-Moore's exquisite 80-yard dash and shot against Arsenal a decade later. By then, Andy Beattie, the former Scottish international full-back, had been appointed to replace Walker – much to Whitefoot's utter ambivalence. "It was a disaster for Forest. He was such a dour Scot, couldn't really get his message across. But he started to chip away at things, for instance we had always gone to the Test Match in West Bridgford for a pre-match meal, steak or whatever, before a home game. Under Andy, that all stopped and he got the lads at a café bar in Central Avenue. I mean, we were all there in our suits and ties and there were punters all around having egg and chips and so on. It wasn't the best preparation for a game, believe me."

In mitigation, Beattie had joined a side already bottom of the First Division having won just two of nine games at the start of the 1960/61 season. Usually the influence of a new boss motivates and invigorates, but Forest were defeated in each of Beattie's first seven league games in charge, a 4-2 win at West Ham United in November being his first and one that, perversely, inspired a seven-match unbeaten sequence through December that included six invaluable victories.

He had inherited a fading squad, although young talent, Peter Grummitt and Henry Newton for example, was on the horizon, but his unpopularity with the fans and players like the now-dropped Whitefoot forced a change. Happily for the latter it was Johnny Carey, a former Manchester United colleague and captain of the famously skilful United side that beat Blackpool in the 1948 FA Cup final. Unlike Allenby Chilton, another United 1948 Cup winner who had fallen out with Whitefoot when in charge of Grimsby, Carey restored 29-year-old Whitefoot to the side and set about rebuilding with his half-back as a pivotal figure. It was during this time that Whitefoot would perform one last significant and honourable service to Forest and football: one which, if for no other reason, should see his name writ large in history. Footballers of a certain vintage may bemoan the lack of financial incentive in the game to play well and win football matches. But what about the incentive to play badly and lose?

The early 1960s were infamous for betting and bribery scandals that infiltrated football, from the very bottom clubs to the top, from Mansfield Town to Doncaster Rovers to Sheffield Wednesday. Though the players received only a tiny fraction of any dodgy money, the jail sentences imposed on Sheffield Wednesday trio Peter Swan, David Layne and Tony Kay and a *sine die* ban on their involvement in professional football was an example to others tempted down that path.

On Tuesday 14 January 1964 temptation came that way for Whitefoot when plumber's merchant and Forest fan Derek Pavis rang him and asked him to call in at his New Basford premises, where he might find something to his advantage. The pair were social friends, both living in West Bridgford, so Pavis's approach was smooth and easy. Contemporaneous clippings from the *Guardian Journal* and *Nottingham Evening Post and News* tell the story of what happened next.

"How would you like to earn £500?" Pavis asked Whitefoot. His task was to ensure Forest lost their next First Division game, at home to Stoke City. To his credit, Whitefoot replied: "I am not interested, not for £500 or £5,000."

Whitefoot duly informed Forest officials, who then tipped off the police about the attempted bribe. Although initially selected in the first XI, he was withdrawn with what was described as a 'back injury'. A late reshuffle in formation restored Henry Newton to half-back and celebrated a debut for 17-year-old Robert 'Sammy' Chapman up front alongside Frank Wignall. Sammy Chapman, ironically, was the same name as one of the Mansfield Town footballers implicated in the nationwide bribery scandal of that year who was also handed a custodial jail sentence.

The lurid details of the Pavis scam emerged as police first investigated the allegations, then brought charges against the 33-year-old plumber's merchant. Bear in mind that £500 represented around half a year's salary for the average professional then. Hard to imagine a poorly-paid plumber, but that sort of money probably translated into a year's salary for most young men qualified in the trade.

Two months later, Pavis's case was heard in Nottingham Shire Hall, where he admitted trying to bribe Whitefoot, whose reputation and good name as a former England Under-23 international and Forest FA Cup winner was unblemished. The web of intrigue was never totally unravelled. Pavis's cut was £200 for what would be called today 'facilitating' the deed. If he had been successful, he claimed, he was to meet a man, identity unknown, at the left hand lion of the Council House.

The defence for Pavis cited Forest's poor form – Frank Wignall's opener against Fulham on 22 February in a 2-0 win was the first City Ground goal of the new year and their first home win in the league for 16 weeks. Yet despite evidence of Pavis's good character and the publicity already inflicted upon his business, the magistrates felt compelled to impose the maximum penalty – a £50 fine in breach of the Prevention of Corruption Act, 1906 which if not paid on time would result in a three-month custodial sentence. Mr AC Flewitt, chairman of the bench, summed up: "We feel that to prevent this sort of thing happening and corrupting British sport and fair play we must inflict the highest fine we are allowed to." Pavis was also ordered to pay £21 costs.

The grubby episode did not tarnish Whitefoot's career; if anything it cemented his place as a decent professional among his peers during anxious times in the industry.

Pavis would return, unsuccessfully, to Forest (see the Brian Clough chapter) and oversee a modicum of success at Notts County. But whatever his achievements in Nottingham sport, the dignified refusal of a humble professional of his tawdry offer should remain an example as a code of conduct for all sportsmen.

WHITEFOOT'S ENDURING GRACEFUL presence as a creative half-back, linking up with Johnny Quigley and Billy Gray, are also memories that many Forest fans will take to the grave. "Looking back, it was a great time to play football. Even when it rained and the balls shipped in water it was bloody hard trying to get the thing in the air and out of the centre circle. I really would like to see some of the modern players having a go with a ball like that, on a quagmire of a pitch and with our boots on. Even at Forest I've known it like a bog in January, and that was a great pitch. Johnny Carey's team talk was always telling us to 'fizz it about boys', but there were some days when you just couldn't do that.

"The game has changed so much. I get invited to Manchester United dinners and I keep telling Fergie [Sir Alex Ferguson, the Manchester United manager] not to play any of the young bucks I see coming through the ranks. One of them being the youngest United player in the first team is going to take my meal ticket away. It is funny, though. I was at one dinner recently and they were auctioning off the chance to shake hands with the United Player of the Year at the annual ceremony. It was going to be Ronaldo and this auction was to help present the prize and shake hands with the winner. Nothing more. Anyway some lunatic at the back eventually coughed up £10,000 for the privilege. And he sent his son to collect the prize because he was too shy!"

Whitefoot is now retired near Melton Mowbray, on the Leicestershire/Rutland border, having spent his final working years in a splendid local boozer in Oakham near the gated entrance of the renowned public school. He stopped going to see Forest during the Matt Gillies regime. "They refused to renew my complimentary ticket allocation, talking about budget restrictions etc. And they were struggling to get 10,000 through the turnstiles. I gave it up after that."

When Forest played Luton Town in the 1989 League Cup final, then sponsored by Littlewoods, the Cup final team of 30 years previous were belatedly honoured at Wembley as guests of the club. Now only the three, Thomson, Gray and Whitefoot, remain. Whitefoot, composed and cunning on the ball, delivers a fittingly incisive verdict on his old mates, those still able to pass wind and water or those passed away.

"It was a team of misfits who gelled and came together in one magical year. Don't ask me how and why, because I don't know. What I do know is that I played in some great sides and with some great players at Manchester United and I've seen the best like Duncan Edwards come through. They set a standard for how football should be played. But I can honestly say that the Forest side of 1959 played the best football I have ever seen, and that includes the fabled Busby Babes of Manchester United. Quite simply it was the best football side I have ever been part of."

Henry Newton

1960-1971: 315 games, 19 goals

HE WAS THE classic cult hero of the 1960s. Wiry in frame, quiet in his demeanour, a thick head of hair and handsome face that disguised a silent sort who kept his own counsel, but seldom had to stray far to find trouble. Mainly because trouble, and plenty of it, would often find him during the course of his weekly performance.

Fortunately, here was one man who knew how to handle himself in the rough and tumble world in which he earned a living. Physical contact was frequent, sometimes brutal, but however many wounds he sustained, Newton always appeared to have the final and decisive word or blow before full time.

Anyone above a certain age reading this will know of course that the enigmatic hero of the piece was McGill, aka actor Richard Bradford, who regularly took the cuts and bruises but still came out on top against the bad guys as the eponymous *Man in a Suitcase*, an ITC production that was screened on the ITV networks during the middle of the decade. A disgraced former CIA agent thrown out of the organisation (of course he was framed), the American McGill plied his trade as a freelance and naturally maverick private investigator helping keep the pendulum of justice swinging in tandem with the decade, trendy London and his brooding temperament.

His christian name was even more cherished than Morse's. Viewers never did discover what it was, but our Transatlantic cousin retains a position of esteem and popularity among audiences whose alternative television included *The Prisoner* and *Adam Adamant*, but not *Crossroads* or *The Saint*. Apart from his angular good looks, McGill filled the role of tacit hard man, patrolling dangerous territory but never afraid of a challenge, never shirking the opportunity to get stuck in and defend a cause, and he was a perfect analogy for Henry Newton.

In fairness, Newton's hair was black, not grey like the American thespian's. And being acknowledged by only his surname might have left him vulnerable to being nicknamed after the Rovers Return's favourite brewery, Newton and Ridley. Then again, intellectuals could have argued against Newton's Law of Gravity on his behalf. Those he kicked up, maliciously or otherwise, were not always destined to fall back down to terra firma. Not without a degree of discomfort at any rate. But in every other sense, Newton was the midfield linchpin who tidied up the mess, covered for others in their absence and was the first on the scene if violence erupted. And by the way, as Bill Shankly once added in gloriously deliberate understatement after dismissing Bobby Moore in an Anfield team talk as a playboy drunk likely to have been inebriated the night before, "the boy can play a bit as well".

EVERY FOREST FAN OF 1960s ilk will talk, and rightly so, about Ian Storey-Moore, Joe Baker and Terry Hennessey, as well as John Barnwell's intricate passing game, but it was Newton's selfless contribution, making him the ultimate team player, that not only inspired his popularity, but also made him the thinking man's cult hero.

I interviewed Newton at his Derby home late in the summer of 2007. Perhaps you can recall the time and date. It was a Thursday, around 2pm and the sun was shining. In between the monsoon, arctic blizzards and persistent gales that otherwise inhabited the British Isles from May to September. Newton was building a house to the front of his immaculate lawned garden, a home for his daughter Sarah and her husband and his grandchildren Harry and Holly. His energy and enthusiasm for the task seemed boundless, matching the relish with which he tackled games and opponents after being signed as an apprentice by Billy Walker the season after the Reds had won the FA Cup against Luton Town in 1959.

Four years later, in December 1964, the young Newton would be one of the pallbearers at Walker's funeral. Storey-Moore, Frank Wignall and Peter Grummitt were among the others.

His stamina and appetite for a battle were immediately striking hallmarks of his game. When Newton returned two weeks late to pre-season training after a hernia operation, far more complicated and extended in recuperation in the early 1960s than today's keyhole surgery, new trainer Tommy Cavanagh, a stickler for fitness, was determined to make him pay for his unavoidably tardy attendance. Despite Cavanagh's best efforts, which often had other players regurgitating ill-advisedly consumed corn flakes earlier that morning along with last night's liquid consumption, Newton proved as fit as the rest despite his fortnight's delay. The pair then became good friends when Cavanagh realised he had a thoroughbred on his hands.

Storey-Moore remembers Newton as a box-to-box player, one whose engine room and ability would see him survive with ease in the Premiership today. "Running just came naturally," says Newton, relaxing with a cold cup of tea as the sound of scaffolding being riveted into place disturbs the afternoon hush and sunshine on his patio. "We'd run behind a horse and cart up around Balloon Woods, potato picking in the summer. You got paid by the bucketload. In the winter, I'd get three paper rounds for after school [William Sharp, at Bilborough] and finish them with a couple of mates before running down to the City Ground if there was a midweek game on then."

Newton is not one to reminisce, mind you. His father Jack died of lung cancer when he was just 14, leaving his mother Nellie to lend the support that took him into the precarious business of professional football. Years later, he met an old teacher from William Sharp who told him it came as no surprise that he moved to Everton (in 1970) because the club was desperate to sign him as a schoolboy. It was Forest, though, who prevailed and Newton suddenly discovered a home from home.

"I suppose it was a unique period in that the likes of Ian [Storey-Moore], Peter [Grummitt] and Peter [Hindley] and John [Winfield] were all coming through the ranks. There was a real family atmosphere about the place. I have to say if I go down to the club nowadays, there isn't that same genuine feeling to it anymore."

The big freeze that saw football postponed in this country for a month around the cusp of 1962/63 deprived Newton of his debut under Andy Beattie. He had to wait until the following season when a Tuesday night home game with the lesser of two devilish east Midlands rivals, Leicester.

"The team sheet went up and my name was on it, which was something of a surprise to say the least. I remember Johnny Carey [who succeeded Beattie] coming into the dressing room and asking me if I felt nervous.

"'A wee bit boss.'

"'Well, I'm not nervous at all. You are ready for this otherwise I wouldn't have picked you.' It made me feel so much better."

A 2-0 victory ensued, goals from Colin Addison and Frank Wignall sending the Foxes home with tails between their legs down the Fosse Way and thus a relationship of trust and reciprocated promise was established between old school manager and aspiring player.

Of course Carey, captain of the 1948 Manchester United side that beat Blackpool 4-2 in one of Wembley's most captivating but unsung FA Cup finals, already knew the potential he possessed with Newton. Jack Burkitt, a Forest institution, but another not feted by the football world at large or recognised by England selectors, had returned to the club as reserve team coach after captaining the 1959 FA Cup final side.

"There were people like Joe Mallet, who was a great influence on me, and Frank Knight at the club as well as Tommy Graham, although he was mostly involved with first team coaching," says Newton. "But the whole place was full of people who made it a family club, like Jeff Whitefoot, who was one of the nicest blokes to walk through the City Ground doors. And then along came Jack Burkitt, who was a massive hero to us all and well respected by the young lads. He was a great player who could pass the ball but also very rarely lost a challenge. He used to show us how to block tackle; he'd ask us to come up and tackle him and you could see with some of the frailer lads, he was being a bit gentle, just resisting. The challenge was to put him on his backside and, even with some of the bigger lads, you could see he was holding back a bit.

"Then he'd tell me to come and tackle him and I knew he wasn't pulling out of anything. I got the full treatment, but gradually I won more than I lost, though I never did put him on his backside. But I think he was proud of that. Because he showed me how to tackle fairly, not late with trailing studs or trying to hurt anyone deliberately. And I think he was proud of that as well."

Johnny Quigley, lately lamented by Forest fans, was one of those who suffered as Newton's boyish zeal went into overdrive. After one Tuesday morning practice match when the novice had been asked to mark the seasoned inside-forward, as he was going to be shadowed in the next First Division game, Quigley hardly had a kick of the ball without the young snapper at his heels. "You know I got into bed last night and I was bloody well looking for you under the blankets," Quigley remarked the following day to his nemesis, who was doubtless brimming with the pride that the old-timer had meant to imbue in him.

THE RECORD BOOKS SHOW that Newton was quickly in the thick of the action as he became a first team regular in the 1963/64 season. Taken off for 15 minutes with a nasty cut above the eye in a 3-2 away win over Wolverhampton Wanderers in January; sidelined for a similar length of time with a rib injury during a 1-0 home defeat to Blackpool. At least Richard Bradford had doubles for his fight scenes!

Newton's and Forest's progress was unrelenting. Amazingly so for a whippet of a lad who had been exiled to the left wing for Nottingham Schoolboys because his tiny frame was considered not meaty enough for the midfield maelstrom, even at that pubescent level. Like Storey-Moore his face appeared on the Esso coins for the preliminary 1970 World Cup final squad. "I remember playing in an England practice match and a report came back that I should be made to shuffle onto my right foot because I was so left-footed," says Newton. "I thought that was interesting because I have always been right-footed. My dad taught me to kick with both feet, that's what you did then."

But let's be honest, it was those midfield contretemps with some of the biggest bruisers in a football industry where men were men and sheep were fearful of the tackle from behind that elevated Newton to cult status in Nottingham.

It was at that time that Newton shared a bedroom with Norman Hunter. Unexpected guests or unwelcome intruders were few and far between. Imagine dropping in on Hannibal 'Bite your legs' Hunter and Henry 'Neutraliser' Newton. Survival chances were not high.

"He's actually a really nice bloke," says Newton. Well they all say that, don't they, though in this case it happens to be true. "To be honest there were a lot of hard men around at the time, but none of them really frightened me. Why should they? I never went in for the Jimmy Case or Graeme Souness style of tackling where they would leave their studs showing. Don't get me wrong, they were hard lads, but it just wasn't necessary.

"Tommy Smith was a genuinely hard full-back, but a bit of a pussycat really. He could hurt people but his growl was far worse than his bite. In my early days, though, I once had to look out for Paddy Crerand. He was coming to the end of a great playing career with Manchester United and I had dumped him on his backside early in the game. It was a fair challenge, but he didn't like it and for the rest of the game I had one eye on him. I felt I had to watch myself, especially as I was just a kid at the time."

Retribution came in many ways, however.

"The hardest man I ever came up against was Andy Lochhead. I mean he was an animal in that no matter how much stick you gave him, he gave more back. In one game, he made an awful gash in Bob McKinlay's leg, and we all know that Bob was such an elegant centre-half, who played it hard but fair. Then he ripped Terry Hennessey's shins to pieces as well. Lochhead took it well, though, but he was one of those blokes who seemed superhuman, that nothing could hurt him.

"Then there was Ron Harris. He was a decent schoolboy international and made his reputation as a hard man. I suppose 'Chopper' was about right for his nickname. I remember at Stamford Bridge he whacked Ian [Storey-Moore] early on. Well that was the tactic in that season we were flying [1966/67], any season come to think of it. We'd try to get the ball out to Mugsy as quickly as possible, but as far as the likes of Ron Harris were concerned, if you could kick him good and proper early on, their job was done.

"He did as much at Stamford Bridge, and I walked over to him. He thought he could stare you out with some bulging eyes and a mean expression.

"'What you staring at, you Mongol?'"

Newton's inquisition did not meet with approval. Neither did his later remark when the by now less anger-inflated Harris ventured over the half-way line.

"Be careful now, you're going to get lost and not find your way back if you're not careful," Newton reminded the full-back normally reticent of departing his defensive domain. Suffice to say, Harris was not amused.

"Some tried to intimidate or frighten you with a bit of a stare. But to be honest, the real hard men just got on with it without the theatrics," recalls Newton. "Peter Storey and Peter Simpson at Arsenal were among those. At Forest we just got on with it as well, but we looked after one another. There were the likes of Peter Hindley and John Winfield. They weren't hard men, but they were fit and they could play. Fans used to have a go at John, who was a decent wing-half. He seemed to be a bit ungainly because of his frame, but he could read the game superbly. He couldn't have survived at left-back so long without that.

"McKinlay was just, well, majestic and John Barnwell played those little triangles where he would pirouette and make the passes. But Terry Hennessey always said he preferred it when I was sitting in there. It gave him a licence to go and play. Barnwell knitted us together and gave us variation; Terry was just world class. But none of us could have played without each other, and the beauty was we all recognised that.

"I think perhaps that I might have scored more goals if I had been more selfish, but that wasn't me. I used to get the ball and give it to the likes of Barney, who I thought could do better with it for the good of the team. It makes me laugh when people say I left Forest just for the money when I went to Everton. If that was the case, I could have gone to Liverpool or Arsenal earlier in my career. Glory never really interested me and when I was with the England squad, I was happy to merge into the background.

"I was annoyed when the club let Terry Hennessey go to Derby. I knew Cloughie had been after me before, but my only dream had been to play for Forest, retire at Forest and then possibly manage them.

"Sounds daft now, but that was how it was for me. I didn't want to leave Forest when I went to Everton, the board had accepted a bid [£150,000 plus Tommy Jackson valued at £10,000 making Newton the third most expensive British footballer behind Martin Peters and Allan Clarke] and I went. But suggestions that I was bitter because I was left out of the final 1970 World Cup squad because I was only with a little club like Forest were simply untrue.

"As a Forest fan, it was great when we brought the likes of John Barnwell, Chris Crowe and later Jim Baxter to the club. There was a buzz about the place. But I carried on playing in the way I had been taught by Jack Burkitt, the right way. I used to apologise to players if I kicked them by accident, I can honestly say that I didn't kick anyone who didn't deserve kicking."

And in the hard men's manual, that has to be the definitive statement of intent.

NEWTON ADMITS THAT he was not one to remonstrate with officials or colleagues, but occasionally a latent but potent anger got the better of him.

"Sammy Chapman was a player who I always felt should have gone further than he did," says Newton. "He had what I would call lapses of concentration. I remember I used to bawl him out on the pitch regularly because of it, then one day he came into the players' bar where my mother-in-law was having a drink. She'd become a football expert by then and Sammy went up to her and said: 'Please tell Henry to stop getting on at me. And would you also tell him that my mother and father are married!'

"Sammy was a great lad. I remember after I left to join Everton I would bump into him as Forest were gradually slipping down the First Division [they were relegated in 1972, two seasons after Newton left]. Sammy had been one of the younger lads when I was there and he told me how those lads, like him and Billy Brindley coming through, looked up to me and the likes of Mugsy [Storey-Moore] and Peter [Hindley]. He said the lads were prepared to take some stick and verbals from us, but they were not going to stand for it from the new lot, he mentioned Tommy Jackson. The club was in decline. It's amazing to think what role models we were to those younger lads and the influence we had on them."

Newton was by then established at Goodison Park, although initially the move to Merseyside was not the smoothest.

Newton had married Hazel, a young Arnold girl he had met at the Locarno at the bottom of St Ann's Wells Road during his formative years at Forest. The ballroom has become a bingo hall and goodness knows what since its heyday, removed like the St Ann's district and its indigenous population from its roots and *raison d'être* by urban development and sponge-minded local council policy many last dances ago.

"Harry Catterick [the Everton manager] knew that I used to play golf at Southport with a group of lads from Nottingham," recalls Newton. "That was a year or more before I joined the club. He had been checking up. The club put me in a hotel just outside Liverpool, great for Goodison, but a long journey to the training ground [Bellefield]. I kept travelling back to Nottingham on a regular basis. I suppose I was a bit homesick because I never really wanted to leave Forest. One day the manager called me in and queried my hotel bills.

"'Usually we're having a go at players for overspending and putting things on expenses but your bills are so low,' Catterick told me.

"'I just keep nipping back home.'

"'Nipping. You can't pop back to Nottingham [these were the days of the Salt Box café and the laborious trek along the single carriageway from the M6 through Derby]. How long does it take you?'

"'About two and a half hours.'

"'I've never done it in less than three. But that's five hours a day. Not good, Henry.'

"Everton moved me into a hotel closer to the city centre and Harry told me to put a few extras on the bill and invite the lads round for a bit of social and game of cards. They could not have been better or more accommodating in trying to help me settle."

IT WAS AT GOODISON that I first met Henry Newton. I was still at Fairham school at Clifton, nurturing ground of Viv Anderson and Peter Wells, and playing for Ilkeston Town in the Southern League north division, and Everton had invited me for a trial.

Much as predicting the denouement in the latest episode of *Z-Cars* in digs near Stanley Park and the prospect of cleaning Howard Kendall's boots were appealing to aspiring apprentices in 1972, it didn't quite do it for someone trying to cope with Russian grammar and the Cyrillic alphabet while trying to overthrow society, or at least the tyrannical lower-sixth careers teacher.

But then there was always the football.

The home dressing room for the reserve team game with Bolton Wanderers was brimming with what panellists on the contemporaneous *New Faces* would call 'star quality'. Jimmy Husband,

Howard Kendall's boots and the dulcet Welsh tones of goalkeeper Dai Davies. And me and Henry Newton.

"When you get the ball, just look up and I'll be around to take it," was Newton's advice once he had discovered a) my Nottingham roots and b) the nervous disposition that was turning into naked fear in one corner of a dressing room that would have housed five Clifton families back in the 1970s. Even with a young chunk of concrete on legs by the name of Sam Allardyce on the opposing side, Newton never flinched from his promise. Five yards away, he was always available for the short pass that extricated this youngster from the mire.

As his old schoolmaster had alluded, it was almost destiny that took Newton to Everton, even though Brian Clough had pressed for his signature as he began to shape Derby County into a side capable of European glory and outstaying Liverpool as a domestic and foreign power during the 1970s.

Forest chairman Tony Wood's dislike of Clough and Hennessey's previous route down the A52 effectively ended that departure route. Yet Catterick's admiration of Newton dated back to what the player believes was his finest moment in a Forest shirt when Everton, the holders, were beaten in that epic FA Cup quarter-final at the City Ground in April 1967.

"It was during that Cup run that you felt the crowd really was beginning to become part of the game, part of the club. I remember running out for the third round game with Plymouth Argyle at the City Ground and you always had the 'Pop' stand and the Trent End giving you vocal support, but suddenly the Main Stand, who never really shouted, were joining in as well. We thought: 'Flipping heck, what's going on here?'

"That carried on for the entire run and reached a crescendo for that Everton game. I've never played in an atmosphere like it.

"It was one of my best games, but the daft thing was I played with a broken toe which I'd done a couple of weeks ago away to Sheffield Wednesday. We'd come back and I went straight to the old General Hospital where our surgeon, Mr Jackson, diagnosed a fractured toe. The manager [Carey] asked if I would be fit to play in the Cup tie and he said that I would have to go into plaster straight away. But there was a compromise and I wore a light plaster cast. On the day, I wore my own boot on the left foot and one of young apprentice Steve

Pegram's on my right. It was about a size too big, so there I was with these odd boots on. On *Match of the Day* Kenneth Wolstenholme was saying about me that one day this boy must play for England. If only he'd known..."

That crushing disappointment of losing to Tottenham Hotspur in the semi-finals, without Joe Baker who was injured in that Everton defeat, still rankles with Newton. Though not as much as it did at Hillsborough that day.

"I know we would have beaten Tottenham with Joe in the side, but then it made matters worse when we lost Wiggy [Frank Wignall] during the game. The worst thing was that I knew it was Dave Mackay's doing, he played a big part in it because Wiggy was giving Mike England a torrid time. For that match I hated Dave Mackay, I wanted to get him off the field one way or another. I don't think I hated a man more in my life. Funny, when he became manager of Derby County after Cloughie signed me then left, I got to know him really well. Of course he was a real hard man, but he never went in with his studs and he was doing what he had to do that day. I now know him as a superb friend and in a different class and one of the people I could call upon if I needed help."

LEAPING IN BETWEEN beams and rafters, climbing precarious ladders, Newton's nimble movement belies his 63 years of age. But then it also disguises a veteran who finished in the game prematurely, virtually a cripple, a midfield player whose weekly ritual was manipulation of an agonising hip injury and the regular cortisone injections that temporarily eased the pain.

By the end of his career with Derby County, then latterly Walsall, both managed by Mackay, Newton was dreading away trips, having to stand upright in the front well of the team coach on long or short haul journeys back from Plymouth or Peterborough as the injection wore off and the jarring bones began to grate and fix rigid inside his body. At 39, he had his first hip operation on his right side which lasted until two years ago. A second has now fully restored movement. His other hip replacement, on his left side, celebrated its seventh birthday in 2007.

It was on a grim Lanarkshire night when Forest lost to Airdrieonians on penalties at Broomfield Park that Newton sustained the original injury that would blight his later career.

"It was hail and wind and the sort of game you just defend most of the time. Peter Grummitt could hardly kick the ball out of our half it was that bad. Somebody just came from behind and clattered me. I played on, concussed as it happened, and don't remember a thing about the rest of the game or the after-match ceremonies." Forest drew 2-2, 4-4 on aggregate, but lost the penalty shoot-out. Two weeks later Newton was an Everton player, his last game a 3-1 home win over Blackpool when John Robertson made his debut for the club.

"The tackle had caused a hairline fracture of my hip, something which didn't come out until I failed a medical for Derby County. But they still signed me anyway and it was only later that their doctor told me about it. Billy Bingham had taken over at Everton, a strange man. I'd been forced to play left-back because of injuries and he promised I'd be back in midfield. Instead he drove me down to Stoke services off the M6 one Friday morning to meet Brian Clough. The press had already nicknamed him 'Billy Liar' and I knew there was no point in staying on with him because he could not be trusted."

Clough had finally got his man, but then departed acrimoniously shortly afterwards, during the Sam Longson fallout fiasco. So it was under Mackay, and the duress of extreme fame, that Newton secured a championship medal with the Rams.

If that does not endear him to the Forest camp, his ten years of unstinting loyalty to the club should persuade them otherwise.

"If I had been selfish, I should have left Forest much earlier than I did," muses Newton. "But it just wasn't in me. My ambition had been to play for my hometown team, retire with them and then manage them. That's how I had seen it although when I left at 26, I had grown so fond of Forest and Nottingham, it was hard to keep away. I missed them both."

As someone who accepted knocks, scrapes and bruises as an occupational hazard, Newton had the admiration of fans and fellow professionals alike. At a gala dinner to raise funds for Joe Baker some years ago, Johnny Quigley and Jeff Whitefoot took him to one side.

"We always knew you were going to make it and Pleaty wouldn't," they agreed in unison, damning David Pleat, the England youth international, who had the world at his feet when he joined Forest around the same time as Newton, Storey-Moore et al.

"And we always liked you better Henry. We never did like Pleaty."
Hard to disagree with such sentiments.

A FAINT RING OF Newton's mobile phone briefly interrupts the rare brilliance and tranquillity of this hot August afternoon. Once the terror of the midfield, Newton is happy to let his granddaughter run rings around him nowadays. His one regret is that his father Jack was not alive to see him play professional football. His mum Nellie, much like Newton, opted to take the silent supportive role.

When he called time, or more appropriately his aching limbs called time on his playing career, offers of management came in from the Potteries and Port Vale to Copenhagen, to which a Danish entrepreneur flew him out in his private jet for talks. The contract was lucrative, more money than he had earned with Everton or Forest. It had been a similar story with Walsall when Mackay had wanted him to extend his playing days in a holding midfield position. As usual, honesty about his physical capabilities got the better of Newton. He declined Mackay's offer and turned down the chance of a small fortune from his Danish suitor even though his own future was far from secure to retire from the game.

"I always had their respect and their friendship. That's something money can't buy," he says now.

Newton springs to his feet. It's time to get on with constructing his daughter's new home. The 'Teddy boy' haircut is no longer, more a sandy shore of a thatch, but the high cheekbones and the integrity simply refuse to disappear.

Nice to know that the good guys can still manage to come out on top – in real life as well as television pap.

Ian Storey-Moore

1961-1972: 271 games, 118 goals

THINK *JAWS*. THE theme tune. Prematurely, of course, because Peter Benchley's marine carnivore would not emerge in the literary world for another three years. It would be a further two years before the plastic inflatable would then surface on the silver screen thanks to a certain Steven Spielberg and thus revolutionise the blow-up doll industry; in certain parts of California at any rate. But five years before its unleashing upon an unsuspecting audience, imagine that dramatic ditty of impending doom that now nags and reverberates infrequently around the darker chasms of Ian Storey-Moore's mind.

7 February 1970, Manchester City versus Nottingham Forest at Maine Road, remains a Groundhog Day for Storey-Moore. Being Manchester, the repetitive intrusion of rain, thick, dense drizzly rain on a grainy Saturday afternoon, will not surprise Mancunians or occasional visitors to Piccadilly Station and Granada Studios. "I can still see it now, remember it vividly in fact," says Storey-Moore. "It was one of those grey, rainy days in Manchester. I'd just had a shot at goal and out of the corner of my eye I could see him coming. Coming and coming...I think he'd already set off to slide tackle me and couldn't stop and suddenly he cleaned me out. I could feel the pain instantly. All my weight was on my standing leg and I thought: 'Bloody hell, this is trouble.'" The shark had bitten.

The 'he' in question was Arthur Mann, the City full-back who had moved south of the border from Heart of Midlothian a couple of years earlier; by coach, as a Dennis Bergkamp-like fear of flying precluded Mann from leaving on a jet plane. It's fair to say that there was not a malicious bone in Mann, a fact I can confirm as someone who would later call him a mate as a Notts County colleague in 1973. Storey-Moore, too, would come to realise the tackle was not conceived in the evil mould of the Leeds midfield or Jack Charlton's 'little black book' of retribution. Even so, it severed the ligaments in Storey-Moore's ankle.

Only the skill, swift reaction and tenacity of a surgeon at Nottingham's old General Hospital, a centre of healing and care for the sick and dying that has since been demolished to be replaced by sterile rabbit-hutch flats and bars that encourage pavement pizzas vomited by the sick and desperate under- and over-age buffoons, saved Moore's career.

It transpired to be a temporary respite. Four years, a hundred headlines and over £200,000 in transfer fees later, his playing days were over at 28 years of age. Manchester United's European Cup-winning centre-half David Sadler jostled for a loose ball in a gentle gym five-a-side and Moore's weakened ligaments gave way once more. The man bought for a then British record fee in a blaze of publicity was forced to say goodbye to Old Trafford and the potential of a glittering swansong during Tommy Docherty's fleeting renaissance.

Docherty, in fact, despite his young braves restoring pride and the FA Cup to Old Trafford, would soon be gone; caught in flagrante delicto with the physio's wife, one Mrs Brown, or, as the old song went as improvised by Billy Hughes and a few players when Docherty was appointed manager of Derby County, *Doc's Up Mrs Brown*. No knees, but a bumps-a-daisy and rapid transfer for Hughes, the former Sunderland forward, whose Scottish sense of humour and adapted lyrics did not appeal to his compatriot manager.

Back with United, though, Docherty had admired Storey-Moore's talents with relish, purring that he didn't know that he was such a good player. "That was some compliment I suppose," recalls Storey-Moore. "But I was flying at the time, just getting my full fitness back. Then bang, I felt the ankle go in training and I knew straight away that it was the same thing. After that, I'd lost a yard. I could never be the player I had been at the top level."

And what a player he was, as Forest fans of a certain generation would say.

Gallingly, his only England appearance had arrived just a few weeks previous to his snaring in the jaws of Arthur Mann's tackle, on 14 January 1970. Alf Ramsey's agora-wing-a-phobia, the medical term for a morbid and irrational fear of wide-open wingers, seemed in remission as he finally selected Storey-Moore on the left flank against the emerging nation that was Holland.

The Wembley audience that Wednesday night, slow handclapping and jeering, clearly did not appreciate the world champions as their preparations to retain the Jules Rimet trophy in Mexico that summer spluttered and stuttered, as they were held to a 0-0 draw. But then the crowd did not appreciate either that the Dutch national side, which included Johan Cruyff, Wim van Hanegem, Piet Kiezer and Ruud Krol, was a whisker away from establishing the tangerine dream team of total football that would captivate and conquer, at European level at least, for the next decade.

For Storey-Moore, the breakthrough debut was deserved if belated recognition for his outstanding club form and incredibly it might have ended with a hat-trick as the prolific winger had two cleared off the line and what appeared a perfectly 'good' headed goal disallowed. Still, with Gordon Banks in goal and Bobby Charlton edging ahead of Storey-Moore's cap count by 98-1, the immediate future was promising. "Alf took me aside afterwards and told me I'd done enough. There was a friendly in Belgium next month and I'd be playing in that, he said. I really thought my chances of making the Mexico squad were good. And then, bang, along came Arthur and the injury."

In fact, avid collectors of football memorabilia should possess Storey-Moore's embossed face as depicted on the Esso coins commissioned by the petrol firm in 1970 that covered the initial 30-man World Cup squad. His injury eventually forced the issue for him and he did not make the final 24 that would lose to West Germany in the quarter-finals.

DESPITE THE SETBACKS, the premature retirement and an infamously convoluted and almost conspiratorial transfer to Manchester United, Storey-Moore's legacy at Forest remains an uplifting tale of the shy Suffolk lad, raised in Scunthorpe, who reflected the club's rising stature during the decade dubbed as 'swinging'.

Any comparisons to London would be apocryphal. Bridlesmith Gate was not the King's Road and Forest could not compete, at least in terms of glamour, with Chelsea, but there was movement away from the old order in the East Midlands city. The Hippo, a dungeon-like nightclub, was establishing a reputation on Bridlesmith Gate, while rowing clubs along the River Trent, adjacent to the City Ground, attracted a younger audience, who suddenly found a voice in the popular music and live groups that frequented the most famous of the venues, the Boat Club.

The pipe and gentlemanly image, as portrayed in Jeff Whitefoot's heyday and epitomised by the 1959 FA Cup-winning side, was vanishing from the game. Also disappearing in the architectural carnage overseen by 1960s town planners was the Black Boy, the Market Square landmark that was demolished to make way for a slab wall of repulsive new bricks that became first a Littlewoods store, then Iceland supermarket. How Watson Fothergill, the Victorian architect born in Mansfield as Fothergill Watson, might have been dismayed as its Bavarian balcony, wooden gables and Gothic chemistry was brought crashing to the ground, one of several Fothergill buildings obliterated in an alarming cull of Nottingham's historic heirlooms that was perpetrated by people – they called themselves 'architects' – whose motives were not entirely honourable. It had laid breakfast for Gregory Peck and told the local authorities to silence Little Tom, the bell on the Council House clock that had kept Don Bradman and his touring Australians awake on the eve of a Trent Bridge Test. But for a few shillings more, the Black Boy's grandeur was reduced to rubble and disappeared forever.

In the world of football, the changing face was more acceptable. George Best's audacious skills and the confrontational rebel in Denis Law held sway as Manchester United forged ahead of their rivals in the domestic game. Somewhere in between, Storey-Moore captured the imagination; a drop of the shoulder, a shimmy here and there and a blinding turn of pace confounded opponents and placed him on a pedestal that he often shared with Joe Baker. Storey-Moore, though, wasn't a bad looking sod either. If he turned full-backs inside out, he also turned the heads of the ladies, whose appearance at games was as rare as it was radical, but nevertheless an irresistible phenomenon.

A nickname of 'Mugsy', which like many players' sobriquets still follows him to this day, emerged with some of his City Ground contemporaries claiming it arose because of his handsome, boyish looks and photogenic appeal. "They got that wrong," insists Storey-Moore. "It was Mugsy Moore from my schooldays. It just fitted."

Those formative years had been spent in Scunthorpe where a friend of his father's tipped off the local Forest scout that here was a young lad who could play a bit and score goals. Storey-Moore arrived in the brighter lights of Nottingham in 1961 as the lad from carrot-crunching territory. He was also saddled with a double-barrelled name, normally the preserve of Tory politicians and the landed gentry, which pretty much amounted to the same thing.

Johnny Cash would later sing about *A Boy Named Sue*, thus christened by his errant father to toughen him up in life, but the combination of those good looks and a posh-sounding name handed the Forest dressing room plenty of ammunition for ridicule, even though Jeff Whitefoot and Johnny Quigley, a pair then heading for veteran status, proved guiding and protective presences. "I tried to drop the Storey and just be Ian Moore later in my career, but it stuck. I suppose everyone knew me as Ian Storey-Moore by then and that was that." After trials and a short spell on the ground staff aged 16 and a half, it was manager Andy Beattie, not exactly regarded with fondness by some of the more senior players, who offered the Ipswich-born teenager the chance to turn professional. In those days, 17 was the watershed of a football career. Potential players were either shown a light blue contract to sign or the door to exit.

It was into these less than glamorous environs that the young Storey-Moore and his aspiring peers were initiated in what was the Notts Thursday League. A traditional Thursday afternoon off was enjoyed by some working men from all walks of life in the city, notably the uniform branch, bus drivers, milkmen and so forth. With Sunday still sacrosanct in England, the midweek Thursday afternoon slot attracted a healthy and talented following, with several leagues brimming with top amateur players from the region.

As well as the Memorial Gardens in honour of World War victims, the Embankment was a vast green swathe of park football and cricket pitches on the fringes of the Meadows, a verdant oasis that induced Sunday strollers to promenade along its wide concourse by the side of the River Trent. It was overlooked by Mundella School, one of those dreadful grammar schools that encouraged meritocracy and discipline among its pupils and high teaching standards among its staff. Small wonder David Cameron and the New Tories despise the concept so much. Amid turning out numerous scholars and over-achievers from less affluent backgrounds, it was responsible for David Pleat's education, a seat of learning that the former Tottenham Hotspur manager is always proud to mention. An England schoolboy international winger who joined Forest at the same time as Storey-Moore, Pleat was among the first children to live on Clifton Estate as his family moved home in the early 1950s. A huge housing project to the south of the city that relocated families in the post-Second World War baby boom generation, either from inner city or the Meadows slum clearance programmes, Pleat lived and played on Farnborough Road among the bricks, mortar and mud of the Wimpey new-build. The A453 road linking Nottingham to junction 24 of the M1 offers a view of his old house, a nostalgic reference he often pointed out when his Spurs players passed by on the team coach en route to the City Ground during his spells in charge, no doubt as a measure of how far he had travelled in life from humble beginnings.

Indeed, of the two raw recruits, it appeared that the former Mundella pupil was destined for greater things in comparison to the Scunthorpe springer. Wiry and seemingly undernourished, Storey-Moore and a clutch of hopefuls were thrown in at the deep end as a Forest A side turned out every week in the Notts Thursday League.

Crowds flocked to the Embankment not for a Sunday stroll, but a Thursday massacre as the precocious talents of the fledgling professionals defeated physical superiority, the occasional malicious tackle from the older and bitter members of City Transport or Nottingham Pork Butchers and the elements of a park pitch that had seen better days. Daylight was at a premium on the touchline or behind the goals as intrigued supporters caught a glimpse of future potential.

If the Embankment staged Forest youth's home games, away trips took them to the bus depot at Chilwell or the site where Goose Fair set up stalls before decamping four days later every October. Then there was the police ground at Carrington, a leafy, thriving suburb of Nottingham just off the Mansfield Road, which has since fallen into disrepair, like the lido that, even on scorching hot summer days, once chilled to the bone the more adventurous bathers. It is not difficult to understand the trepidation that was integral to the preparation for a visit to Carrington. Before it merged with the county later in the decade, the city police force recruited only constables who stood over 6ft tall, a rugged bunch of shrinking violets who were scarcely naïve in the art of self-defence. Bob Raynor, a goalkeeper with attitude and a real character who once had trials with Forest, epitomised the spirit of the force and its traditions. That was partly a legacy of the old Chief of Police Athelstan Popkess, who during several decades assembled bobbies on the beat who just happened to be marginally failed pugilists. The plethora of divisional boxing trophies at Central HQ were a delight to behold, no doubt. "Kick the little bastard," was about as fair and legal as City Police could muster, although friendships were forged in between the insults and abuse that inevitably ended with a Forest youth victory.

The local constabulary stopped short of deploying Tug Wilson in battle. The handlebar moustachioed constable, standing almost as tall as the Council House clock in the Market Square, was a legendary figure on the beat in the city centre. Crime may still have paid in the 1960s and maybe the past does materialise with a rose-tint hue, but the few who picked an argument with Tug Wilson, night or day, never finished on the winning side.

Against this background, Storey-Moore was starting to find his feet and expand his fragile frame. "Looking back, it was a tough learning curve because it taught us the realities of playing against men," says Storey-Moore. "They were big lads as well, even if we always managed to beat them." However, sharing digs with Peter Hindley on Loughborough Road in West Bridgford, another leafy suburb nicknamed Bread and Lard Island because of the parsimonious nature of its indigenous population, did little to expedite the toughening-up process. For £4 a week, the pair had their washing and ironing on tap and a meal at any time of the day. "She was a lovely lady who ran it. Mind you it was a freezing cold, old Victorian house."

Strangely, footballers remain impervious to inclement conditions when it comes to queueing after midnight to gain entry to nightclubs, a tradition now extinct with the emergence of VIP rooms, Sugar Lounges and the Vacant Areas that inhabit them. Back then, the equivalent was a nod and a wink that took Forest players to the front of the queue and into the warmth of a basement club to be greeted by rum and coke and the sounds of Tamla Motown. If that was an erotic combination for the 1960s in-crowd, the height of chic even, their lust was further fuelled by a Forest club that was starting to become sexy, the only available and attractive sporting team in town in fact.

Across the Trent, the once pre-eminent Notts County's decline was now an acute embarrassment, their black and white stripes reflecting a dreary, old-fashioned image that contrasted poorly with the technicolour widescreen action on view on the south bank. Mind you, if there was an Achilles heel at Forest it was the hideous music that the players and fans had to endure as the team ran out before kick-off. "Roben Hud, Roben Hud, riding through the glen," was how the American twang of Dick James sang about the Sherwood Forest outlaw. The theme tune from a dated 1950s black and white TV series starring Richard Greene as the eponymous bandit hero in Lincoln green was the one anachronism that betrayed a club looking to its future.

Even that was not sufficient to drag County into the swing of things. A team of perennial relegation dodgers, watched by persistent coffin dodgers, had entered into the realms of stand-up comedy. True, unlike Bradford Park Avenue and Hartlepools United, they did not need to rely on the outrageously absurd vagaries of the re-election system and benevolence of other clubs who were likely to call in a favour when their turn came to flounder in the bottom four. Nevertheless, there was a gap far wider than the Trent that separated the two local teams where once County, with Tommy Lawton at his imposing, imperious best, had held sway. That gap grew to gulf status during Storey-Moore's and Forest's most memorable season from the 1960s, a campaign that included that FA Cup quarter-final against Everton.

THE TEAM OF mid-sixties vintage was without doubt Forest's best and most consistent team for decades, arguably ever – to that point. Storey-Moore concedes that the club had certainly been dormant since the historic 1959 FA Cup triumph, but with the immaculate Bobby McKinlay at centre-half and flanked by Welshman Terry Hennessey, plus the fearsome tackling of Henry Newton, Forest had consistency, guile and considerable grit across the park.

In any other generation, Peter Grummitt would have won countless England caps as a goalkeeper, his misfortune being that he played in the same era as Gordon Banks and Peter Bonetti. With the fleet-footed Joe Baker and the granite target man Frank Wignall up front, John Barnwell in midfield, Barry Lyons on the wing and full-backs Peter 'Tank' Hindley and John Winfield bombing down either flank, all Forest required was a free spirit with a knack for scoring goals and unravelling tales of the unexpected. Enter Storey-Moore and the blue half of Merseyside, Everton, to the City Ground on 8 April 1967 with a place in the FA Cup semi-finals as the winner's prize.

A few weeks earlier, it had taken a magnificent, trademark piece of opportunism by Denis Law to end a sequence of 13 games unbeaten and stretch Manchester United's cushion over Forest at the top of the First Division with a 1-0 win at Old Trafford.

Despite that, Forest still stalked the league leaders with an almost inconceivable Double remaining in their grasp. "The whole city was buzzing, the Trent End had suddenly become the place to be on a Saturday afternoon," recalls Storey-Moore. "You couldn't experience the weekend game properly unless you were there."

Anyone who witnessed this particular Cup tie need not embellish the story to younger listeners. Events unfolded so dramatically in Nottingham that Saturday afternoon that *Match of the Day* cameras could barely condense the highlights for their evening transmission. After less than two minutes, Joe Baker, the intrepid fulcrum of the Forest attack, had been reduced to casualty status courtesy of a Brian Labone tackle that would have stopped a tank in its tracks. Baker said later it was the most painful injury he'd ever had and for him, the war with Everton was over. With Alan Hinton on as substitute, Forest trailed to Jimmy Husband's goal at the interval and the Cup holders seemed certain to progress to another semi-final. But Storey-Moore's elevation to play alongside Frank Wignall proved critical. The latter's long-range shot was parried by keeper Andy Rankin and Storey-Moore pounced for his first. His second was an instinctive effort from distance, but Husband's second of the tie, in the 78th minute, dampened the Forest revival. "All I could think was 'Here we go, a replay at Goodison Park,' which I didn't fancy and the last thing we needed going for the Double," recalls Storey-Moore.

In the last minute, however, Storey-Moore scored again, a finish that lives forever with those who witnessed it either live at the ground or on the BBC later that night. Denied in a hectic frenzy by Everton full-back Ray Wilson, then Rankin, then the bar, Storey-Moore finally flung himself at the ball and headed it over the line. 3-2 and time was up. "It was probably our finest hour as a team if not my finest game," Storey-Moore explains. "I remember the atmosphere was electric and they allowed the kids to come over the terracing and stands and sit beside the pitch. Great memories. That last goal was fortuitous to say the least, but Frank Wignall was the Man of the Match for me. He caused them so many problems and had a hand in all three of my goals."

The first hat trick of his career would bring him the 22-year-old winger the accolade of 'Sheriff of Nottingham' from some commentators. In fact, the sheriff's badge, the star award in the *Sunday People*'s marks out of ten the following day, was as close as he came to public office. "It's daft when you look back and think we couldn't wait to get a copy of the *People* to see if reporters, who had never really played the game, were going to give us six, seven, eight or nine out of ten. Then again, it wasn't about the money then really. Our win bonus was £4 the year we almost did the Double. No kidding, so we weren't going to make a fortune that was for sure. Everyone at the club was on about the same basic, around £40 a week. But if someone else like Terry Hennessey, a really talented player who I'd say was world class, was on a bit more, nobody moaned. There was no jealousy really."

Fame and kudos were most definitely high on the agenda of motivation along with the pure enjoyment of playing the game to win.

'GIVE IT TO MOORE, he will score' the Trent End gleefully chanted and their fervent wish was often granted, the right hand going up rigidly á la Denis Law to signal another Storey-Moore conversion. In all, he scored 24 goals that season, an outstanding strikerate for a wide player.

In celebration, Storey-Moore and Hindley, plus wives and girlfriends, headed for the Parkside Club on the night of the classic Everton quarter-final victory. It was a fashionable cabaret club that mixed exotic strippers with acts like comedian Dave Allen and Val Doonican, the rocking chair crooner's woollen attire probably addressing the balance of the preceding floor show of flesh. "I got absolutely pissed," Storey-Moore admits. "But then if you couldn't do it that night, you couldn't do it ever."

In the unlikely event of selective memory loss, Storey-Moore has a black and white video of the game at his home today. Some other images best forgotten are some dodgy fashion shoots with young girls in newspapers and magazines, sporting the sort of abstract clothes, flowery shirts and coiffured hair that made the 1970s almost respectable. Even so, the playboy footballer, as patented by George Best, suited Storey-Moore and Forest well.

Unfortunately, progress to the FA Cup semi-final had come at a price. Baker's injury meant he would not play again that season. His reflexes and eye for goal had been key elements in Forest's unlikely assault on two fronts, but just when the critical period of battle came into sight, his presence, or lack of it, was sorely missed.

Forest lost to Tottenham Hotspur, the eventual winners, at Hillsborough as a mistake by Hennessey, of all people, allowed Greaves to pinch what was a customary goal against the East Midlands side. As Manchester United continued to score goals at will – they amassed 84 in the league that season, 20 more than Forest – the upstart pretenders to the throne faltered. "I felt it was a massive tragedy for the club that we didn't win something that year." Still, two goals by Robert 'Sammy' Chapman at Craven Cottage on the final day of the season meant Forest retained runners-up position ahead of Tottenham, Leeds United and Liverpool, four points adrift of United.

They had gone close, but in effect finished three wins short of toppling the champions. Such an achievement normally would inspire a club to consolidate for the present and invest in the future. In Forest's case, the reverse happened. Hennessey and Newton were sold and Hinton, an underrated and unappreciated winger, was also allowed to leave. The timescale may have been two or three seasons, but the effect was demoralising for Storey-Moore. "I couldn't understand why we were not building on that team instead of selling our best players," he laments. A feeling of déjà vu greeted him when he returned to the City Ground as a coach in Dave Bassett's regime, as striker Kevin Campbell was sold without the manager's consent as the club was asset-stripped by its owners. "We'd just finished second to United in the league, nearly reached the FA Cup final with a great team and suddenly overnight it was being dismantled. It was sheer lunacy."

BY NATURE STOREY-MOORE was slightly reserved and a little shy, but his goalscoring exploits instilled more confidence in the waif signed from Scunthorpe United. In the days when referees considered themselves peripheral figures without recourse to writing drivelling memoirs about their 'careers', match officials routinely inspected the studs of players' boots to detect any illegal filing of sharpened objects.

"Any questions lads?" the man in black would always finish on.

"Yes," piped up Storey-Moore. "What won the 2.30 at Haydock Park, ref?"

That warped sense of schoolboy humour, a facet of dressing room life, has never left Storey-Moore, who at the time of our interview was chief scout at Aston Villa working alongside former Forest team-mates Martin O'Neill and John Robertson. When O'Neill first came over from Northern Ireland it was Storey-Moore who, as Jeff Whitefoot and Johnny Quigley had done for him in 1961, tended to look after the young Irishman. That friendship has remained constant over three decades. "Now and again Robbo will say to one of the young lads at Villa, 'Hey son, come over here, I want a quick word.'

"'Yes John, what is it?'

"'Alacrity,' Robbo replies. It's just silly schoolboy humour. My wife tells me I'll never grow up. Perhaps she's right.'"

That growing up process continued at a sluggish pace as Forest declined. The main stand fire of August 1968, taking hold with Leeds United drawing 1-1 at the City Ground, was followed by a fire sale of the club's best players. By 1971, only Storey-Moore, disaffected and, in the eyes of some colleagues, disruptive, remained as a saleable asset. Talk of a record transfer and powerhouse Derby County looming on the horizon undoubtedly turned Storey-Moore's head, but with Forest hurtling towards the Second Division and cementing their reputation as a selling club, few could blame the rising star, still only 26 and surely not yet at his peak, for wanting to pursue his football path elsewhere.

BEFORE HIS DEPARTURE, though, Ian Storey-Moore left one last golden memory.

Aptly, nearly 43,000 crammed into the City Ground to witness it. That may have been 5,000 short of the Everton Cup tie crowd, yet those among the festive audience who gathered on 27 December 1971 for the visit of Arsenal cannot forget the moment. "It has to rank as my best goal," says Storey-Moore, who picked up the ball on the edge of his own penalty area from a throw-out by Jim Barron, the Forest goalkeeper with the model looks which compared favourably with the recipient of his short throw.

Like Tommy Lawton's goal at the City Ground 20 years earlier, estimates vary as to the distance travelled by the hero before the ball hit the back of the net. In Lawton's case, it was a towering header that might have originated anywhere between the halfway line and edge of the penalty area. In Storey-Moore's scenario, the run that carried him into the Arsenal 18-yard box measured at least 70 yards. This was the day when Tommy Gemmell, the former Celtic full-back and one of the Lisbon Lions, made his debut for Forest. On the other side in the yellow away strip was a ginger firebrand by the name of Alan Ball, recently transferred to Highbury for a British record £220,000 from Everton. "The thing I remember most is being chased for quite a way by a pair of white boots," smiles Storey-Moore. "They belonged to Bally and all I could see was these boots trying to catch up with me. Suddenly I seemed to be on the edge of the Arsenal penalty box confronted by about six or seven yellow shirts and I thought: 'What the bloody hell do I do now? How am I going to get past this lot?' So I went this way and that and it all opened up and there was Bob Wilson [the Arsenal goalkeeper] and I thought: 'I'd better not mess this one up now.'"

He didn't. As Duncan McKenzie, Storey-Moore's successor in many ways, tells it, he beat Wilson at his near post; reference the goalkeeper's angular gaffe when he had allowed Liverpool's Steve Heighway to beat him at the near post during extra time of the 1971 FA Cup final.

Although he was to score twice more for Forest, in defeats to Leicester City and Southampton, it was in effect a farewell gift to the club and the Trent End, a comfort zone during the inevitable descent to Division Two that lay in wait that season. That home defeat by Leicester attracted just over 27,000 to the City Ground, confirmation of the team's form and plight.

It was another defeat by another East Midlands rival, Derby County on 19 February 1972, that was to be Storey-Moore's swansong. It was an ironic ending, for what followed was the stuff of farce and legend combined. A case of when rather than if, Storey-Moore's transfer, a proposed British record of £225,000 – eclipsing Arsenal's fee for Ball by £5,000 – began in earnest at the Edwalton Hotel on a Friday in late February, when he met Frank O'Farrell, the Manchester United manager. "We talked for quite a while, but could not come to an agreement about terms," Storey-Moore reveals. "Then Matt Gillies [the Forest manager] got up and told me I could talk to Brian Clough [the Derby manager]. He dialled the number for me from the phone in the hotel and put it to my ear. To say I was overawed is putting it mildly.

"'Hello Mr Clough.'

"'You stay there young man [imagine the Clough accent]. I'll be there in ten minutes.'

And with that Gillies and the secretary stood up and left the lounge area.

"'But Brian Clough's coming here in a few minutes,' I said.

"'Is he?' replied Gilleis.

"'You know he is, you just dialled his bloody number!'"

But Gillies did not respond. He carried on walking out, leaving Storey-Moore on his own to negotiate the biggest deal in the club's history for the largest British transfer on record.

Less than ten minutes later, the solid glass doors at the Edwalton swung open, Storey-Moore took a deep breath and in waltzed the Sopranos, or at least Clough and Peter Taylor in full battle regalia, armed with jackets, ties and rapid-fire Wrigley's chewing gum. "Any young player would have been intimidated. But they sat me down and gave me all the bullshit. 'Just sign lad, I'll look after you.'"

Clough was a master of getting players to sign blank contracts, although he seldom broke a promise. "Take him to Derby, Peter," Clough said. "I'm going down the City Ground to sort this out."

It was 9 o'clock in the evening when Clough turned up at the Midland Hotel in Derby, the habitual venue for the Derby squad the night before a home game. "It's sorted. You're a Derby player now, son. Peter, get the lads up and we'll celebrate with some champagne." Even Archie Gemmill, always tucked up and half asleep by that hour, was the reluctant recipient of a glass of bubbly as the players, destined to lift the title that season, toasted the new acquisition.

History has recorded how Clough displayed Storey-Moore to the Derby faithful at half-time of the following day's home game against

Wolverhampton Wanderers, a premature parade. In fact Storey-Moore signed for Manchester United, leaving Clough, an outspoken and confrontational leader who was already unpopular with the game's ruling bodies, to face Football League charges of contractual irregularities. The rumours flowed fast and furious, with spurious suggestions that the player's wife had been influential, her dislike of Clough being pivotal in steering him towards Old Trafford. "Absolute garbage," confirms Storey-Moore. "They tried every trick in the book to save face."

It was, in fact, chairman Tony Wood, one of many with Forest connections whose wealth derived from Nottingham's once thriving rag trade, who vetoed the move. He had been on holiday during Clough's opening gambit, but vital contracts had been left unsigned. Although he had overseen the Derby-bound departures of Terry Hennessey and Henry Newton, waving off a third star asset down the A52 to the Baseball Ground apparently was unacceptable. "Eventually, Cloughie asked me to speak on his behalf when the League brought charges," says Storey-Moore. "He said it would save the club a bob or two and who was I to argue? So I did. And you know from that day on, he never spoke a word to me. No, I tell a lie. He was speaking at a gala evening at the City Ground years later, when I was a coach at the club. He saw me standing in the doorway, turned and said: 'I hear you're not as big a shithouse as I thought you were then.' And that was that. But he must have known none of it was my fault. I would gladly have signed for Derby. They had some terrific players, but the Forest chairman was adamant and that was that."

On 11 March 1972, Storey-Moore duly made his debut for Manchester United against Huddersfield Town. On the same day, normal service was restored for Derby, who ground out a 1-0 win against Tottenham Hotspur at White Hart Lane on their way to the championship trophy. At the City Ground, the lowest crowd since November 1955, just 9,872, turned up to grimace at Forest, who were beaten 2-0 by Ipswich Town on their way to 21st position and relegation.

Someone on the City Ground Tannoy clearly had a perverse sense of humour. With the home team toiling desperately, it announced that Manchester United had taken the lead at Old Trafford. "And the scorer is Ian Storey-Moore on his debut!" Oh happy days.

Like George Best, at Old Trafford Storey-Moore weaved his talents all over the pitch, rather than being a traditional winger who hugged the touchline; and that during a period when football was at its most vicious and cynical. "You had to commit mini-murder to get booked," grimaces Storey-Moore. "There were the likes of Tommy Smith, Ron Harris and Norman Hunter, who you were always looking out for. I remember a game against Leeds at the City Ground. We beat them 1-0 and I scored. I think it was the only kick, at least of the ball, that I got during the match."

AS WITH MANY OF HIS contemporaries and successors, Storey-Moore is dismayed at Forest's plight in more recent seasons. He left in acrimonious circumstances as chief coach during the disastrous Gary Megson era, and worries at the direction the game has taken. "I know it's a cliché," he says. "But the money has not changed football for the better. I just loved playing and seeing my name in print, Storey-Moore, 89th minute."

Scoring goals and pleasing the crowd; a timeless football concept that seems so terribly old-fashioned in the context of today.

Joe Baker

1966-1969: 134 games, 49 goals

MAY 1967. THE SUMMER of love was about to descend upon the planet. Well the west coast of California, which is as good as being on a different planet at the best of times. But if the anthem of Flower Power urged people: 'let's go to San Francisco' or indeed the Monterey Pop Music Festival, with the obligatory flowers, as in 'peace man', in their hair, Nottingham Forest headed for a few days in sunny Spain where straw, as in donkeys, plodded the coastline from Valencia to Barcelona.

Such a brief Spanish excursion was the scantest reward for a season that had seen the Reds menacingly stalk Manchester United all the way to their seventh First Division title, while falling at the penultimate hurdle in the FA Cup as Tottenham Hotspur, the eventual winners of the trophy, squeezed past them in the semi-finals.

Neil Footitt, a young Forest fan at the time, was also on Spain's east coast during the summer of love, having hopped on a train at Midland Station with Meadows pal Tony Baker to soak up both the sun and Watney's Red Barrel in Lloret de Mar.

"I told everybody back home I'd got a job in advertising. In fact I carried a sandwich board on the beach around Lloret," says Footitt, now a property developer and still fervent Forest supporter. "Eventually I got promoted to head barman at a local pub. The manager came onto the beach one day with a red jacket and asked the four of us on sandwich boards to try it on. It fitted me and so I got the job."

The colour of the jacket is apposite as is Footitt's Cinderella-moment because he did get to go to the ball and see Forest beat Barcelona in the Nou Camp. His childhood friendship with Billy Brindley, the Forest defender and also Meadows born and bred, took him and his friends to Barcelona and the Forest hotel. John Barnwell, Terry Hennessey and Henry Newton were among the players on the mini-tour, but there was only one person who the sandwich board delegation, expanded to three by Peter 'Nobby' Stevenson, wanted to see. Joe Baker, idolised by Footitt and all of the Trent End. It could be argued that Baker was the first, in the modern way of thinking, and ultimate Forest cult hero ever to have worn the Garibaldi red.

Lightning quick over five yards, fearless in the penalty area, a predator's eye for goal allied with a flair for the sensational, it was small wonder that the man and boy on the terrace could relate to Baker. This in a period when the boots that were flying in the 18-yard box were made of unforgiving leather underpinned by metal screw-in studs that were often more pointed than oval-tipped. This may have been accidentally by wear and tear, or by files and other sharp objects with a more sinister intent. In comparison with the carpet slippers sometimes called boots today with moulded man-made fibre soles, it was heavy artillery that Baker breached on a regular basis. Should the two boot cultures ever collide in a parallel universe, the carnage is certain to resemble the Doc Marten-wearing cast of *A Clockwork Orange* crushing a battalion of *Guardian* reader sandals underfoot. Messy, naughty but nice.

Baker, often nattily dressed in mohair coat and boasting a flowing head of hair, exuded a man of the world presence. His time in Turin with Denis Law had only added to his mystique, while his behaviour constituted that of a maverick, who, by universal consent, could 'handle himself'. While at Torino, he had launched a photographer into a Venetian canal as he was being trailed following a sending-off and a missed training session. The end was nigh when he crashed his Alfa Romeo and had to recover on a drip in hospital for six weeks. Law, a front seat passenger, walked away with little more than a scratch on his nose, but Baker almost lost his life that night.

A broad Scottish accent courtesy of his upbringing in Motherwell (Baker was born in Liverpool to English parents, who moved north to seek work when he was young) did little to enhance his credibility as an

England centre-forward. He was capped eight times by his country by virtue of his birthright and there were those who believed he had done enough when with Arsenal to merit inclusion in Alf Ramsey's World Cup-winning squad of 1966. A goal and a match-winning performance against Spain in Madrid in December 1965 had persuaded many, but not Ramsey, of his worth to the England side. Now, almost two years later, back in Spain, he was once more the centre of attention, albeit from goggle-eyed fans fresh off the beach at Lloret.

Some complimentary tickets courtesy of Forest manager Johnny Carey ensured that Footitt and his two mates got into the Nou Camp, where they saw goals from Frank Wignall and a cracking 30-yard shot from Barry Lyons secure a deserved 2-1 win over Barcelona. Theirs were isolated English cheers among the 45,000 mostly Spanish fans, cheers raised to a higher volume when their pal Brindley made a 20-minute cameo as a second half substitute.

Back at the team hotel, Footitt and friends returned to find the squad ready for a night out. Since the maximum wage of a sandwich board carrier or even red-coated barman, even one fluent in the virtually native Lloret tongue of English, was scarcely a king's ransom, the pair declined to join the party, whereupon Baker, Barnwell and club officials on the trip pitched in with a kitty which raised 1,000 pesetas each for the trio. Hardly a fortune, but enough to buy a few rounds of San Miguel and frites, and still have enough left for a bus ride back to Lloret the following morning.

Even that wasn't necessary. The players shifted rooms to accommodate the Meadows contingent, Footitt sleeping on the settee in Brindley's room. The following morning, he sneaked some fruit up from the breakfast table; feeble hangover tuck maybe but nourishment for a sore head and Spanish tummy nevertheless.

"As we were going it was John Barnwell who turned around to us and told us to join the players on the team coach [headed for Valencia and the second and final game in Spain, a 0-0 draw as it transpired]," Footitt recalls. "We had to say no. We told them we had to be back at work! Which was true – and we needed the money."

Footitt and friends' summer sojourn would reach a dead end and empty pocket in Casablanca – but they would always have Barcelona. It's a story that would be impossible to relate today and for fans and players alike to comprehend. The second best team in England and

FA Cup semi-finalists having a whip-round for a couple of young fans to join them on a night out in a European city? Chances are Frank Lampard would need to consult with his agent first to see if it was tax deductible. And would Ashley Cole be inviting the riff-raff on the team bus/private jet to share a can of beer and a meaningful conversation? Come on. Girls allowed maybe, but certainly not those nasty hoi polloi who live in grubby back-to-back housing and can't even afford an inside loo.

If the tale evokes a vague innocence of distant past lost in the modern sporting genre, it also confirms why the idols and cult heroes of the working class hordes who, by and large comprised football's devotees, were truly genuine, tangible and in touch with the people who paid their wages. The sort of audience whose idea of live entertainment was to be found at the ground where it was happening rather than slumped in the corner of a bar en masse trying to focus on a digital image through the haze of several pints of lager. Thus when Forest returned to domestic duties and a new season brimming with hope and expectancy in August 1967, the Trent End stood in eager expectation, excited about the prospect of the new campaign, ready to grumble and moan about the standard of play rather than the quality of a rump steak and prawn salad sandwich.

The clever crooners among the notoriously vociferous Trent Enders had also dreamed up a new anthem for Joe Baker. With a finger on the pulse of hippiedom and a youth culture that was expanding and breaching hitherto forbidden boundaries and taboos, Keith West released a single called *Excerpt from a Teenage Opera*, or *Grocer Jack*, as it became known popularly. West was also a member of Tomorrow, (for pop enthusiasts and anoraks its line-up included future Yes guitarist Steve Howe) a psychedelic band which in terms of 1967 street cred was every bit as compulsory as having an oddball theory about the *Sgt Pepper* album cover, the meaning of its portentous tracks played backwards and, of course, being on nodding terms with Maharishi Mahesh Yogi, Ravi Shankar and the Dalai Lama (only the Beatles were able to master all five).

As Forest opened their campaign on 12 August with a 3-1 City Ground victory over Sheffield United, Baker, Ian Storey-Moore and Alan Hinton scoring, Scott McKenzie's *San Francisco* was still at the top of the charts, but West's playground ditty had made an inauspicious entry into the top 50. When it reached its peak, fittingly at No.2 the following month, the position in which Forest had finished the previous season, the Trent End had voted it their own No.1.

> "Joe Ba-ker, Joe Ba-ker, you are the king,
> of the Trent End, oh yeah yeah…"

And it scanned pretty well, too.

A generation or more later, the young Forest fans would chant "We all live in a flat in Hyson Green" (to the tune of The Beatles' *Yellow Submarine*) to demonstrate that some of the better seeds of lyrical ingenuity had been passed down the genetic line.

The Trent End's tribute to Baker was as fond as it was novel, West's original concept apart that is. It had been the previous season that the famous "Zigger-zagger-zigger-zagger, Joe Ba-ker" chants had resonated around the concrete terracing and tin roof at the most boisterous side of the City Ground, where occupants would often feel the chill winds blowing in from the River Trent. Two songs dedicated to one man reveals the depth of feeling which the little feller generated amongst his loyal followers.

SIGNED IN FEBRUARY 1966, Baker made an immediate and dramatic impact, and not just with fans and opponents. "You really felt as if the club was trying to achieve something when they started signing quality players," recalls Henry Newton, a Forest fan as a Bilborough schoolboy and whose affinity and love of the club was unwavering as he was nurtured from ground staff skivvy to the England World Cup squad in 1970. "The likes of Terry Hennessey and Chris Crowe had come in, but when I heard Joe Baker was being signed, well it was a really exciting time to be at Forest, and not just for me. The other lads felt that we were actually going somewhere and Joe, coming from Arsenal and having played in Italy, was a really big name for us."

In fact manager Johnny Carey had twice broken the club record fee in recent memory, firstly to acquire Crowe, from Wolverhampton Wanderers for £30,000 in August 1964. Carey topped that by persuading Hennessey to join him in November 1965, paying Birmingham City £50,000 for the accomplished Welsh half-back, but he exceeded that effort when Arsenal received £60,000 for their restless centre-forward, who had demanded a transfer, along with another England international George Eastham, after the pair were dropped by Billy Wright following an FA Cup defeat to Blackburn Rovers.

Actually Forest had tried to bring him north of London the previous season, but negotiations had faltered on personal terms. In an era when the only way players could capitalise on their talent was a transfer, Baker had also been courted by Chelsea just a few weeks previous to this second attempt to sign him by Forest. With no Russian oligarch on the horizon, Baker declined Chelsea's terms and headed instead to the Norman Cross Motel on the A1 at Peterborough, where he met Carey, chairman Fred Sisson and vice-chairman Tony Wood. Behind closed doors, the deal was swiftly concluded.

His Italian reputation as a fractious, potentially disruptive element did not deter Forest or Carey. On the field, he had established his stock in trade as a goalscorer with Hibernian, for whom he once bagged nine goals against Peebles Rovers. To call the Scottish FA Cup fixture a tie, game or match would of course be a misnomer. It ended 15-1 to Hibs at Easter Road that Saturday, 11 February 1961, and Baker was well on his way to claiming 42 goals that season and a lucrative £85,000 move to Torino. Strangely enough, his feat has been bettered by only one player, who scored ten goals in the same competition in January 1960. His brother Gerry delivered the record tally as St Mirren hammered Glasgow University 15-0.

It was Joe's predatory powers that were needed most by Forest, though. The team had slumped badly since the false dawn of a 3-0 away win over West Ham United to welcome the new year of 1966. Four league defeats, including a 4-0 drubbing administered by a ruthlessly clinical Leeds United at the City Ground, had intensified pressure on the Irishman Carey as supporters formed an 'Action Committee' designed to raise 10,000 signatures in favour of signing Baker. It soon became an inaction committee, but the fallout from a fourth round FA Cup defeat at Hull City lingered in the Forest camp.

In truth, Hull at Boothferry Park in front of a capacity 38,000 crowd was never going to be an easy proposition. The Humberside club was flying at the top of the Third Division with former Mansfield Town player Ken Wagstaff the sharp edge of a formidable forward line that included Chris Chilton, Ken Houghton, Ian Butler and Ray

Henderson. Forest were brushed aside 2-0, but the absence of Bob McKinlay and Colin Addison from the starting line-up stirred the rumour factory back in Nottingham. To this day, almost like a self-perpetuating urban myth, local gossip insists that fighting had broken out on the coach en route to Humberside, fuelled by allegations of adulterous wives. Addison, McKinlay and Peter Grummitt were all implicated, according to the Forest drums that replaced the more familiar jungle ones during that period.

However, talk to any of those players who travelled that day, and they will tell you that the allegations carry no substance. Addison was already injured and McKinlay was suffering from a stomach bug. End of story – if not the urban myth.

Rather than the salaciously juicy tales, Forest's true stories revolved around players who liked a drink or two, but did their socialising away from the public gaze, often retiring to the lawn green bowling club at Wilford village for a few pints, a game of cards and gentle banter among its members. It was nothing new and the tradition continued a Forest generation later as the likes of Kenny Burns would prefer to drink in the shadows of cue balls and the green baize at a local snooker club rather than be dazzled by the strobe lighting while dodging handbags on the disco floor at the Palais or Madison's. Unusually sensible beyond his years in retrospect was Burns – at least in that particular marginalised field.

It was to Wilford BC that Gordon Banks and Richie Norman, the Leicester City players, occasionally would drive after watching one of Forest's midweek games, to be joined later by some of the participants. "We always went over there to watch them as well, but somehow never quite managed to drink as much as Banksy and Norman!" recalls Henry Newton.

Into that environment Baker was thrust, although his scheduled debut against Sheffield Wednesday on 26 February was delayed because the City Ground pitch was waterlogged. When he finally did play against the Owls, on 7 May, he scored the only goal of the game. On 8 March, his debut finally arrived in a 1-0 home win over Burnley – 28,246 fans revelling in the moment. It was hardly a classic, even if Ian Storey-Moore did score the winner.

Baker's second game brought two goals, away to a Northampton Town team that, though the club did not know it, was heading back down the divisions as swiftly as it had ascended them. At least John Kurila's last kick of the game salvaged a point for the Cobblers in an undulating 3-3 draw at the County Ground's open-sided venue that also accommodated the county cricket club's square and pavilion.

There were only three more goals for Baker before the end of the season, including that Wednesday effort and one in a 4-1 defeat away to a Burnley inspired by a Willie Irvine hat-trick. But the die had been cast, in Garibaldi red. Baker had captured the imagination of the Forest public and players alike.

COLIN ADDISON WAS moving in the opposite direction in the summer of 1966; on to Arsenal after several years as a gifted inside-forward for Forest, having signed from York City in January 1961. Addison would later become assistant manager to Ronnie Fenton at Notts County, where he was removed more or less on a whim by chairman Jack Dunnett, but his association with the city survives strongly through family and friends he visits regularly from his Hereford home.

Though they passed like ships in the night, Baker and his motion left an undercurrent that Addison recalls to this day. "He was just lightning quick. His pace was the thing that we all gasped about," says Addison, who masterminded one of the most famous FA Cup upsets as player/manager of Hereford United when they beat Newcastle United in 1972. "He could score goals as well. Used to pass the ball into the net, not blast it, like Jimmy Greaves. I remember playing against him when he was at Arsenal with George Eastham in midfield just opening up defences with his passes and Joe's pace. They were unstoppable on the day we played them."

Addison's Forest swansong coincided with Baker's first club tour, to Belgium and France at the end of the season. It was a close shave, however. "I remember sitting on the team coach at the City Ground waiting to get off to London airport," laughs Addison. "All the players and staff were there and the manager, everybody except one – Joe. They tried everything to get hold of him, but there was no reply. The talk among the lads was that his wife had gone back to Scotland knowing we were going on tour for ten days and Joe had been for a night on the town because he liked a drink or two.

"In the end, Johnny Carey says in that Irish accent of his: 'Ah come on, we'll pick him up on the way.' So we set off and drove to Joe's house in Wollaton, pipping the horn and everything outside his house with all the curtains drawn and no sign of life. Then, after about ten minutes of knocking on the door, Joe comes out looking a bit worse for wear. All he's carrying is the tiniest holdall I have ever seen, just enough room for a shaving brush, toothbrush and perhaps a pair of shorts. He got some stick from the older lads, but then that was Joe, always a glint in his eye and full of fun.

"After the first match [a 4-3 defeat by Standard Liege, Crowe, Addison and Baker scoring] we went back to the hotel and ordered a meal in the restaurant. Joe orders spaghetti because of his Italian days and we all sat around, John Barnwell, Bob McKinlay and myself, having a glass of wine and chatting. Not once did Joe look down at his meal. He twirled and twisted it around his fork and rolled it up into balls and ate the lot without once stopping the conversation or having his wine. At the end, the entire table had to give him a round of applause. 'That was different class, Joe,' we told him.

"He loved a joke, too. But the funny thing was he had to carry around a couple of handkerchiefs in his pocket. When he became excited, and he often did telling a joke or having a laugh, apparently his eye ducts were not quite right and he wasn't able to stem the flow properly without mopping up. Not tears exactly, but the moisture. It was a legacy of that accident in Italy. He came so close to death then, but the surgeons repaired everything except that."

IT WAS TO BE MORE tears of joy that Baker would induce in the following 1966/67 season in the audience that idolised him. A sluggish start, two defeats in the opening two games, and a 0-0 home draw with Chelsea scarcely foretold a season that transpired to be truly unforgettable for all those who stayed the course of the journey either side of the terrace and main stand walls. Gradually Forest, and Baker, began to find a stride that was to keep pace with the finest Manchester United team perhaps of all time.

While Frank Wignall might have lost a yard of pace, his aerial menace and shrewd positional sense allowed the time and space that encouraged Baker's instinctive play to blossom, while Ian Storey-Moore, out on the left or drifting across the penalty area, vied with Baker in the Trent End's popularity polls.

"It makes me laugh now when they talk about strikers not getting the right service or complaining that they are being starved of a decent pass," says Storey-Moore, formerly chief scout at Forest and then Aston Villa. "I see the valuation of some forwards and I can't believe it. In comparison, Joe was priceless because he didn't make excuses or wait for openings to come along. He fashioned them himself, making runs to create space and spotting when to get on the wrong side of defenders at just the right time. He was brilliant in that respect."

But as Forest chased United and an elusive Double, it was the brilliance of Denis Law that saw off Carey's side in a crucial league defeat at Old Trafford in February 1967. "I always remember Johnny Quigley [the former Forest player whose semi-final goal against Aston Villa had eased Forest into the 1959 FA Cup final] coming into the dressing room after the game and telling us that we were by far the better side," Henry Newton recalls.

A far more devastating blow arrived two months later, ironically during Storey-Moore's finest Forest hour and arguably one of the best FA Cup ties in the competition's history. Storey-Moore's hat-trick did defeat Everton at the City Ground, but Forest paid a hefty price. With just three minutes played, Brian Labone's crunching tackle laid Baker low and the centre-forward, although bravely hobbling on as a passenger for a little while, was forced to limp drearily to the dressing room to be replaced by Alan Hinton. What appeared to be nothing more than a routine 'dead leg' turned nasty and the bone around the injury calcified. Instead of a couple of games, Baker was out for the remainder of the season.

"It was a team without big stars, but there was no doubt that, without Joe, the pressure told on what was a thin squad," insists Henry Newton. "With Joe's pace, you knew you always had an outlet. It gave us confidence that if we were under the cosh, we could absorb that and Joe would always nick us a goal. He could catch anyone on the break and with Barry Lyons and Ian Storey-Moore on the wings with their own pace, we had a nice balance. But we lost that for the semi-final against Tottenham. I know for certain we would have beaten them on the day if Joe had played and, had we performed anything like that in the final, we would probably have beaten Chelsea. But history says different and you have to accept that."

The trip to sunny Spain followed the disappointment of missing out so cruelly on at least one trophy. Those games in Barcelona and Valencia were interspersed by essential rest and relaxation.

"There was a great story I heard about Joe in Valencia," recalls Duncan McKenzie, a young professional in Baker's final season at Forest. "He and John Barnwell were having a drink in one of the shadier bars in the city when this bloke walks in and tells them he wants the 'Scotsia' to leave. 'I'll go right enough,' Joe says in that broad Scottish accent. 'When I've finished my drink.' Barney was crapping his trousers, but Joe didn't budge. He was as hard as they came. Anyone who could chin Ron Yeats [the man mountain Liverpool centre-half who Baker punched during his Arsenal days] and put him on the deck must have been pretty handy with his fists."

McKenzie remembers Baker bringing his dog to training sessions and his Jaguar car that turned heads. "He'd leave his dog in the car. I jumped over it, the car that is, for a bet once. He was a fantastic man and that car…it had that gold Jaguar badge and a silver plate on the inside near the glove compartment with an inscription. 'Don't open the windows in excess of 125mph'. Said it all really."

When Baker returned the following season there were no signs that he had suffered irretrievable damage from his Labone-induced injury. Three goals against Eintracht Frankfurt over two legs in a 5-0 Inter Cities Fairs Cup demolition of the Germans indicated normal service had been resumed. Elimination by FC Zurich in the second round came as a nasty shock for Forest, who had battered the Swiss at the City Ground without translating their possession and supremacy into goals. A 1-0 reverse in the second leg knocked out Forest on the away goals rule despite drawing 2-2 on aggregate. Further embarrassment on the night was instigated by Barnwell and Carey, who insisted that the players remain on the pitch after 90 minutes, erroneously convinced that they had earned extra time.

An FA Cup defeat at Leeds United at the fourth round stage, with Baker scoring in a 2-1 defeat, ensured there would be no repeat of those epic Cup efforts. There was repetition by Baker duplicating the 16 First Division goals he had claimed the previous season, but the general consensus of opinion was that 'the king', as he had now become known, had lost a yard of his exhilarating pace.

Only four goals in 30 league appearances as Forest clung to their top flight status the following season confirmed the Trent End's worst fears.

BAKER MOVED ON TO Sunderland in June 1969 for £50,000 and finished his playing career back with Hibernian, then Raith Rovers.

If his heart belonged to Edinburgh, though, there was part of his soul that lingered in Nottingham. He returned for John Winfield's testimonial in the 1970s and a decade later, responded to an invite that was addressed: 'Joe Baker – via Scotland' to attend the club's centenary celebrations.

When he suffered a second heart attack in 1995, it was a measure of the affection and esteem in which he was held by a generation of Forest fans that some of them organised a timetable of events to celebrate Baker and his time at Forest, sending a personal invitation to the former player.

Again he came 'like a shot' when asked, saying he felt butterflies on the train journey down from Scotland. Back at the City Ground, strolling around the players' tunnel and patrolling the 18-yard box he had demonised for opposing defenders, the emotions of that 1966/67 season returned vividly.

"You'd sit in the dressing room and there would be a hum from the crowd coming through the walls," he said at the time. "The noise from the Trent End was incredible. They used to draw the ball into the net."

That tells you everything you need to know about the man who became a snapshot of that successful Forest team. Joe Baker was a man of the people, one who took the time to talk to the supporters and one whose every touch seemed to put a smile on their faces.

"The fans idolised him, but then so did quite a few of the players," admits Henry Newton in heartfelt tribute.

In October 2003, Baker passed away. The King of the Trent End was dead – but his legacy lives on. A working class hero with attitude. Zigger-zagger, zigger-zagger…

Jim Baxter

1967-1969: 49 games, 3 goals

THE SHINDIG IN the south Notts village was swinging, as befitting a decade known to tilt from side to side on occasion. Nothing to do with keys in the middle of the table, mind you. This was Ruddington and a gathering of players' wives far removed from the self-indulgent and promiscuous image promoted by a fanciful drama series nearly 40 years later.

A small enclave of Nottingham Forest players had moved en masse into the village known affectionately as 'Rudd'. A home to framework knitters and textile workers a century before, the new blood arriving now relied on the dexterity of their feet and legs rather than fingers and thumbs, allied to an alert mind and body. Dexterity in any part of his body had deserted one of the revellers among the Forest couples and their friends and neighbours.

It could have been a Tamla Motown vinyl revolving around the latest record player in the front room of one the 1960s' finest examples of Wimpey new-build. Smokey Robinson's *Tears Of A Clown* was certain to have got them on their feet; Cream's *Strange Brew* might have been less disco, but perhaps more apposite as one of the guests descended the staircase in an unsteady fashion. Upstairs an empty bottle of Bacardi revealed just a fraction of the truth behind the rubber legs that struggled across the flock carpet. With a head and a room spinning as swiftly as the single record at 45rpm, his hand reached out to steady himself and all of a sudden the good ship Jim Baxter capsized, his suction dragging down a new pair of curtain rails and curtains recently purchased from Nottingham's toffest department store, Griffin and Spalding.

"I think it's time you were on your way home Jim," came the immortal words that Baxter must have heard, or at least half recalled through the fuzz of alcohol, hundreds of times. "I'll call a taxi." The 'I' in question could have been Terry Hennessey, Henry Newton, John Barnwell or any number of Forest players living locally and partying that evening.

It could have been that night when Baxter failed to make it back home. There must have been plenty of those occasions, but on one in particular, the Scotland wing-half ended up having smashed his torso through a display window at C & A Modes, a cut-price department store for the masses which stood just around the corner from the old Broadmarsh bus station when the depot was a vast landscape open to the elements. En route to his early hours rendezvous with C & A, Baxter might have stumbled up Drury Hill, one of Nottingham's oldest thoroughfares dating back to medieval times, a historical gem demolished by the usual suspects in Council House HQ to make way for the grotesque shopping centre that stands there today. So narrow was the street that Baxter would have rebounded up and down it off the walls of the tiny premises like a pinball heading for oblivion. His final destination was somewhat perverse. How many dummies had he sold to opponents during his dazzling career and now here was a motley ensemble of inanimate mannequins in third-rate attire sneering over the immobile, unconscious and glassed-up drunken Scotsman on the floor beneath them?

From Govan to Gunthorpe, someone seems to have an off-the-field and off-the-cuff tale about 'Slim' Jim Baxter, mostly inspired by copious amounts of alcohol. On it, they are all inspired by his genius as a footballer. Yet whatever gutter he fell into, whatever shop window he gate-crashed before opening hours, in fact whatever trail of devastation he left behind, neither his peers nor his supporters have anything less than fond memories of Slim Jim Baxter.

The loveable rogue, the generous layabout or the itinerant drunk. Take your pick. He was a legend at Ibrox with Glasgow Rangers and, though his time was brief – just 18 months at the City Ground – he remains an extraordinary cult figure, still talked about eagerly by friend and foe alike.

FOR A MOMENT FORGET the indiscretions, and there are plenty, but recall how Tony Wood, then Forest chairman, gushed about Baxter when he signed him from Sunderland in December 1967. At £100,000 Baxter was only the seventh British player to command a six-figure sum.

"He is the best Christmas present I have given to any club," chirped Wood, who made his money from the thriving textile industry that still flourished in Nottingham then. "The thought of paying out such a big fee does not worry me at all. This is not a gamble. Baxter is a world class player and he will make a tremendous difference to us."

Wood clearly knew a thing or two about the rag trade, but it seemed everybody in football knew that the gullible Forest chairman had been well and truly stitched up when he agreed to splash out a club record fee for Baxter. He was 28 and it was not so much the water under the bridge that blighted Baxter but the amount of Scotch he'd mixed in with it.

Money earned from the previous campaign, when Forest reached the semi-finals of the FA Cup and failed narrowly as runners-up to Manchester United in the league, was lavished on one player who Wood and manager Johnny Carey thought could elevate the side to secure at least one of those trophies that had been so tantalisingly snatched from their grasp.

To some contemporaries, Baxter's signature had been a feather in the cap for Wood, a trophy signing to impress his social set of friends. True or not, it backfired in disastrous fashion, both in terms of finances and football for the club.

His stock, at least at the City Ground, had risen with an impressive performance for Sunderland at Roker Park against the Reds the previous month but in truth it was only an incongruous star billing during a downward spiral. His debut, on 16 December, saw Sheffield United beaten 1-0 at the City Ground, Dave Hilley scoring the only goal of the game, and, to celebrate the passing of 1967, Baxter scored a spectacular effort himself in a 3-1 win over Stoke City at the Victoria Ground on the 30th, completing a rapid double over the Potteries club after a 3-0 home win on Boxing Day.

It was fleeting success and by the end of the following season both Carey and Baxter had departed Forest. From being genuine title contenders, they had descended to relegation dodgers. Amidst the freefall, Baxter's immense reputation as a player, at least among colleagues, seldom wavered. Sammy Chapman and Billy Brindley recalled players fearful of going near Baxter in five-a-sides, even on the ash-laden car park where the Scotsman's ability to nutmeg and ridicule an opponent still ruled.

With the ball at his feet, he was mesmerising. Asked to run a few laps without it, less so.

"He used to come in most mornings with his eyes a bit bloodshot," says Jeff Whitefoot, the stylish former Manchester United wing-half and FA Cup winner with Forest, whose own career was ending when Baxter joined the club. "Tommy Cavanagh [the fearsome but inspiring Forest trainer] was determined to make him sick as a dog through training, although in fairness he tried to do that with most of us." Baxter would oblige more often than not on behalf of the others. "He had incredible skill, but had that self-destruct button which players like that seem to have."

During his phenomenal rise from Raith Rovers through to Rangers and then his national team, the comparisons with the incredible abilities of George Best were inevitable, both in terms of dribbling and drinking capacity.

Duncan McKenzie would never set himself among those legends, but the young Forest professional who etched his name with pride and panache at the City Ground and other clubs, was one of the first to understand the legend that was Baxter.

"I think it was one of the most flattering things that happened to me when I was a young professional," McKenzie recalls. "The lads would come in at the end of training and ask if anyone wanted a game of head tennis with Jim. Not many wanted to take him on, but they always put me forward for a game with him if he fancied it." Some accolade. "Problem was that by the time Jim came to us he was pregnant, wasn't he?" quips McKenzie. Certainly Baxter was overweight and out of condition. "But he was one of the only footballers that I knew that got ten out of ten in the player ratings in the *Sunday People* for two consecutive games."

Given Baxter's obvious physical deficiencies that was a pretty remarkable effort.

"He was such a generous bloke, particularly with the young lads," says McKenzie. "We all loved him because he'd come into the Trent Bridge café at the top of the street from the ground and we'd be tucking into beans on toast or a fry-up after training. He'd get out a ten bob note or whatever on the table and pay for the lot of us, about four meals, and that meant a lot to us then because we were on a relative pittance.

"I was the one who had to deal with his fan mail and believe me he got an inordinate amount of that. Before e-mails and the internet, mobile phones, texting and all the stuff that comes with football clubs nowadays, the fans wrote to Jim at the ground and it was my job to open the mail and pass it on to him. It was mostly fans asking for autographs on photographs, which he was happy to sign.

"Then one day an envelope arrived from Sunderland and I opened it. It was a final pay-out from the club after his transfer to Forest. Remember I was on about £16 a week then. The cheque was made out to Mr Jim Baxter. For £8,000. I couldn't believe it. I'd never seen that amount of money written out like that in my life. Can you imagine? I remember I took it with me back to my digs where I was staying on Loughborough Road and put it under my pillow. I slept on that cheque all weekend then on the Monday I gave it to Jim. He was totally unfazed. As far as I knew he took it and put in some drawer for a few weeks. He didn't need to cash it, that's for certain. Just shows the value and how he was rated at the time.

"I was glad I had the chance to see him again many years later. Then, shortly before he died, I spoke to him on the mobile phone. I wanted him to know how much we really loved him at Forest. And we did."

IF BAXTER LIKED A drink, he also liked to gamble. Were there any vices that passed him by? Apparently not. His rapacious thirst for a 'bevvy' was equalled by a penchant for a card game. Not just the odd penny blind at three card brag, either, more £10 and £20 minimum stakes for all-night poker and ku khan sessions.

Of course, there is that famous old chestnut of a quote on this subject attributed to Jim, who, when asked if having been paid the huge sums of money footballers received in later decades would have made a difference to his lifestyle, replied, "Definitely. I'd have spent £50,000 a week at the bookies instead of £100."

He was only half joking. Apprentices and professionals alike would glare agog when Baxter rolled up to the City Ground car park, opening the boot of his car to reveal a bundle of notes that would have been enough to confirm that somebody had just robbed a bank.

The self-indulgence, already in its advanced stage, took an inevitable toll. Tales of him being ejected from the Hippo, the trendiest club in Nottingham on Bridlesmith Gate, for urinating on the dance floor, enhanced dressing room gossip but scarcely improved performances on the pitch. Peter Hindley had to be restrained on one occasion from trying to remonstrate with several bouncers as Baxter, not without some justification, was shown the exit door.

Yet what was to be his final season began in August 1969 so promisingly with a goal in a 2-2 draw with a decent Burnley side in front of 30,000 fans at the City Ground. Joe Baker scored the other, but it was a desperately false dawn. It would be Baxter's only goal of the campaign and his compatriot, at least linguistically (Baker had been capped for England with a broad Scottish accent), would add only three more in the league. By the end of the month, the main stand had disappeared following a half-time fire during the game with Leeds United. While Forest were accommodated at Meadow Lane for six 'home' games, they failed to win a solitary match. By February of the following year, Carey had gone too, replaced by Matt Gillies, the former Leicester City manager who had guided Forest's East Midlands rivals to two FA Cup finals and a League Cup final victory against Stoke City over two legs in 1964. One of his first signings was Alan Hill, the Rotherham United goalkeeper who quickly made his debut in a 3-0 victory over West Bromwich Albion in March.

Hill doubled his wages when he joined Forest and was also given five star treatment by being lodged in the Bridgford Hotel overlooking the River Trent and the City Ground, the building today that is offices of the local district council but was then a luxury hotel replete with rooms with views. "I was in awe of the likes of Hennessey, but none more so than Baxter," Hill says. "He'd sit in the dressing room and tell one of the kids: 'Go and get me my magic wand, son. I need my left boot.' He made my eyes pop out when I saw some of the money he was gambling. Anything from £500 to £3,000 a night playing for a £1 spot at ku khan. There was a lot of it going among the players then. It was unbelievable because I was on £65 a week and thought that was a lot of money.

"Jim used to come into training laughing and joking whether he'd won or lost. Unshaven and usually chewing the last bits of a bacon butty. His attitude used to make Tommy Cavanagh foam at the mouth! It was his mission to make him throw up every morning!

"When I first signed, I was booked into the Bridgford for three months. I was living in Barnsley then with Janice [Hill's wife] and we needed to sort things out about moving down. We had been on the verge of taking a newspaper shop but the Forest offer came right out of the blue and changed everything. Anyway I hadn't been there long when I got a call from the gaffer [Gillies] to meet him in his office.

"'Alan, I'd like a quiet word.'

"'What's the matter boss?' a nervous Hill replied, only too aware that he had been offered a great chance to establish himself in a First Division side.

"'We've just got the drinks bill back from the hotel.'

"'And?'

"'Well, it's a little high to say the least. Around £30 a night seems a bit excessive.'

"'But I only have the odd glass of lemonade, maybe a shandy now and again. Nothing more.'

"'But there's lager and all sorts on here.'

"'But I don't drink lager, boss, and I don't put my drinks on the bar bill anyway. I pay for them myself.'

"'Well what's this then? Is this your signature?'

"'No, bloody hell it's not.'"

With that, Gillies stormed into the dressing room and demanded an explanation from the squad.

"Jim was the first to put his hand up," said Hill. "He'd been going back to the hotel with some girls after a night out at the 99 [a club frequented by players from both sides of the River Trent that adjoined the Bridgford Hotel]. When it came to paying, he knew I was staying there and forged my signature and put it on my room tab!"

DESPITE ALL THE SHENANIGANS, Henry Newton remembers a player who could drift past markers with a sublime body swerve, even though his better days were well behind him.

"There were some mornings when we trained in front of the stands, doing doggies, weights and running. Jim would excel at some of the sprinting work," says Newton, himself probably the fittest all-round athlete in that Forest squad. "I thought then that he must have been a pretty fit bloke when he was younger in his prime.

"When he was going through a bad time in that last season, I asked him how he did it; how he just seemed to get possession of the ball and almost walk past players without really trying. It was a gift. But he didn't have an answer. 'I don't know' was all he could say."

Once Baxter had lost that shining talent, with his pace decimated by the ravages of time and alcohol, he was a mere shadow of the Slim Jim that had tormented England at Wembley in both 1963 and 1967 and the one which gleamed in the Rest of the World XI that faced England, also in 1963.

"In my opinion he was up there with Besty. He was a genius," insists Hill. "Wonderful ability and the ball seemed to be on a string when he had it at his feet. And didn't he score some great goals with that left foot?! Regardless of what I thought of him off the pitch, I always had the highest regard for his talent, but I was never sure of him as a team player. Then, near the end of that season, we played at Coventry [April 19] and needed a point to be certain of avoiding relegation. Jim left the field with a massive gash in his head, this in the days before substitutes, and I thought that would be the last we saw of him. Then, after a few minutes, he was back on the park with stitches and a head bandage and he stayed on for the rest of the game. We got a 1-1 draw and were safe and I had the utmost respect for him as a player in every way after that."

Newton also recalls another game that season in the frozen wastes of Merseyside when Liverpool manager Bill Shankly was anxious to get the game played on February 15.

"They had European games coming thick and fast and Shankly probably thought this was going to be an easy two points for them, so he did everything in his power to persuade the referee to get the game played, which it duly was. Matt Gillies took us all into the dressing room beforehand and said that if anyone didn't fancy it out there, they should say so now and they would not be picked.

"Of course none of us wanted that, but we thought Jim might walk just to be awkward. In fact he played one of his best games for us. Barry Lyons got two and we nicked a 2-0 win! That was very pleasing."

That sort of Anfield slip-up was the sort of result that helped Leeds United secure their first league title by the end of the season with a record haul of 67 points. They celebrated by beating Forest in the final game of the season at Elland Road, 1-0 before over 46,000 fans.

It was to prove to be Baxter's last match for Forest. Afterwards, Leeds manager Don Revie sent bottles of champagne into the away team dressing room to congratulate the visitors on avoiding relegation by three points and to assist them to join the trophy-winning party which the Leeds boys were instigating, a gracious gesture equally graciously received and imbibed no doubt.

Being a Wednesday night match, the Forest players continued to celebrate long into the early hours back in Nottingham at the 99 club and then at the Bridgford Hotel. Officials joined the party, no doubt relieved to have survived in the First Division for another season.

Baxter, high on bubbly, Bacardi and goodness knows what else, confronted Tony Wood, the chairman who had bought him. Words were exchanged, to the effect that Baxter called Wood a "stingy bastard", alluding to the chairman's reluctance to invest in the transfer market and strengthen the squad. The £100,000 he had paid for Baxter might have been one reason for the lack of activity. Certainly it was a case of biting the hand that feeds you and Baxter was destined never to kick a ball for Forest again.

Such was Wood's chagrin, and as most people in football know hell hath no fury like a chairman's ego scorned, Baxter was allowed to leave the club on a free transfer, the equivalent of the 'soccer scrapheap' as it was referred to then.

In truth no other club would have paid a fee for Baxter and have been able to match his wages, in the region of £150 a week at Forest. For Wood and Forest, it was an embarrassing fiscal performance. *Après moi le déluge?* Possibly, since Forest's decline was not arrested and Hennessey, Newton and Storey-Moore were all sold as the club sank into the Second Division over the next four years.

For Baxter, there was temporary respite.

Rangers took him back briefly, but not even afternoon sessions in a sweat box to lose weight earned an extension of his short term contract. A few skirmishes with the law and drink-driving offences headlined his years immediately after leaving Forest before he settled down to make a living as, what else, a publican in Glasgow.

The lad born in the Fifeshire village Hill O'Beath, who had walked four miles a day to work down the pit at Fordell Colliery, following in his father's footsteps, seemed to find a certain contentment on the other side of the bar for a time. His drinking past, however, caught up with him and, in another echo of his link with George Best, two liver transplants in the 1990s saved his life before he died of cancer in April 2001, aged 61.

If he was mourned deeply and widely at Ibrox where he had won three titles, three Scottish Cups and four League Cups, there was more than a tinge of regret at the City Ground where Baxter had doubled the gate when recovering from injury in the Central League side.

A drinker, a gambler, a womaniser and a towering talent bordering on genius during an era enriched with players of genuine ability and star quality. Who could fail to cast an envious and admiring glance his way?

Interviewed behind his Glasgow bar in 1974, aged 35 and not having kicked a ball in anger for four years, he wrote his own epitaph, to be read out in a defiant but elegant Caledonian lilt.

"I live for today. What's gone has gone. There is no point looking over your shoulder at things that have happened or might have been."

Duncan McKenzie

1969-1974: 111 games, 41 goals

IT WAS A DILEMMA. Not much of one admittedly. More a question of priorities really. Like that depressingly dreary Noel Edmonds show, *Deal Or No Deal?*, depressing because its compulsive attraction leaves you wondering about the meaning of your own disturbing existence when it loses another half an hour when there is, in fact, an alternative. The last Tuesday in February 1974 threw up such a conundrum. But it was, thankfully, solved. "Come on lads, we're going over to the City Ground to see them play Orient."

The invitation came from the senior professionals at Notts County to the younger generation of 1974. Only a fraction younger in the great scheme of things, but six or seven years in football terms was considerable; although, if it meant the difference between being royally whacked by the right boot of Sam Ellis – in the early '70s – or Sam Allardyce – in the late '70s – the generation gap was not quite as wide as it might have been perceived. The choices were: a) upmarket Second Division football fodder at the City Ground or b) an early doors drinking session in town which may lead to a week's wages fine and possible disciplinary action.

About to enter my last year as a teenager the following week, there seemed only one course of action. But we ended up at the City Ground that night anyway, cajoled by the small print and menace implied in case of a refusal by the Meadow Lane old lags society. What greater tribute can anyone pay to a fellow professional than to sacrifice their Tuesday night out on the lash and lay down their weary limbs in the Forest main stand to watch one man perform, well, his one-man show?

Duncan McKenzie most certainly has had higher accolades from his peer groups, respected scribes and discerning supporters, but no matter the purple prose or platitudes, surely no gesture could have been more heartfelt or sincere than when a team comprised of thirsty seasoned pros and hedonistic youths – from a rival club no less – settled down to watch the moustachioed Dave Serella and John Winfield attempt to quell the combined threat of Barrie Fairbrother and Gerry Queen; among other sideshow attractions that evening.

Fine professionals though all those aforementioned were, it was McKenzie who we went to study; the bag of tricks that had ignited Forest's quest for promotion under the dour Allan Brown regime and carried the side into the quarter-finals of the FA Cup.

In fact, while McKenzie swivelled, dummied and shimmied his way through his impressive repertoire, an otherwise dull affair suddenly became interesting when Tommy Jackson, Forest's Northern Irish midfield player, and Ricky Heppolette, Orient's Bombay-born, Bolton-reared midfield anchor, found themselves having a very public difference of opinion that swiftly descended into farce. Had it been a Thursday night at the Goose Fair in Sillitoe's Nottingham, the sparring duo would have been in the freak show marked Midget Mayhem: the world's two smallest men fight it out to the death overlooked by the bearded lady (in this case the poor old referee Keith Styles in drag). Next door, McKenzie Magic would be dragging them in like the old Roaring Twenties, the naughty peep show where the breasts were anything but midget-sized and the apples even larger as some of Barnsley's finest set about re-enacting Eve's early struggles with haute couture in the Garden of Eden. Eventually after Heppolette and Jackson had glowered menacingly at one another for long enough, Styles sent them off. "And a good thing too," Heppolette, later a colleague and friend at Peterborough United, once told me. "Once I'd raised my fists I didn't have a clue what to do next. I was just hoping Tommy wasn't handy with his. We had a laugh about it afterwards!"

Goals from Neil Martin and George Lyall, another flame-haired pocket battleship on parade that night, settled the game 2-1 in Forest's favour against the side who were second in the table. With Jack

Charlton's Middlesbrough streets ahead at the top, realistically it was a scramble for the remaining two places, this in the days before the play-off system, and those two vital points had thrust Forest firmly in the frame.

WHAT HAD ENHANCED their promotion credentials most, though, was McKenzie's scintillating form. He was slight of frame, sleight of shoulder and sly in body movement. The zenith of his Forest career had arrived just a month previously. "You know we won the league and two European Cups and all some of them ever talk about is that match against Manchester City," is how John Robertson, architect of those European triumphs, often greets McKenzie. It is indicative of how fans recall the mercurial, waspish runs which created merry hell in opponents' defences and chances aplenty for his forwards. McKenzie was the archetypal underachieving entertainer in many ways; a maverick, blessed with ability to wow crowds with a feint or shimmy that has small boys and grown men wishing it was they blessed with such talent.

The winter of discontent was declared officially in 1979, but Ted Heath's government could claim a patent as the miners' strikes, a hike in petrol prices, Gary Glitter's aerosol demands and the wattage required to stage a Yes concert saw the introduction of the three-day week and power cuts in the winter of 1974. Football obliged by cancelling midweek fixtures and kicking off early on Sundays to negate the use of floodlights.

Forest's first Sunday match at the City Ground enticed just over 23,000 from the lunchtime boozer, well worth the trip as the home side edged Bristol Rovers out of the FA Cup third round 4-3 on 6 January. Their next opponents were Manchester City, hardly pulling up trees in the First Division, but still a glamour club that included Rodney Marsh, Mike Summerbee, Denis Law, Frannie Lee and Colin Bell among an admittedly ageing squad that new manager Ron Saunders had inherited. Their visit proved a watershed for McKenzie.

"Every kick, every nutmeg, every flick, they all came off, I just felt that if I went at them in the box, I could not be stopped," McKenzie recalls of that incredible Sunday lunchtime when City were put to the sword in front of a disbelieving crowd, both *Blue Moon* and *Over the Moon* factions, of 41,472. "They tried to kick me, but I just kept going inside and out. It was amazing." Ian Bowyer scored two against his old club, Lyall another and one from McKenzie, the thin controller who pulled all the levers and strings at precisely the right time, completed a 4-1 rout.

The following week Middlesbrough, runaway leaders of the division, were thrashed 5-1, just over 18,000 turning up for the league fixture. Perversely, in terms of modern football fads, the punters packed in once more when the FA Cup returned to town, again on a Sunday, this time with the visit of Portsmouth. Rubbish game, but a McKenzie penalty was sufficient to get Forest through to the quarter-final, where Newcastle United awaited.

In keeping with a languid style and easy-going exterior, it seemed to all the world as though McKenzie's elevation to the Forest elite had been executed with consummate ease, that his fame must have delivered his fortune, and that everything in the Forest garden was tickety boo, Garibaldi rose-red tinted and destined to end in harmony and success by the end of the season.

But then this is football. This is Nottingham Forest. There was much heartache, soul searching and pain to come before May was out, not to mention something which was symptomatic of the era and virtually de rigueur for the oppressed working classes fighting first the old Tory 'Grocer' Heath, then the old Labour Harold Wilson; a mass demonstration by the workers and a downing of tools as a mark of solidarity. But at least Abba won the Eurovision Song Contest, so that made everybody feel a whole lot better!

FOR MCKENZIE, THE media exposure and recognition of talent was in some ways just the beginning of an illustrious career that would embrace Brian Clough's fling with Leeds United, thence Everton, Anderlecht, Chelsea and Blackburn Rovers. Yet it was also the conclusion of a long journey from the backwaters of Grimsby that had found diversions in Mansfield more than once along the way. Schooled in an era when religious segregation was irrelevant, some of his classmates ranged from Russian Orthodox to agnostic. McKenzie played for the local Notre Dame Catholic Boys side despite having no affinity to their faith. "We went everywhere, from Glasgow to the Channel Islands and Dublin which was great for a lad like me from a relatively sheltered background." His headmaster Norman Harvard was at loggerheads with his father when Forest came calling after some impressive games for a Sunday morning men's side called Clee Rovers. "My dad worked on the docks in Grimsby when the fishing fleet was everything. He'd seen a lot of ex-Grimsby youngsters come down and work there and didn't want me wasting my life away. I was in my first year doing A-levels at the time, some boring subjects (Geography, History, Economics), and didn't know which way to turn. Mr Harvard said: 'Look, go to Forest. If it doesn't work out, you can always come back and take your A-levels again. I'll talk to your dad about it.'"

He was ferried by his father to several A team games. The crunch, literally, came in the new year of 1968. McKenzie's dilemma was acute, with exams pending. "I didn't need ifs and buts, I needed to know then and there, but I was injured after half an hour on the day Johnny Carey [the Forest manager] came to see me. He came into the treatment room puffing on his pipe and said: 'Son, I've seen enough to make my mind up. We'll offer you a contract.'"

In the summer of that year, McKenzie decamped to the Loughborough Road digs that Ian Storey-Moore was vacating in favour of marital bliss, and shared with Colin Hall, a winger in the Franz Carr mould minus the latter's curiously inaccurate sat nav system that was disabled when trying to find the location named Penalty Area.

McKenzie moved from Grimsby to a club and city with a vibrant youth culture that included, respectively, John Cottam, Graham Collier, Alan Buckley and John Robertson, the Boat, Union and Britannia rowing clubs. Martin O'Neill and Liam O'Kane ('always going to be a world beater, great pace and touch') would join later on.

"Our idea of a night out in Grimsby was the jazz club near the river front, what locals called the 'town head'," recalls McKenzie. "Every Friday and Saturday night it was the Rumble Band. They were good, but never anyone else, no guests or anything; just the Rumble Band. So Nottingham was an eye opener.

"The TBI [Trent Bridge Inn] was incredibly fashionable then, although most of the young lads preferred the rowing clubs or ice skating. Can you imagine that now? We thought we were invincible, we'd never get injured, so we went every Wednesday to the ice stadium, a gang of us and a few girls in tow. Fortunately the manager never got to hear about it. I think he would have had kittens if he had.

"There was something about the club at the time. Tony Wood was the chairman, from the rag trade and there were a lot of wealthy types knocking around. They liked having a chat, even with someone like me, a young professional but nobody really. It made you feel special and that you and the club was going somewhere. There was an undercurrent, a kudos about wearing the red shirt and it fitted in with that time. There was glamour about the place and even someone like myself playing in the A team felt like a celebrity in the town. I felt it was on the verge of buzzing."

The sight of Rolls-Royces purchased on the back of what was then a reasonably thriving textile industry in the Lace Market was enough to turn the head of any young man who aspired to increase his bank balance and make a name for himself.

For McKenzie, however, the path to betterment took him initially no further than Field Mill. A sequel, McKenzie II; Set Free in Mansfield, would follow some three years later and prove pivotal to progress. However in March 1970, the short skip down the A60 to the Stags' ground appeared more akin to punishment than a learning curve. "Matt Gillies [Carey's successor] was a strange man in the fact that he hated anybody in his team who was over 30. He implied that I would be getting a free transfer at the end of the season, so I'd better be prepared. Tommy Eggleston was the manager at Mansfield. They were on the fringes of the promotion race at the time. Frank Wignall was there, Malcolm Partridge, Phil Waller and Jimmy Goodfellow, a left winger from Leicester, too, and Stuart Boam at centre-half.

"I was doing so well that Tommy had to stop playing me because he knew my fee might go up and he wanted to sign me permanently. David Herd, who was manager at Lincoln City, was also showing an interest and so Gillies recalled me. I think he realised his own lack of ability because other managers were prepared to pay a fee for me. I always remember the advice dear old Johnny Quigley gave me when I was at Mansfield, though. Quigs was still playing then and he told me: 'Look Duncan, any fool can come down and play at this level. You're better than that son. Go back and fight for your place at Forest. You can go and play in the First Division and if the chance comes, take my word, reach for the highest possible point.'"

McKenzie had actually made his Forest first team debut in a 2-1 defeat at Sunderland in September 1969, but festered in the reserves upon returning from exile up north of the county in the mining roughlands of Mansfield. He would have to wait until April 1971 before he scored his first goals for the club, in a 3-1 away win at Manchester City that clearly was a taste of things to come.

It was the arrival of Dave Mackay from Swindon in November 1972, replacing Gillies whose stewardship had seen Forest relegated to the Second Division, that revived faltering ambitions. That and another trek to Mansfield. A trip that took in the inviting vistas of the Home Ales brewery at Daybrook, the Wagon and Horses at Redhill, the splendid boozer owned by Forest's Cup-winning full-back Bill Whare, and the Hutt public house nearer the Blidworth turn-off. It was a hazardous route lined with liquid temptation at almost every corner. Fortunately McKenzie was also in the Forest drinking reserve team. "Dave Mackay was such a brilliant inspiration, for me at any rate. He transformed my career," McKenzie affirms. "I remember the first day he took charge, he got us all out on the pitch in the centre circle at the City Ground. 'Look,' he told us. 'I don't expect your respect for what I've done as a manager because I've done nothing yet. But I expect it for what I've done as a player.'

"After that he told Des Anderson [his assistant] to throw him three footballs. He drove the first into the back of the net without bouncing and then said he'd hit the crossbar with the next one. Whack, half volley onto the crossbar. And the last one he volleyed down the players' tunnel and told us all to go home and get changed. 'Bastard,' I thought. But what bloody talent.

"He sat me down and told me he wanted me to play left wing with Martin O'Neill on the right. I explained it wasn't for me, but he'd got Neil Martin and John Galley and he wanted to play with two big lads down the middle and two wingers supplying them."

The combination didn't work, at least for McKenzie. Back to the drawing board translated into a loan spell with Mansfield Town, this time at the recommendation of Jimmy McCaffrey, a former Forest aspirant and old mate of McKenzie's.

"Jimmy was like shit off the shovel and again Mansfield were trying to get promotion, so he advised Danny Williams [the Stags' manager] to come and get me for a month when he knew I was available. Dave Mackay thought it was a good idea, so I was allowed out. The first training session I was stuck out on the right and Jimmy said to the manager: 'Just give him a free role. Trust me.' So Danny Williams said 'go and play a free role.' I picked up the ball, zipped past two or three and put it in the back of the net. That was the end of the session."

McKenzie scored seven goals in six games in his second spell at Field Mill, a double-edged sword for the lower league club. "I remember Danny banging his head on the desk when he got the call from Dave Mackay that they wanted me back.

"'Why didn't you do that for me' Mackay asked me when I got back.

"'Because you never asked.'"

At the next team meeting, Mackay roused up his troops by telling Sammy Chapman that he was doing a grand job, kicking opponents, heading the ball and winning his fair share of tackles, but now the system was going to revolve around McKenzie.

"Suddenly I was being given star billing, a free role. I owed that to Dave Mackay and even after he left to take the Derby job, there was no way new manager Allan Brown could change it. Only a numbskull would do that. He must have thought he'd woken up in paradise when he got the job. We were flying near the top of the league and the side was in good shape. Mackay was the only man who could take the Derby job after Clough. For all Sam Longson's faults [the Derby chairman who ousted Clough], he did his homework there and got it right.

"Dave took no stick from anyone. Only a character as strong as he was could tell the likes of Roy McFarland, Colin Todd and Kevin Hector that if they didn't want to play for him or Derby they could rot in the reserves. The youngsters might get beat 10-0 every week, but they'll be giving their best for Derby County. It was a great strategy and it worked brilliantly.

"The only thing I've got against him is that he didn't let any of us know that he'd got the job. We could have made a killing at the bookies."

There are two pertinent references in those latter paragraphs. The numbskull that Allan Brown might have been and the paucity of readies that was a feature of McKenzie's Forest career. The two are inextricably intertwined with the player's acrimonious departure and indeed the manager's subsequent failings and sacking that ushered in a certain Mr B Clough.

SO BACK TO 1974 and a buoyant Forest about to tackle a couple of Magpies. The Geordie hordes at St James' Park could wait, but the black and white stripes of Notts County and a small issue of local pride were more pressing matters on 3 March, another milestone encounter being the first Sunday league game at the City Ground.

Although just a couple of points behind Forest, County manager Jimmy Sirrel knew that any hope of promotion had been squandered with some slipshod displays and having played at least two games more than their adjacent rivals, he sensed a chance to make a statement to County supporters who for so long had slouched in the shadow of their illustrious neighbours.

The opportunity had been lost on Boxing Day 1973 when McKenzie earned a penalty even less deserving than John O'Hare's gravity and belief-defying launch that was rewarded with a hairline decision in the 1980 League Cup final replay with Liverpool. George Lyall smacked in the spot-kick and Forest, with their jubilant fans swaying joyously on Meadow Lane's incongruously brim full Spion Kop, claimed the first Trentside derby in 16 years.

More galling for Sirrel was his pre-match instruction to his trusty left-back Bob Worthington re McKenzie. "He has this trick, Robert," Sirrel had revealed, continuing to demonstrate how McKenzie would shimmy this way and that when the ball was played at pace to feet, spinning and turning to run on beyond the bemused marker with the ball skimming its way tantalisingly towards the opponent's penalty area.

Within a minute of the kick-off, Bob's database had been erased and McKenzie was scampering off to the County 18-yard box, where Ian Bowyer managed to head over his cross under severe pressure from David Needham and Brian Stubbs, while Bob was under severe pressure from Jimmy's guttural Glaswegian expletives emanating from the dugout.

Perhaps determined not to have a repeat and driven to match the enemy on the doorstep, Sirrel asked me, actually told me for a week before the clubs' next meeting, to stop McKenzie. Man-to-man marking that would embarrass even George Michael and friends in any public convenience. We drew 0-0, job done and the Sunday proved historic for football.

The first PFA awards took place that night in London's Hilton Hotel on Park Lane with McKenzie named in the Second Division's best XI selected by his professional peers. Under normal circumstances that should have been no more than a blip on Forest's season. Enter the second Magpies, Newcastle United of the First Division, the following week in the FA Cup quarter-final. The myth of friendly, sporting fair play Geordies was dispelled forever when Forest raced into a 3-1 lead and, seemingly destined for the semi-finals, with Newcastle defender Pat Howard already sent off for dissent, so a recovery from the home side seemed a remote possibility. Until, that is, the Leazes End decided to invade the pitch and the players retreated to the dressing rooms for their own safety.

"Nobody wanted to go back out in that atmosphere, it was a nonsense, the whole thing," McKenzie recalls. "It was ugly. The linesmen didn't move off the halfway line when we came back out. All the officials were intimidated." Lord Westwood, the League President and Newcastle chairman famous for his eye patch, was in the stands. After Newcastle rallied following the restart to win 4-3, Forest appealed. Surprise, surprise, instead of Newcastle being booted out of the competition, the game was declared void and a replay ordered. "Clearly Westwood had his eye patch over his good eye that day," McKenzie laughs. Maybez, as they say up there in the north east, Newcastle had learned from Rangers fans in the semi-finals of the UEFA Cup a few years earlier in 1969. Two-nil down in the second leg of the tie at St James' Park and seemingly out of the competition, the Glaswegian visitors trampled onto the pitch with 20 minutes remaining, about the same time as the Newcastle louts intruded.

Frank Clark, later Forest defender and manager, was the Newcastle left-back on that balmy, barmy May night. "All hell broke loose and Willie McFaul [the Newcastle goalkeeper] ran down the tunnel with me when he stopped suddenly and told us he'd left his gloves and stuff in the back of the net. As he turned back to get them, I grabbed a hold of him. 'Get in there and don't be so bloody daft.' To be fair to the Rangers chairman, he came into our dressing room and told us that they would forfeit the match no matter the outcome. In the end, we went back out and played the last few minutes with police and their dogs surrounding the playing area and held on to win. The atmosphere was something else."

Unfortunately Westwood and his cronies did not have the good grace to grant the game to Forest despite the appalling behaviour of their fans. It was a rotten way to carry on. "To this day I don't know how they got away with it. Couldn't happen today with television replays and everything. They would be thrown out. Let's just say for the first and possibly last time everyone in Nottingham was a Liverpool fan on Cup final day." [Newcastle got their comeuppance with an abject performance as Liverpool won 3-0. Poetic justice?]

McKenzie did score to beat promotion rivals Blackpool 2-0 the following Saturday but the League's blatantly arrogant prejudice meant that Forest had to replay Newcastle on the Monday, at Goodison Park. That one finished 0-0 before an extra time goal by Malcolm Macdonald ended Forest's stirring Cup exploits three nights later in the second replay at the same venue. It was cruel and unjust. And to twist the knife into open wounds, a George Lyall free-kick that scorched its way into the Newcastle net was disallowed by Gordon Kew, the referee in charge for all three ties. "Ungentlemanly conduct," Kew called it as Paul Richardson diverted and distracted traffic in a practised set-piece routine. The irony was probably lost on the man in black.

A 2-0 away defeat to Fulham on the following Saturday just about ended dispirited Forest's promotion ambitions. Four games in a week, how would the Special Ones have whinge about that these days?

FOREST'S ASPIRATIONS HAD vanished inside seven days at the end of that 1973/74 season. Now their fortunes were about to deteriorate rapidly in tandem with McKenzie's own, felled by his increasing frustration with the prevarication tactics employed by Brown and his paymasters. "It began to turn nasty after we were knocked out of the Cup. We were all gutted enough, but all through the run, the chairman [Jim Wilmer] and manager had promised us our bonuses. After all, they were getting full houses and reaping the rewards and we were told that we had earned our money. We were going to get this and that, but then gradually it dawned on us that we were not going to get anything at all.

"Remember in those days I'd signed as a young lad for £12 a week with £4 for a win and £2 for a draw. But I was always brassick, never had any money but as a young lad you didn't mind too much. But I was married [to Dorothy] and we were expecting our first child later that year. People thought I was on a fortune, around £200 a week, but at the height of all that Cup stuff I was on £30 a week, no kidding. I used to drive around in an old NSU Princess, paid for by money we'd borrowed from Dot's mum. The bin men and window cleaners were earning more than me on average. They upped it to £50 when I kicked up a fuss, but, even so, most of my mates outside the game were on the same or more. They didn't understand."

The acrimony spread to dissolution on the terraces and gates dropped to 12,000 and below. It did not prevent McKenzie, who was being touted as a target for just about every First Division team, from doing what he did best – scoring goals and, to the delight of the spartan few on the terraces, extracting the Michael out of opponents. "I read somewhere that Frank McLintock loathed me because of my arrogance and John Bond [the Norwich City manager] couldn't understand why I was always taking the piss out of players when I got the ball. Anyone who knows me knows that I'm a regular sort of bloke off the pitch, happy to mix with the lads and not be the centre of attention. On the pitch was different. It's a Jekyll and Hyde thing, I suppose, I just couldn't help doing stuff when I got the ball to feet. I used to have this trick where I'd flick it up and over a defender and I remember doing that to Bob Moncur at Newcastle only he wasn't going to let me pass at any cost, so some opponents did get their own back.

"The analogy I use is Franz Beckenbauer; he was the best in the world at what he did but everyone wanted him to play more forward, more this or more that. They wanted to change him and his position. People won't be happy until they have spotted some kind of weakness in you so they can pick fault."

The enigmatic forward finished with seven goals in the last seven matches, scoring in each of the last five, including a couple at Portsmouth on the final day of the season, nudging his total up to 28 (2 FA Cup) for the season. "The lads had all got together and decided we had to do the best for one another, a unified front," McKenzie recalls. "In the meantime Wilmer and Brown were making noises that we'd all get our bonuses if we signed new contracts for next season. I remember the pair of them asking me to have contract talks with them in the chairman's office on the Monday after our last training session. I fully expected to be a Nottingham Forest player the following season, and a Forest player on a decent wage at last. So I went in only to find that the manager was golfing at Royal Birkdale that day. So we couldn't have talks. That's how much they wanted Duncan McKenzie to stay at Forest. The pair of them led me down the garden path. They had no intention of trying to keep me there.

"Then Wilmer tells me that if I want a transfer, I've got to put it in writing. Well that was the final straw. They'd paid me a pittance at the club, reneged on cup bonuses and now they wanted to take the five per cent cut I might get out of any fee off me as well. I thought: 'Stuff this. If this is the way football is being run, I'm better off out of it.'"

McKenzie stormed into the office of secretary Ken Smales and demanded his cards.

"Don't give him them," Des Anderson, the assistant manager, warned.

"Do you want the police down here? They're his cards and he's entitled to them. I can't refuse him," Smales replied and gave McKenzie his due. The mercurial player walked out refusing to play for Forest ever again, effectively going on strike.

In retrospect, the conclusion to the stand-off and McKenzie's radical action was always going to be a positive one for the player, but at the time he recalls he genuinely felt like turning his back on the game.

"It was a traumatic time because I was no big-time Charlie with contacts here and there. Not a soul had been in touch, by mail or phone and Dot was seven months pregnant with our son [Andrew; a daughter Rhia, Wendy Craig's character in *Butterflies*, would complete their family] and although we were in no danger of starving, we had to be careful with the bills and everything."

AT A LOOSE END, McKenzie kept himself fit by training with his local amateur side, Borrowash Victoria, and idly thought that he might open a newsagent's shop, even though as a vocation it sounded like Nigel Mansell giving up the day job to drive buses. "The manager was a phoney and he'd lost the dressing room by the end of the season. I could not understand his attitude or the chairman's. They were trying to lose this reputation as a selling club and you would have thought they'd have learnt from selling Henry Newton, Terry Hennessey and then Ian Storey-Moore because that blew right up in their faces when Forest were relegated."

McKenzie went six weeks without wages during his one-man 'strike'. Years later Pierre van Hooijdonk observed that Forest tradition with one tiny difference – Forest were actually going down that season and really could have done with the petulant Dutchman at his place of work. Eventually, a curt phone call from Allan Brown in mid-July brought the impasse to a close. "They had tried to squeeze the life out of me and then Brown called me and told me that they were going to allow Brian Clough to speak to me and then put the phone down. I hardly got the two words in I wanted to say to Brown. God, I would have killed him if I'd seen him face to face after that. He was supposed to be my manager looking after my interests and he was so condescending, and I'd been playing out of my skin for him, scoring him goals and now the club was going to get a quarter of a million pounds when I moved. And still they wanted me to leave without anything myself.

"I used to see John McSeveny [Brown's assistant] over the years and he tried to persuade me that Brown was not as bad as I made out. Well, I beg to differ. You speak as you find and he was a disgrace."

Freddie Goodwin at Birmingham, Dave Mackay (Derby County) and Bill Nicholson (Tottenham Hotspur) were among the eager suitors who asked about McKenzie once Forest had granted permission for their most valuable asset to talk to potential buyers.

In the end, the words of Johnny Quigley echoed around his brain as he mulled over his options. "'Go for the top,' he'd told me at Mansfield," says McKenzie. "And they didn't get any higher than the champions of England, Leeds United. Of course I was intimidated by Clough. I'd only met him once before when me, Jimmy McCaffrey and some of the groundstaff went over to the Baseball Ground to see Derby play. They were just the best team around then, but we didn't have any tickets. We told the ticket office who we were and Cloughie came out with three tickets. 'Mind you, young men, I expect the same treatment when I come to your place.'

"When he wanted me at Leeds, he took me for lunch to the Victoria Hotel in Huddersfield with his wife and family and I signed three blank contracts there and then. He honoured the lot and gave me everything I asked for. He said when I signed: 'Don't go walking out on me' so I warned him: 'If you do to me what those lot did to me, I will make no bones about it.'"

It never happened. Clough went in 44 days, but he'd helped McKenzie hit the jackpot.

"Keith Archer, the Leeds secretary, called me in to sign something," says McKenzie. "And there was a cheque for £3,333.33p, the first of four instalments.

"'What do I do with this?' I said.

"'Spend it,' he laughed. 'It's not taxable yet because you haven't been paid any wages.'"

McKenzie was also now earning £200 a week, quadruple his last Forest salary.

"It changed my life because it was a relative fortune to a Grimsby lad like me, but I like to think I never became a poser, just a normal bloke with normal friends."

NORMALITY IS RELATIVE, of course. His penchant for leapfrogging minis in the Forest car park and hurling golf balls vast distances brought Brian Moore and the ITV cameras to the City Ground during his final season there. "We used to train at Boots' sports ground on Lady Bay. There was a stile there where you had to file through Indian fashion, but being one of the younger lads then, the senior pros took precedence and were first back at the ground, so you had no chance of a bottle of milk or lemonade. One day I just up and hopped over this five bar gate, about 5ft high it was, beside the stile. It became a thing at the club, I was like one of those sheepdogs on the trials, always springing up and over it.

"It was Brian Williamson, who came to us from Fulham, who took it a stage further when he bet me a fiver that I couldn't get over Tommy Cavanagh's blue mini in one go. I took a step back and over I went. But he never did pay up. The golf ball came when I was throwing stones across the River Trent when we were walking back from training. Most of mine were reaching the other bank, but when the rest of the lads had a go, it barely got past halfway. It just went from there. They were just little tricks."

Despite his fame and fortune, McKenzie reflects on a career that never quite fulfilled potential and an empty trophy cabinet, with not even a solitary England cap to show for one of the game's great entertainers. "During that last season with Forest I must have hit the bar and post even more times than I scored, it was amazing.

Then I got the call for England from Sir Alf, me just a lowly Second Division player among the Alan Balls and Roy McFarlands. I think it was Harold Allcock, who was a Forest director and on the Under-23 selection committee who recommended me. Was that how it worked then?

"Anyway we went to Portugal. Can you imagine, Duncan McKenzie from Grimsby docks and Forest being feted at a garden party at the British Embassy in Lisbon. I remember it because it was Phil Parkes's only England cap. After about ten minutes, Malcolm Macdonald was struggling with a hamstring strain and I'm looking around the bench and thinking: 'Hey up Duncan, you're the only forward here. You'll be on in a second.' I was jumping through hoops.

"Then Sir Alf stands up and looks over to Alan Ball. 'We're having a spot of trouble in the middle of the park' [McKenzie mimics Ramsey with a BBC World Service news announcer reporting on a *Horse and Hound* convention in Roehampton]. 'Bally; get stripped and get in there and sort it out.' And that was my chance blown. It ended up a 0-0 draw and on the way home I was sitting next to Dave Watson, the Manchester City centre-half, on the plane. Sir Alf came over and waved Dave away. 'I'm frightfully sorry for dragging you all the way here without giving you game,' he said. Then it was my turn to say how much I'd enjoyed the experience and what a privilege it was to be called up by my country. Which it was and it was what he wanted to hear.

"'We'll get you on next time,' were his parting words."

That was April 1974 and there were not many next times for Sir Alf Ramsey, whose management was effectively over after England's failure to beat Poland the previous October and qualify for the World Cup finals in West Germany.

McKenzie came perilously close to winning a cap during Joe Mercer's brief tenure and there was even talk of Clough wanting to take him back to the City Ground when he was appointed manager in January 1975. "John O'Hare and John McGovern were allowed to leave [Elland Road] to join Forest, but not me. I don't think they could have afforded me then. Besides, would they have won the European Cup twice and the league with me? Who can tell?

"I remember Jimmy Armfield leaving me and Trevor Cherry out of the side that lost to Bayern Munich in the European Cup final in 1975. He said he wanted Don Revie's players to play that night out of respect to their former manager [then England manager] and even asked him to lead the side out that night in Paris. Revie declined, but he, again, told me my time would come. Oh really? I'd been top scorer for Leeds and how many European Cup finals would there be again for me, I asked him. Crazy."

There are compensations for McKenzie.

His fiscal security has allowed him to live with Dot in a charming Lancashire retreat just a few furlongs from Haydock Park racecourse. His reputation as an after-dinner speaker is impressive and in his spare time he tends a lush garden, piled high with compost and other horticultural artefacts which suggest fingers turned green with the passing of years. In other moments not contemplating his navel, McKenzie has taken up oil painting as well as auctioning portraits for deserving charities. A player of perpetual motion and a body language that yielded an obsession to dink, dally, dummy, shimmy and shuffle, has found new ways to occupy the waking hours.

McKenzie still has his quirks and tricks and an ability to deceive. The battered old Mercedes he drives around the country to his dinner engagements might betray a yearning to return to the £30 a week halcyon days of Nottingham Forest, but I doubt it.

"Punters remember and I'm grateful that they do. Nottingham Forest and that final year in particular was such a special time for me. It was essential to my whole life and everything I have today and can give to my family is a result of that one season. I've had a fabulous life on the back of it. In some respects I'm something of a nearly man, should have done this and achieved that, but I would have been not even close, none of this would have ever happened with Forest. I look back and thank Dave Mackay for giving me that free role, I owe him so much. And people like Johnny Quigley and Frank Wignall, who I learned from. But there would have been no Duncan McKenzie and the player I became at Nottingham Forest if it wasn't for the Sammy Chapmans, Dave Serellas and John Cottams of this world."

MCKENZIE WAS LIKE THE conjuror with the new trick, desperate to ingratiate himself with his audience while bemusing an unsuspecting and unwilling volunteer from the opposition.

Having myself been nutmegged, kicked in the head and suffered neck pains trying to quell his revolving door act, and seen those spring-heeled, jack-in-the-penalty-box antics from close quarters, there is little doubt McKenzie was, first and foremost, an entertainer who gave value for money. And he was adored for it, brief though his sojourn at the City Ground was. "It was nice to know that I was mentioned in the same breath as Marsh, Bowles, Currie, Worthington and George Best. Sometimes more George Formby actually than Best. Let's be honest, there was only one George Best. The rest of us were just names to make up the numbers, but now and again, you could be George Best for a day."

Brian Clough

1975-1993: 907 games, 411 wins

THE ENGINE WAS idling as the team coach awaited its departure from the City Ground car park. On board, a mixture of callow youth and a few old lags contemplated an evening's entertainment at Fellows Park and a reserve team fixture against Walsall. 'Surely there were better ways to spend a Tuesday night than dodging studded tackles and tackling dodgy grub in the Black Country?' most of the disparate assembled throng probably thought.

Except one George Waterhouse. Freshly appointed as a director from the laughing stock of over 200 members that passed for a committee at the City Ground, the Nottingham accountant was determined to make the trip to Walsall, riding shotgun if necessary since he had introduced himself as a 'troubleshooter'.

"What does that mean?" Alan Hill, trusty assistant to Brian Clough, had asked on first meeting the new director in a hotel foyer whilst on a scouting mission with youth team coach Paul Hart in Italy. Hill, like all football folk, was wary of boardroom people, particularly those with an inquiring mind, big nose and hell bent on intervention.

"I'm going to sort Brian out, he won't be getting away with the sort of stuff he has been doing," boasted Waterhouse. With that, Hill and Hart told the troubleshooting Waterhouse that anything he bought on the trip, he must keep a receipt. "We are all on club business," Hill confirmed, as Waterhouse raised an eyebrow.

It was not many days after that Italian meeting that Hill boarded the coach bound for Walsall to be confronted once more by Waterhouse.

"Hello again, Mr Waterhouse," greeted Hill. "Where are you going?"

"I'm going to watch the reserves at Walsall," replied Waterhouse.

Hill returned to the main offices where Clough was still in situ. "Brian, he's on the coach," Hill informed his boss in hushed tones. Don't ask why, but coaches and managers could be immersed in a soundproof closet inside Fort Knox discussing a secret that no-one within 500 miles could possibly eavesdrop – and still they would be inclined to communicate in reverential whispers. Upon hearing the news, Clough jumped up out of his seat in the manager's office, his familiar green top a little the worse for wear after an afternoon lazing around the ground. The jade, jaded tracksuit climbed up the steps of the coach, its owner suddenly reinvigorated with the prospect of a battle and a director's scalp as the spoils of victory.

"Hello Mr Waterhouse," Clough smiled. "What are you doing on this bus?"

"I'm going to see the reserves at Walsall."

"Are you? Do you have a car?"

"Yes I do."

"Then get off this bus."

"What do you mean, 'Get off this bus'?"

Clough now sterner, brimming with intent and arms resting on the chair tops on either side of the coach's aisle, leant forward. "No directors are allowed on this bus. Not even the directors I like. And I don't fucking like you. So you have no chance. Now get off my bus."

At which Waterhouse trotted tamely away, never to be seen on the team coach again. Before they had scarcely begun, Mr Waterhouse's troubleshooting days were over.

IF THERE WAS ONE quality that was essential to the pedestal upon which the football classes, then mostly working or aspiring middle of the range types, placed Brian Clough, it was his unerring appetite to ridicule the pompous and pious, the simpering and sycophantic.

He had been doing it for most of his playing life and so it became a natural transition when he had entered management at Hartlepools

United, where he encountered the first of several awkward opponents in the vertically challenged figure of Ernest Ord. Clough could not help but notice how Ord's feet failed to touch the ground as he sat on his magisterial throne, the north east club's seat of power, his little legs flailing about in a vain attempt to ground his leather soles and reach terra firma in the Victoria Park boardroom.

The ultimately acrimonious relationship with Sam Longson at Derby County may have soured Clough, as did his 44 days of failure at Leeds United, but he retained that instinct to expose, unnerve and eventually extinguish pomposity and puerility. When he arrived at the City Ground in the winter of 1975, he was not short of raw material in that respect, but gradually, rather than eliminate his rivals, he choose to infiltrate them and play 'the long game' from within. As a consequence, a succession of 'puppet' or 'muppet' directors and chairmen came and went as Clough continued, impervious to their presence, unhindered by their authority and crucially assisted in equal measure by Peter Taylor, to deliver trophies on demand to the south bank of the River Trent.

Did the fans care who ran the club? Of course not. Did they think Cloughie was on the take, running around with brown paper bags full of cash for services rendered by his team? Definitely. But were they in the least bit bothered, in the main stand, at the Bridgford or Trent End or in the East stand, who was running the shop and its business ethics as long as championship titles, League and European Cups and a whole legion of largely irrelevant and now defunct trophies came their way, and with them some unforgettable journeys to Wembley, Berlin and the Bernabeu in Madrid amongst their souvenirs and hangovers? Were they bollocks.

"Come and look at this," Clough once beckoned Hill at the height of the club's fame. Just a few days earlier, the master manager had fallen out with his daughter Elizabeth and, desperately wanting to heal the rift, had asked Hill to drive him to the nearby kennels at Gamston Bridge.

"And what can I do for you, Mr Clough?" inquired one of the kennels' staff desperately trying to suppress an urge to a) ask for an autograph and b) lavish praise on the man who had made more than a few of his sporting dreams come true.

"Do you have any Golden Retrievers?"

"We have anything you want, Mr Clough."

"Well show me the runt of the litter."

With that, Clough took the pup back to the City Ground and held him aloft, repeating: "You haven't half dropped for a life of luxury, little one." And he had. Instead of honing their footballing skills on the training ground opposite Holme Pierrepoint, a succession of Forest apprentices were commanded each morning by their own master's voice. "Young man, get over here and take Del Boy (as the dog was christened) for a walk." The ritual morning promenade may have cost the aspiring teenagers valuable time in terms of their football education, but it earned them a fiver for an extra portion of tuck at the Trent Bridge café or an extra pint at the Trent Bridge Inn come Saturday night, depending in which direction their career path was hurtling. Del Boy's barking alerted everyone in the ground that Clough was in the building somewhere and the mutual appreciation society was cemented because father and daughter had been reconciled.

"Get in here," Clough continued as he shouted down the corridor to Hill, sitting in an adjacent office. Hill moved cautiously towards the manager's door and pushed it open. There, sitting at the great man's desk, bolt upright in his chair, was Del Boy, sporting another piece of Clough's trademark and symbolic attire, the flat cloth cap that he doffed to no-one.

"You see, I told you so. Anybody can manage this fucking football club," Clough, standing behind the door, announced in fits of laughter to his captive audience.

Huge egos frequently merit their status, but in Brian Clough's case, the man was equal to the rapacious celebrity that had absorbed his character during the 1970s. Undeterred by two conspicuous and emotionally draining departures from Derby and Leeds, he re-emerged with Forest on 5 January 1975, replacing the dour Allan Brown, whose nemesis had been the foe across the Trent. Notts County's ascendancy back to the top of the Trentside football ladder had been a slow process, a position they had long ago surrendered when the legendary Tommy Lawton left Meadow Lane and Nottingham in the early 1950s. An exceptionally convoluted and elongated period of mourning saw managers come and go at the Lane thereafter with the frequency of the No.43 trolleybus that yo-yoed up and down Arkwright Street on Saturday afternoons to and from Midland Station to its terminal on the Victoria Embankment, a halfway house for supporters who alighted churning, clanking rattles and sporting either the black and white of the Magpies or red and white of the Garibaldi Reds. But the natural order, at least in the eyes of County fans, had been restored by Jimmy Sirrel's remarkable and idiosyncratic presence at Meadow Lane since 1969 as the Magpies relinquished their alter ego as perennial re-election seekers at the foot of the Fourth Division with two rapid promotions in 1971 and 1973.

The seismic reading on the Richter scale was perhaps not particularly significant; nevertheless a quantum leap had been noted in Nottingham as the balance of power began to shift gradually north of the Trent. Confirmation of this trend came on 28 December 1974 at the City Ground when goals by the impressive Steve Carter, who was running amok on both flanks, and Les Bradd, County's record goalscorer, inflicted a 2-0 defeat.

"Possibly the worst result we ever had in our history," John Mounteney, lifelong County supporter, director and sometime saviour of the club, reflected with hindsight some years later as Clough's incredible impact began to take shape.

Brown was gone by the New Year without a solitary token of appreciation. He had been in charge for just over 12 months, his first game resulting in a 0-0 draw with Sunderland on 24 November. He had presided over that exhilarating, Duncan McKenzie-inspired FA Cup adventure that ended amid controversy in the quarter-finals, but when he left, Brown was granted only a cardboard box full of his personal possessions from the manager's office and a few sentimental artefacts as his leaving gifts.

Eighteen years and umpteen glittering prizes later, it is astonishing to reflect that Clough's departure was eerily, and most poignantly, similar.

"Make sure you fetch my stuff out of the office in boxes and bring it to my home," he told Hill after the latter revealed to the outgoing manager that former player Frank Clark was in secret talks with chairman Fred Reacher.

How could it be so?

SUCH A DEMEANING denouement was a distant and implausible one as Clough strode, more swaggered really, into

Forest. If it was the author Alan Sillitoe who put Nottingham on the map with his book *Saturday Night and Sunday Morning* it was Clough who brought detail and colour to the Lace City's grid reference. In January 1975, the Queen of the Midlands was ripe for change and a vibrant transformation that was in vivid contrast to the glum back-to-back housing and the production line monotony of factory life at the bicycle manufacturer Raleigh, as depicted in Sillitoe's seminal work. Paul Smith, the fashion designer, had opened up some small premises in Byard Lane, while slum clearance programmes and new housing developments were redefining the landscape. Amid such shifting sands, Clough moved in and first established stability at the faltering Second Division club and then built a legend that almost eclipsed that of Robin Hood, the bandit of Sherwood Forest and Hollywood.

Almost a year before his arrival, I was treated to some familiar Clough punditry following the Nottingham derby with Forest at the City Ground. As a lumbering Notts County centre-half, I had been asked to mark Duncan McKenzie, the sprightly and gifted Forest forward, at close quarters and as a 0-0 draw ensued, it was mission accomplished from my own and the visiting team's perspective.

"If McKenzie is worth £200,000, how much is that McVay worth?" Clough opined in a national newspaper the following day. Not nearly as much as McKenzie as it transpired, and Clough, shrewd as ever, bought the Forest winger, not yours truly, for £250,000 during the brief encounter that was his managerial tenure at Leeds United. Had Clough felt compelled to bring McKenzie back to Forest when he slipped his feet under the manager's table, his ambitions were thwarted by his own valuation of the spring-heeled prodigy. Price, though, was not an issue in restoring his alliance with John McGovern and John O'Hare, also late of Elland Road. The former always considered Clough, his mentor at Hartlepools, Derby, Leeds and Forest, to be a father figure; one of many, including Hill, who shared that emotion. Unsurprisingly so, since Clough could be sporadically a fraternal or avuncular influence on youngsters and peers alike. "I always tried to conduct myself with the sort of discipline he would have wanted," said McGovern following Clough's death in September 2004. "I lost my dad at 11, but Cloughie was always strict with me. Not as strict as me mam sometimes, though."

But if O'Hare and McGovern represented the old guard, Viv Anderson, Tony Woodcock and Garry Birtles became synonymous with the wind of change sweeping through the club.

There were others, far from household names perhaps, but fledgling professionals who owe a debt of gratitude to Clough. Peter Wells and Steve Burke were local youngsters who graduated through the apprentice ranks, Wells being a classmate of Anderson's during their time at Fairham Comprehensive on Clifton Estate. Bert Bowery, who hailed from the Meadows area before its destiny lay in rubbles at the hands of demolition squads, was signed later in his career from Midland League side Worksop Town. All three had varying degrees of success in their later careers, but it was Clough who gave them their league debuts and opened the door of opportunity on which they had been knocking for so long.

The same could be said of Bryn Gunn and Jimmy McCann, the latter a dedicated Scotsman, but a naturalised Nottinghamite these days, who still lives and works in the county that first witnessed his talents both as a football player and frequent nocturnal partner and confidant of John Robertson on the city's increasingly lively social scene.

INEVITABLY CLOUGH'S FIRST game in charge inspired a win. What else? A 1-0 FA Cup replay victory over Tottenham Hotspur at White Hart Lane. It was against the odds, against a glamour club and against generally pronounced predictions and perceived wisdom. Nostradamus could not have scripted a more prophetic opening gambit.

What followed was the embryonic stage of Clough's modus operandi – mimicked, but never replicated – melding and moulding a collection of misfits, mishaps and miscreants into a football team. Keeping them out of trouble or keeping their minds focused on the task ahead, the two went hand-in-hand with the job really and nobody in the game man-managed the misdemeanours of players better, both on and off the pitch, than Clough. Even when his charges had achieved heights beyond perhaps even his own expectations, he was relentless in asserting the basic principles that had lifted him and the players to unprecedented success. His Forest team won promotion back to the top flight in his first full season in charge, then, unbelievably, inexplicably, lifted the league championship in their first season back. They also added the League Cup for good measure, seeing off double European champions Liverpool in both competitions. As if wired to prove to the Liverpudlians that anything they could do smalltown Forest could do too, Clough next led his charges to back-to-back European Cups. More League Cups and high-placed league finishes followed as Clough regenerated his team throughout his 17-year reign, all the while retaining his other undying principle of entertaining his adoring crowd with the most attractive football around.

His one-liners became the stuff of legend. On club chairmen: "Football hooligans? Well, there are 92 club chairmen for a start." When questioned about dispute resolution with players: "We talk about it for 20 minutes and then we decide I was right." Of West Ham midfielder Trevor Brooking: "He floats like a butterfly, and stings like one too." And of himself: "I wouldn't say I'm the best manager in the business, but I'm in the top one." All delivered with the famous, dead-pan north-eastern drawl, followed by a pause and a twinkling smile.

There were downs as well as the many ups; the punches Clough landed on pitch-invading QPR fans and, later, on errant young Irishman Roy Keane landed him in hot water, and then there was the drinking which left him with an increasingly claret nose. And, of course, famously, on the pitch, he never won an FA Cup. But it didn't really matter. There were the two European Cups, one league title, promotion from Division Two and four League Cups to celebrate, not to mention some sparkling football. And anyway Cloughie was, well Cloughie.

At the height of their pomp, Kenny Burns, the former Birmingham City reprobate centre-forward, and Larry Lloyd, a former Liverpool and England centre-half on the downward slope, had their cards marked by the unforgiving Clough.

At Forest, Burns had developed into a stylish, but tough centre-back foil to Lloyd's rough and ready defensive instincts, a partnership born out of necessity for both players whose careers had been written off before they arrived at the City Ground. A couple of wilder elements in what was anyway a pretty wild decade for professional footballers, erratic behaviour combined with a reputation for being oversubscribed members of the drinks culture that was virtually mandatory in the game then, Forest was their last chance saloon.

The pair grabbed it willingly with a steady, firm grip belying their fabled exploits, Burns in particular cementing a seamless transition from a centre-forward whose finishing was as wayward as his character to the very model of calm and poise sweeping up alongside and behind the imposing figure of Lloyd.

When County briefly held sway on Trentside in the mid-70s, the bedrock at the hub of their back four had been David Needham and Brian Stubbs, a similar goodish cop, bad cop alliance that played or scared the living daylights out of the opposition with Stubbs the enforcer and Needham the silent, more cunning, avenger. Now Burns and Lloyd had taken the concept to a different level, largely thanks to Taylor's eye for a bargain and, eventually after persuasion by the latter, Clough's belief in them. The long and short of it was that the pair became the most feared double act since the Krankies played Morecambe Hippodrome.

But like every single one of their dressing room colleagues, Burns and Lloyd, much like their televisual contemporaries Starsky and Hutch sheepishly facing the bullish Captain Dobey, had felt the wrath of Clough on more than one occasion. It was the manager's way of demonstrating exactly who was in charge; who was boss. Nothing new about the technique, but as usual Clough found novel ways to execute it.

Burns carelessly passed across his own 18-yard area one Saturday afternoon, the ball being intercepted by Manchester City's Dennis Tueart who, fortunately, could only head wide. At half-time Clough told Liam O'Kane, one of his coaches, to sort something out. By the final whistle, an envelope with the red tree of Forest was handed to Burns. It's contents read: "Defenders must not pass the ball across their own penalty area. You have been fined £50."

"It's your career, now learn from it," came the advice.

Clough was more abrasive and confrontational with Lloyd, who he regarded as self-opinionated with far too much 'gob'. In short, he thought Lloyd should be seen and not heard and do the job for which he had been bought from Coventry City; to stop opponents playing. As a stopper Lloyd was almost flawless, but his tendency to having running feuds with the bigger names knocking around the Second Division in 1976 – England forwards Mike Channon and Peter Osgood of Southampton for example – invited trouble and a plethora of cautions. Clough dropped him from the side, refusing to accept Lloyd's conciliatory offer to pay a fine instead, even though he knew it might jeopardise Forest's promotion chances. "Because whether I am manager of Forest, England or Nottingham Pork Butchers I am determined to preserve my standards of team behaviour and discipline," ranted Clough at the time.

That was March 1976 and it was two and a half years before what might be perceived as a repressed simmering rivalry between player and manager flared up again after a 2-1 European Cup win over AEK Athens in the Greek capital. The incident, where Lloyd boarded the team coach the morning after the second round first leg victory wearing jeans and sweat shirt, but minus his club blazer, has passed into Forest folklore. Lloyd repeatedly refused to get the blazer out of his bag in the boot; Clough told him that each time he said 'no', his fine would increase by £50. Even a clapped-out old nag at the Royal Show gets away with just four points for a refusal but this veteran chaser accumulated £500 before he jumped to it and conformed with the dress code. The conclusion was never in doubt, but the result illustrates how Clough controlled his leading men, even those with a physique eclipsed by their ego. That edge was a double-sided one because it earned respect from both players and fans alike.

AND YET THE dichotomy was that, for a man who demanded an almost blind faith from his staff and commanded obedience, Clough himself bent rules and persistently challenged authority. He was a determined socialist who backed *Nottingham Evening Post* journalists in their strike of 1978, banning the local paper from talking to him and his players, while revealing exclusives to John Lawson, one of the striking writers who was also working for the newly-formed *Nottingham News*. And yet, did he take bungs for favours and hike up the price when the club struck domestic and European gold like any good capitalist? No doubt. But the double standards, hypocrisy, cunning or perception, whatever the facet may be called, perversely endeared him to his dressing room and adoring audience.

When a dashing young winger by the name of Terry Curran was turning full-backs inside out at Belle Vue as a Doncaster Rovers player, Clough spotted something that would enhance considerably his promotion prospects from the Second Division. Despite Allan

Brown's failings, Clough had not inherited a bad side, but it lacked genuine pace and wingers and Curran, although something of a rogue by reputation, possessed speed in abundance, even if his final ball tended to terrorise the Trent End rather than opposing penalty areas. Never mind, that might come with careful nurturing. In the meantime, it was vital that Curran's head was not turned elsewhere. Thus during the spring and summer of 1975, Clough deputised a posse of club officials to drive to Bawtry on a weekly basis. Normally the quaint old Crown Hotel in the south Yorkshire market town was a stop-off for pre-match meals for clubs travelling by coach to and from the east coast and further north to the Midlands and beyond. But for Forest and Curran it was a rendezvous where £20 exchanged hands – in cash. The extra tax-free money topped up Curran's wages, kept him happy and was also a sign of intent from Clough. It worked. The Doncaster player signed in August 1975, though in hindsight, Franz Carr's erratic contributions from the flanks were half decent in comparison to Curran's wayward delivery that matched his somewhat turbulent personality.

Everyone, it seems, has been touched by Clough and his gestures. Whether it be demeaning, damning, detrimental or more often that not philanthropic. Like Chic Thomson, Forest's 1959 Cup-winning goalkeeper, whose opinion changed when he saw Clough mopping out the floor and toilets at a residential home near Sandiacre. "Mucking in with the rest, just being one of the people," recalls Thompson, who along with his wife was performing their regular charity work at the centre. Chatting up old ladies in a checkout queue might sound like an offence for which even Plod might turn out in full body armour, but in Clough's case, he was prone to end up paying for the shopping and carrying the whole lot to the car.

He just couldn't help his paternalistic shows. The team coach returning from Sunderland in the mid-1970s normally would have arrowed straight from the Mackems' territory to Nottingham, but Clough had other ideas. Two young lads, waifs and strays almost, were standing outside Roker Park trying to poach an autograph when Clough emerged from the entrance doors and swept them onto the coach.

"Where do you two buggers live then?" he asked.

"Not far away."

"Then show us the way and we'll drop you off. Albert [the Forest coach driver], take these two home."

Imagine the consternation in the row of terrace houses when the plush first team coach pulls up.

"These two could do with a good wash and sommat to eat, missus," Clough addressed the lady of the house and mother of the two lads.

The lady of the house could have been offended, but instead, her maternal instincts made her warm to the smiling Forest manager, joining a huge club of admirers smitten by his charm. After all, Clough had wooed hundreds of mums when trying to sign precocious talent. All in the line of duty really.

"The upshot was we took the pair to Nottingham and Cloughie kept them for a week," reveals Alan Hill. "They had a good bath at the City Ground, stayed in digs and he kitted them out with clothing at what was the Oxford Clothing Company in West Bridgford. For years the two of them would come back and visit either in the holidays or during the season. They grew from young scruffs to men in the meantime."

Only some were welcome on the team coach, as the unfortunate troubleshooting Mr Waterhouse discovered.

Another who found out that Clough's autonomy was not to be tampered with was Derek Pavis. His exploits on football coaches were already infamous in Nottingham circles, but once allowed back into those circles, the former plumber's merchant continued to drop almighty turds wherever he laid his posterior. Pavis had become one of the committee members at Forest, one of just over 200 people, some of whom were inexplicably more delusionary in their ambition than even Waterhouse. To paraphrase Jim Hacker's character in *Yes Minister* with some journalistic licence, *Daily Mirror* readers think they run the club, *Guardian* readers think they ought to run the club, *Times* readers actually do run the club, while *Sun* readers don't really care who runs the club as long as she's got big tits. If Clough, metaphorically, was the *Times* reader, the committee's reading habits belonged somewhere between the other three, with Pavis perhaps erring towards the Guardianistos. Unfortunately for him, he laid a wager with a fellow committee member, as they travelled by coach (not first team) to a game at Old Trafford, that a young Forest team would be defeated by Manchester United that day. As it turned out, Forest won and Clough got whiff of the wager. It was an understatement to say he was not amused.

Shortly afterwards the annual voting to elect board members from the overblown committee ranks took place and Pavis, with several influential friends, was a firm favourite to succeed. The first round of votes saw him comfortably in front of his rivals, but unusually that night, Clough had attended the meeting. "Let everyone know if that bastard gets elected, I'm down the road," he told his faithful cohorts during the interval before the second ballot. Result, if it were ever in doubt, Pavis lost – by a landslide majority. Eventually, he sold his plumbing company and bought out Notts County chairman Jack Dunnett to try and emulate Clough's achievements on the north bank of the River Trent. Had he stumped up a few bob with his local turf accountant on him completing that mission implausible, Pavis, as with the Forest bet and his attempt to join the board, would have ended up with a losing ticket.

Whether it was directors, players or the media, Clough manipulated supremely. In 1988, he announced that he had been offered the job as manager of the Wales national team. Welsh officials were so steamed up about it that they scurried to Nottingham with contracts in hands hoping to finalise the deal. Alan Hill, who had joined Pavis at Notts County as academy director at the start of that season, had been invited by Clough to be his No.2 in the Welsh connection. On the Thursday morning, five days after his initial statement, Clough held a press conference at the City Ground. He had had a change of heart. He could not devote enough time to juggling the Forest and Wales jobs in tandem. Nor could he leave his beloved Forest. He declined the Welsh FA's kind offer. But by then, he'd negotiated a new, improved deal for himself as the Forest board panicked. And he'd also prised Hill away from County and Pavis, restoring him as a coach on improved wages at the City Ground.

In the game of bluff, Clough was master.

IT WAS A FLABBERGASTED Manchester City manager Alan Ball who held his arms up in despair at half-time as his team trailed 3-0 and thought: "How am I going to motivate a team of millionaires?"

During Clough's career, that was almost exclusively played out before the Premiership, the association of a million pounds and football conjured up pools winners, not FA Cup ones. If he were still operating today, could he work with the boardroom perma-tans, often heavily perfumed and daintily manicured, who lavish Sky money, but never their own on the glad-shaking scavengers, otherwise known as agents, loitering with intent for the next handout?

Perhaps not. But could he handle them? Could he manipulate and motivate simultaneously and navigate a path, crooked or not, through the labyrinth of corruption and claptrap that courses through the game today? Without a doubt. And take it from me, there would be none better.

A Friday night out in the Flying Horse Hotel, the pride and epicentre of Nottingham's social scene in the 1970s, reveals how Clough would have survived and flourished with consummate ease. The old tavern represents an allegorical tale of lost youth and the desperately sad and obsessive pursuit of style over substance that fixates society presently. One of the oldest watering holes in the city, its origins dating back to Tudor times, a generation of hopeful teens, trendy young things and aspiring middle classes or pimps depending on horizons, congregated at the Flying Horse before embarking on a night on the town before the pubs shut at 10.30pm sharp. Its clientele was as diverse as its myriad bars, a heady cocktail of the heterosexual and homosexual (often to be found in the 'Queers' Bar', nicknamed pre-political correctness, but nevertheless suitably situated towards the rear of the building).

Then there were the 'ladies of the night' who mostly frequented the Exchange public house next door, but who sometimes strayed in for a Babycham and a peek at the inmates when business was slack. Its intoxicating mix of Bavarian lager, as strong as the women who drank it and as potent as their perfume, the rich tobacco smoke and undiluted spirits served at the double upstairs may have proved irresistible to a young working class lad and it remained solidly the place to be seen during the 1970s before wine bars and licensing hours altered the format and rules of social drinking forever.

So there I stood on Friday 9 February 1979, while other good professionals were tucked up in bed at home or sterile Posthouse hotels dotted around the country, ready for a few drinks and a few drinks more. With the exit door being held wide and inviting on my career at Meadow Lane and only a Midlands Youth League game for the A team the following morning to whet the appetite, what better way to spend the night before than consuming double figures of lager and a red hot vindaloo at one of the less salubrious curry houses down Arkwright Street? As much as anyone can be sure of these things, it is pretty certain that the social and gourmet arrangements for the world's most expensive player, Trevor Francis, on the same night did not include copious amounts of alcohol, ill-advised Asian cuisine or a sleepless few hours on the floor of a Siberian cold flat somewhere in Nottingham. Having been bought for a penny less than £1 million that day by Clough (the VAT took it over the groundbreaking figure), the former Birmingham City wonderkid was most likely dreaming of a fabulous career ahead amid soft furnishings and dimmed lights at his west Midlands home.

Funny, though, how fate has its way of polarising people from the diametrically opposed beliefs and backgrounds, witness the Crusaders, starring Richard I, Coeur de Lion, versus the Moslems, circa 1188. Massacres not far removed from those holy wars were very much in prospect on Saturday morning February 10 when a Notts County A side, comprising two professional players (yours truly included) and nine schoolboys on trial, took to the field to play Nottingham Forest A at a windswept Grove Farm. County had changed in the ramshackle remains of the original farmhouse, the communal dressing rooms for hundreds of park players who played, come rain or shine, on the facility's many pitches.

Since a huge errant punt, a frequent visitor to the amateur game in these parts, could easily deposit the ball into the adjacent River Trent with the wind blowing in the wrong direction, it is best to call the complex an open plan one, vulnerable to the prevailing weather. My body was feeling more than a little vulnerable from head, especially the head, to toe, with a few dodgy functions in between. Instead of being tucked up warm in bed nursing a hangover and thoughts of Sally James on *Tiswas*, here I was on a pitch as rutted and frozen as the flat that had been my temporary bed the night before. Huge solid divots in the penalty areas did not augur well for precious limbs or ankle bones.

Any hopes of a warm-up subsided when the winter chill and a force ten from nearby Beeston and Clifton Estate pummelled the flimsy black and white shirts. It was then, with kick-off approaching, that Forest turned up. In their team coach, wisely having changed at the

City Ground. Had it been a battle for territorial rights, the black and white army would have turned and run right then as names such as Frank Clark, David Needham, John O'Hare, Ian Bowyer and others who had helped secure the championship for Forest the previous season alighted in pristine kit from their team transport, nice and snug and thermally heated throughout. Bowyer, in fact, would be substitute for the first team later that afternoon.

The schoolboy trialists, many of them drop-jawed, did not know whether to make a dash for their pens and autograph books back in the dressing room or shake hands with some of their heroes. I felt a dash coming on, too... of the pebble variety and a sudden urge to relocate in the shoddy toilets of the ageing dressing rooms. Happily, the visit was not necessary, although whether Trevor Francis was grateful, who will ever know. Like Richard I taking the field of battle, here was Britain's first £1 million footballer, the knight in shining armour about to help Forest and Clough conquer Europe. Unfortunately, he appeared to have taken a wrong turning at Dover and ended up at rural Lenton via the Skegness sleeper.

There was a man, naturally, and a dog, the expected crowd level that could be tolerated at such games without the presence of mounted police, an army of fluorescently-clad stewards and several SPG units, but it was not until a man in green turned that the penny dropped. Clough, patrolling the touchline and barking orders, had actually sent his £1 million man into football's version of the Wall of Death. Without a helmet. It should have alerted a generation to a new genre of virtual reality television shows, the pilot episode shot at windswept Grove Farm entitled 'I'm the only bloody celebrity, get me the fuck out of here.'

Was he insured for injury? No-one was quite sure. Was it legal to hand him his debut in this way? Again, pass. And was physical contact allowed should he enter our radar? No-one dared ask.

Suffice to say that Francis' biggest scare that morning came from the draught of a size 11 boot trying to make some meaningful challenge on the fleet of foot forward and the toxic fallout of bad breath composed of stale hops, garlic and extra strong curry powder that most probably wrenched a gap in the ozone layer far more damaging than a fleet of Chelsea tractors on the morning school run. At times the man of the moment resembled a frightened kangaroo trapped in the headlights of an Outback bushwhacker as Clough growled and prowled, verbally prodded and praised in equal measure the young man he had suddenly thrust into the football annals overnight.

Had anyone before or has anyone since contrived such a debut for their most expensive signing? Of course not. And could it happen today, given that not one national newspaper or, heaven forbid, a television camera, turned up to witness it? Not a chance.

Francis graduated to tea boy in Clough's unique academy before scoring the winning goal in his only European Cup tie. By the time they had beaten Malmo in the final at Munich on 30 May 1979, Forest had played 76 league, cup and friendly games that season. They had lifted the League Cup, lost to Arsenal in the fifth round of the FA Cup and pushed champions Liverpool in the title race before settling for the runner-up position. All this having sold Peter Withe, the club's leading scorer the previous season, in August, to Aston Villa and relying on a nucleus of 15 players, including the rookie forward pairing of Tony Woodcock and Garry Birtles. A parochial East Midlands club, whose previously biggest claim to fame had been that they were the only team to win the FA Cup with ten men back in 1959, were now champions of Europe. It was as absurd as it was addictive.

"For me, it was his finest hour, his greatest achievement at Forest," reflects Frank Clark, whose swansong as a Forest player was that Munich final. "Normally when a side was chasing the European Cup after winning the league, during the old format of the competition and before clubs like Chelsea and Manchester United became so strong, they would struggle in the league. But it was testament to the players and the management that we chased Liverpool all the way, never mind winning the other trophies on top."

When Clark departed that summer, earning twice his wages as assistant to Ken Knighton at Second Division Sunderland, who might have guessed that 14 years later he would return as replacement for the deposed Clough?

"COME TO MY house and meet the new manager," chairman Fred Reacher told Alan Hill, by now Clough's right hand man, as a sad finale loomed in May 1993. Weeks earlier, with Forest doomed to relegation from the Premiership in its inaugural season, Reacher had announced Clough's plans to retire with all the diplomacy and tact he must have gleaned as a beat bobby and publican during the 1960s.

It seemed a clumsy smokescreen following allegations by a Forest director that emerged in a Sunday newspaper that there had been plans to sack Clough at board level, an unthinkable chain of events some years previously.

No longer in his prime, ravaged by drink and with the club in decline, Clough suddenly became fragile, mortal. Walking on water held no fears; terra firma? Well that was a different challenge.

Hill met Frank Clark that night at Reacher's house and returned to a reserve game to relay the news to Clough, who was still in charge of the club and had not been told of the appointment.

"You're telling me they've appointed a new manager," an irate Clough boomed as Hill took his place next to him in the near deserted stands.

"Do you know who he is? You mean you fucking know and I don't?"

"Yes gaffer."

"Who is it?"

"Frank Clark."

"Our Frank?"

There was a momentary pause for reflection.

A trip to Cala Millor, his favourite Majorcan haunt, with Denis 'Sinatra' Moss, his favourite impressionist of his favourite singer, had been arranged for the following day. The Forest squad were flying out for one farewell party to the gaffer, but Hill knew he would not be there. Still he needed the gaffer's blessing.

"You stop here and make sure you look after Frank," Clough told Hill. And with that, he duly went berserk at a few players as Stoke City reserves toiled at the City Ground. Lou Macari, the Stoke manager, who was in attendance, heard the news and stormed into the boardroom to remonstrate with anyone who would listen. Strangely enough, not many from the corridors of increasing power attended that evening. "You're a fucking disgrace," the familiar Scottish lullaby echoed around the boardroom after the final whistle. "The fucking lot of you. After all he has done for you."

Clough asked Hill to clear out his office. "Do me a favour, put my things in boxes and bring them round to my house." Eighteen years previously, Allan Brown collected his own belongings in boxes before shuffling off with his P-45.

"The whole episode was unbelievably sad," Hill said.

Hill, like McGovern and countless others, recalled that Clough had always been like a dad to him, even though in later years following an FA investigation into illegal payments, the pair fell out. Ultimately, the autonomy that had secured unprecedented success had been Clough's downfall as his judgement of a player suffered and his ability to ride the storm and hold his drink diminished.

Clough left the building that night – and with his departure went the last of football's mavericks and a managerial genius that can never be surpassed.

Peter Taylor

1976-1982: 347 games, 177 wins

THE LIGHT WAS fading rapidly in Majorca as evening shade began to consume the Balearic isle. In his coastal villa, a great and eternal darkness was about to descend over Peter Taylor. Laid low on the living room floor by a fatal heart attack, he was cradled by his wife Lilian, herself frantic with the worry of one who knows how desperate is the need, but how impotent the carer. In the certain knowledge that his final hour was almost over, Taylor looked up at his wife.

"Come on, give us a smile," he cajoled. The man of mirth who had engendered a habit of laughter and success in the Nottingham Forest dressing room wanted his wife to let him know she was all right; that she would cope without him. His final gesture to his soul buddy.

Seconds later, Taylor closed his eyes and passed away, calmly, peacefully and without pain. A death in vivid contrast to a life that was every bit as controversial and influential as the other half of football's most successful partnership.

Less than an hour before, Taylor had ushered his house guests out, insisting they take a stroll down the road to a local restaurant and celebrate the weather or whatever flimsy excuse was necessary to consume chilled white wine and lightly grilled sea bass or local prawns. His diners were Taylor's own brother and his two sisters, a select and close family unit that he had gathered at his favourite holiday location. His daughter recalls it was a rather prophetic last trip with his siblings.

"It was as if he knew something was wrong and that something was about to happen," recalls Wendy Dickinson, wife of broadcaster, journalist and producer John. "It was all quite weird. He had been talking with Dr Annersley, who he had known for years in his Keyworth practice, before flying out. Dad had a rare lung disease that was putting strain on a heart already weakened by an attack [when at Derby] in his forties."

Wendy drove her father to East Midlands airport and waved him goodbye, bursting into tears as soon as he began to take his familiarly giant strides towards the plane. The parochial airport had grown in stature along with Forest and had been the triumphant setting for many a returning hero after glorious European nights. Now it was the stage for a final farewell. For some reason, Wendy could not bear to look back as she left the airport terminal.

"I didn't dare turn around because I knew I would lose it. We were an affectionate family and I'd given him a hug, but for some reason when I got back to the car I started sobbing uncontrollably. Don't know why. I just cried my eyes out. Then I said to myself: 'Get a grip, don't be stupid.'"

That was in late September 1990 and on 4 October Peter Taylor died, the night before his daughter was due to pick him up from East Midlands. His sister Joan, the surrogate mother of the family once their own mother had died at an early age, was among those who had reluctantly left the villa.

Such finality, a desperate parting of the ways, is apposite in the context of Taylor's contribution to Nottingham Forest. When he arrived, in the summer of 1976, they were largely an embryonic work in progress that Brian Clough had initiated, leading lights only in the nether regions of the Second Division. To plagiarise John Lennon, were they the best team in England and Europe? They weren't even the best team in Nottingham!

When he departed six years later, though, the plodding Ringo Starrs of Division Two had evolved audaciously, a stirring drum roll of expectation that another trick might be conjured up, another rabbit grasped from the hat in conquering just about every football frontier that they encountered. All that heady success and skilful football brought to the boil by the alchemy between Taylor and Clough.

And then came that split, an irreconcilable parting that saw Clough's hubris triggered into warp factor mode when Taylor, having resigned from Forest in 1982, re-emerged as Derby County manager and signed John Robertson during the following summer.

How could it all go that wrong?

DAVID STAPLETON RECALLS one of Taylor's many City Ground stunts. Stapleton was a reporter first for the now defunct *Nottingham Evening News*, then latterly the *Evening Post*, following in his father Albert's footsteps as a journalist who charted the changing face of local sport with an eye for detail and an empathy born out of admiration and having well established roots in the city. Stapleton witnessed Clough's early majesty at the Baseball Ground, reported on the feted championship boxing bouts that regularly adorned the Nottingham Ice Arena, often with Henry Cooper, Wally Swift, David Needham (not the Forest stopper), Herol Graham and Kirkland Laing shedding blood, sweat and tears for a world, British or Commonwealth crown. But it was the Clough and Taylor-inspired Forest renaissance that Stapleton marvelled at first hand as a reporter on some of their finest hours.

"One day we were stood in Brian's office, waiting for an interview when Peter Taylor burst through the door. He was carrying John Robertson in his arms, as you would a little child. By then Robbo was a Scotland international and probably one of the greatest left-wingers in the game. 'So what do you think Brian?' Taylor exclaimed. 'Here's one for the future. A few rough edges, but I think he'll make a player.' Robbo, of course, was looking on in that bemused manner of his. Enjoying the joke, but not quite sure why."

The bonhomie of that Clough–Taylor rapport had endured from their playing days at Middlesbrough in the 1950s and it was frequently Taylor, more adventurous by nature, who chanced his luck on potential players. Therein lay his genius, one perhaps only now gaining full appreciation. He persuaded Clough to give striker Tony Woodcock a second chance, an almighty power of persuasion not because the mop-haired permster had been up for grabs at £5,000 when on loan at Doncaster Rovers, but more so because Stan Anderson, then the Donnie manager, refused to pay Clough the requisite further £5,000 in readies in addition to what was already being demanded to secure Woodcock's permanency at Belle Vue.

At least Clough did not hold the grudge against the player, nor Garry Birtles, another one of Taylor's finds. Coming second best to a mug of tepid Bovril on a double bill popularity contest at Enderby Town did not augur well for Birtles' future (the assessment, long before Simon Cowell's acerbic regime, was Clough's after seeing the Long Eaton United forward in action).

But Taylor persisted.

"We ended up going over to Coventry," recalls his widow Lilian. "Terrible night for weather, but Peter went in and paid and sat at the back of the stands, just me and him with nobody aware he was there. We didn't stay long. He saw something in the player and we left shortly after."

How fitting was Taylor's incognito role. Someone who flitted in and out of the picture, no-one really sure if he was there at all, cameo appearances that seemed to mirror how he was perceived by others in his partnership with Clough. And yet, as always, he left an indelible influence on the object of his purpose. In this case, to raise Birtles' profile and convince Clough that he was good enough to sign on professional forms.

Woodcock and Birtles aside, the list of Forest players to whom Taylor can lay genuine claim is astonishing, especially so since they were pivotal in shaping and moulding the club's remarkable success in the ensuing years after 1976. Peter Withe, Peter Shilton, Kenny Burns, Larry Lloyd, Archie Gemmill. And Trevor Francis and David Needham; not all of them unknown elements from the lower leagues or amateur games, of course, but it was Taylor's eye to recognise who could or who could not meld into a disparate Forest dressing room. In there lurked on the one side novices such as Birtles, Woodcock and Anderson, who had ascended to a first team that was still suffering from an identity crisis, alongside Robertson, O'Neill, Bowyer and McGovern, then scarcely names that would reduce opponents to the screaming hab-dabs in mortal fear of a sound thrashing. In fact it was Taylor, not Clough, who delivered the withering verbal attack that brought Robertson to his senses on a pre-season tour of Bavaria; the 'living out of a chip pan' line allied with 'fatness and a spotty face' being sufficient for the 22-year-old Scot to consider serious introspection.

Yet despite those well-documented stories, Taylor remains an enigma within the Forest equation, never fully appreciated while he was there and reviled by Clough when he was gone. Nottingham folk, too, appear to have memories even shorter than some politicians; a shame because Taylor was most certainly one of their own.

He was the son of a Lincolnshire engineer whose father had relocated to the Meadows district of Nottingham during the early 1950s, working at the Royal Ordnance Factory, formerly owned by Cammell Lairds, on King's Meadow Road. The ROF, as it was known, was a huge leviathan whose tentacles absorbed not only its workers in myriad sheds and warehouses, smoke bilging out of every orifice to fuel an almost perpetual production line, but also the indigenous working class population of the region that it, for the most part, sustained and nourished.

There were some awful slum areas in the Meadows, but by and large, the locals loved the back-to-back terracing, outside loos and its oddly defined recreational areas, mostly flattened spaces encrusted with rubble and reminders of the night the Luftwaffe bombed the city by mistake, offloading incendiary bombs meant for Hull or Derby during the Nottingham Blitz of May 1941. It was that Nazi fascism that so promoted communism in England as an attractive alternative to socialism after the rigours of the Second World War. With the mundanity and fatigue of post-war working life in industrial Britain and the imposition of rationing, the idea of a communist nirvana in these green and pleasant lands most likely became less wishful thinking and more a social expedient for the converted.

Doubtless Taylor, brought up in a Meadows house along with his seven brothers and sisters, saw plenty around him to nurture his leanings to the left and beyond. Even as a young goalkeeper with Coventry City, he could see the vagaries of lower class existence in a city dominated by motor car production and still recovering, even almost a decade on, from the habitual German bombing raids. It was those communist ideals that he would discuss and dissect with Clough after the striker was signed by Middlesbrough manager Bob Dennison in 1955. That and the burgeoning power, grace and unbridled talent that the Hungarians, Ferenc Puskas, Nandor Hidegkuti, Gyula Grosics, Sandor Kocsis and all, had injected into international football.

Clough, the young forward playing for his hometown team, was a captive audience, who also harboured similar dreams and ambitions, one of which was to play in and win the European Cup, a competition that was in its infancy in the late 1950s. The arguments of Taylor, older and a little wiser, carried more weight and tended to veer on the more radical side of politics, a stronger conviction than Clough's socialism and one which influenced the younger man considerably.

"At the end of a long night talking about this or that, it was always back to Taylor's house for fish and chips, 'the best fish and chips in Middlesbrough' Brian used to say," Lilian recalls. In the bitter aftermath of their parting, Lilian will not comment badly on Clough or his behaviour. "She remembers them as two young men arguing and talking so passionately about life and politics in the tiny front room of her club house opposite the old John Collier factory in Middlesbrough," Wendy says. "As my father's daughter I have always been more critical of Brian."

To this day, Lilian retains a letter sent by Clough's wife Barbara following the death of Peter. Her condolences and her wishes that it could have been different reflect a heartfelt sentiment that can only be shared now by two widows who have had much cause for separate yet united grieving.

SO WHAT OF THE Taylor that the public eye did not greet or meet?

Anyone of his Meadows upbringing was able to call a spade a spade and in a game where being ruthless demands 24-hour attention, Taylor did not suffer fools gladly and was aware of his significance. When the chance came to join up with his old mate, maybe he felt a tinge of vulnerability when he was reunited with Clough at the City Ground in the summer of 1976. The pair, dynamic, daring and dashing at Derby County, had enjoyed fleeting rapprochement after resigning from the Baseball Ground, during a brief encounter at Brighton and Hove Albion. But then Clough was tempted to opt for his disruptive, but ultimately lucrative 44 days with Leeds United, leaving Taylor behind to pick up the pieces for a couple of seasons, cementing firmer foundations for Brighton on the south coast.

"So you're the one nobody has a bad word to say about then," was how Taylor greeted Alan Hill when the two met under Clough's supervision, and as the trio entered the manager's office, Taylor shut the door in Hill's face. A former Forest goalkeeper, whose career was ended prematurely after a collision with Everton's Joe Royle in February 1970, Hill, youth team coach since Dave Mackay's brief tenure, had been asked by Clough to help him out after he took charge at the City Ground. The simmering rivalry escalated and reached its nadir when Hill, talking as a pundit on BBC Radio Nottingham, opined that much of the basic ground work had been laid at Forest and Taylor's arrival was now 'the icing on the cake'. It touched a nerve in Taylor's psyche and he tackled Hill in his office the morning following the broadcast. The contretemps would not subside. Taylor argued it was a slur on him, Hill countered saying that there was no malice in his observation. As a result, Hill walked away from his job.

"I can't work with that bloke," he told Clough.

"You and whose army!" the manager retorted.

The impasse was to last four years – until just a few days after Forest had lost what had become virtually their annual March prize, the League Cup. Winners for the previous two years, a defensive cock-up between Peter Shilton and David Needham presented Wolves' Andy Gray with the only goal of the game at Wembley Stadium and an unlikely trophy to the underdogs. Taylor and Hill, still working as a radio pundit, crossed swords in the Wembley tunnel before the game, but it was after the defeat that word came, through director Stuart Dryden, that Clough wanted the pair of them to sort out their differences on Tuesday morning at the ground.

"We went into a room together and to be fair to Peter, he shook my hand straight away, apologised and said we'd just got off on the wrong foot," Hill recalls. "And that was the end of that. It was never mentioned again."

In between radio punditry, Hill had made a living as a landlord, owning several pubs around south Nottinghamshire, with his wife Janice. Perhaps their most famous hostelry was the Rancliffe Arms at Bunny, a cult venue in itself. Taylor banned players and coaching staff from visiting the place after the fall-out with Hill, but it was still one that Clough frequented for a pre-match meal. Despite their closeness professionally at the time, Taylor and Clough seldom mixed socially. "I'm a bit shy of strangers," Taylor admitted once. A fastidious person whose office was always immaculate, Taylor was also renowned for liking a punt on the horses as a neatly folded copy of the *Racing Post* that decorated his desk daily confirmed. He enjoyed the company of trainers, notoriously the worst tipsters in the racing fraternity, but that did not deter him from despatching all and sundry to the bookies to get a bet laid on a horse at a favourable price.

If he was not exactly the man the bookies feared, Taylor's insider knowledge did tend to intimidate on-course bookmakers and often he'd dodge a trip himself to Southwell races and ask others to lay a few bets. "At the best prices you can get," he once urged John Dickinson. As it happened, the horse that Dickinson was despatched to back won, at reasonably short odds, but he had ventured to several outlets and obtained the best prices possible. Come reckoning, Dickinson returned to his prospective father-in-law with a wedge of cash and the tickets to confirm the various prices.

"Just a minute John, I think you're £20 short," said Taylor after tallying up the money against the odds in rapid time. Dickinson was flabbergasted because as far as he knew, he'd handed the entire pot over. It was not until he returned to his car that he found two £10 notes stuffed down the side of the driving seat. His dilemma was acute. Would he be thought of as cheat if he did not return the money? And if he did give it back, would he be as a cheat that had been caught out and forced to confess? "I gave it back and admitted it was an honest mistake," says Dickinson. "Peter was on the ball with his calculations, but I think in the end he believed me."

As the 1980s dawned and Thatcherism began to grip Britain, Taylor and Forest turned to less fickle market forces, more to the fundamental entrepreneurial doctrine of capitalism; speculate to accumulate. Unfortunately only the first half of the adage applied on the City Ground stock exchange.

The European Cup triumph in Madrid over Hamburg SV, retaining the trophy in style with Robertson's solitary effort, had lifted Forest to a new plane, but a disappointing domestic season followed. Supporters who once viewed a treat as a decent FA Cup run in between keeping a grip on a mid-table berth in the Second Division had had their expectations hoisted to a hitherto unparalleled plateau. Suddenly a seventh-placed finish in the First Division was not considered adequate compensation after being eliminated from all three knockout competitions, the European Cup (CSKA Sofia, 1st round), League Cup (Watford, 4th round) and FA Cup, (Ipswich Town, 6th round after a replay). Moreover, the popular Tony Woodcock had departed (to FC Cologne), while strike partner Garry Birtles (to Manchester United) followed shortly after.

Two of Taylor's most inspirational protégés had reaped around £1.5 million in transfer fees. Their replacements, Peter Ward, whom

Taylor had known at Brighton, and Ian Wallace, a ginger fireball from Coventry City, were unable to fill the void. For the first time during his Forest career, and perhaps for the first time since the pair moved into Hartlepools as a management team in 1965, Taylor was beginning to feel the strain. His weakened heart condition, first diagnosed at Derby, did little to ease his worries. The same could be said of the arrival of Willie Young, the Arsenal centre-back, but worse, far worse, had pre-empted the error-prone defender's transfer to Nottingham.

To this day, no-one is quite sure why Taylor went on a scouting mission to Norwich, purportedly to run his eye over Craig Johnston, Middlesbrough's promising Australian midfield player. At any rate, Johnston eventually went to Liverpool and Taylor came back from East Anglia with England Under-21 striker Justin Fashanu, Britain's first black £1 million player and an unmitigated disaster for Forest. If Taylor had contemplated an early retirement from the game, a different life from the incestuous, intrusive and insidious rat race that can be football when displaying its ugliest face, then Fashanu's hopeless form and Clough's bellicose lambasting of the player surely hastened that day.

AND YET THE SEEDS of discontent had already been sown; the cracks in the relationship, tiny fractures to be sure at this stage, were beginning to appear. Clough's flamboyant style and media-friendly approach, or unfriendly depending on where you sat in the press conference, was the obvious focus of attention. Inwardly Taylor, while not resenting it, perhaps felt he was due a tad more credit than he was receiving.

"Why does Brian Clough get all the publicity?" Taylor queried rhetorically in his 1980 autobiography, *With Clough*, itself perversely enough a homage to his partner by its very title, but also a testament to Taylor's own importance in the equation. It was also a source of revenue, a statement that Clough alone should not always have the divine right to earn the lion's share of income earned outside the game, even though his name in the title probably enhanced sales.

"It's your team too, isn't it?" continued Taylor's musings. "I'm not particularly worried about this. I'm certainly not resentful of Brian's renown, but I sometimes wonder why he never says to Bell's Whisky, for instance, when they're handing out Manager of the Month awards, 'You'll have to present an extra gallon bottle. There are two of us.'"

With Clough at the helm, Forest had become football's equivalent of gypsy travellers, uprooting their caravans and pitching up just about anywhere around the world, from Dubai to Denmark, from King's Lynn to Kuwait. At a price, naturally. But then came a friendly in Dublin that would see those cracks widen, the wounds deepen. Paddy Mulligan, the former Chelsea, Crystal Palace and West Bromwich Albion defender, was the recipient of Forest's grandeur and their first team for his testimonial match against a Dublin XI in the Irish capital on 5 August 1981. Forest won 3-2, but the real consequence came when Mulligan blabbed to the *Sunday Times* about how he had been made to hand over cash, on the morning of the game, in a brown paper bag in the back of a taxi cab, to ensure his match went ahead.

Apart from portraying Forest as grubby, grasping and money-grabbing chancers, the article cast Taylor in the light of the debt collector, the sly, manipulative and hardened figure. His daughter Wendy awoke to the disturbing portrait on a weekend away in London.

"I picked up the papers, including the *Sunday Times*, as normal and was utterly shocked by the article. Dad was, too, although he was a realist and knew this sort of thing might happen now and again. But what upset him most was that he was portrayed as some sort of Rachman character, going around doing the dirty work and picking up the pound notes off everyone in some sort of sleazy way, in the back seat of cars and taxis. Whatever did or didn't happen over that match, Brian was just as guilty...or as innocent, as Dad, but he was quite happy to let him take the flak and not stand shoulder to shoulder with him – a moral coward, in my view."

Was there a grain of truth in the story? Probably so. The Clough–Taylor modus operandi was common knowledge inside the game, although, like the old 'boot money' amateurs, most people accepted that tax-free cash was a frequent bartering tool in the game. Besides, Mulligan had earned his pile of cash from Forest's appearance, so why take the moral high ground?

Clough was equally angry when Mulligan went public although he was not tainted in quite the same way. Nevertheless, he promised Taylor that they would fight the allegations and drag the paper and Mulligan to court, kicking and screaming if necessary, but apparently a telephone call to a London QC was as far it went.

As in many long-term marriages, the bitterness and enmity lingered and deepened. The final separation was not long in coming. Taylor announced his retirement in 1982, mainly on health reasons. He had known Clough since his Middlesbrough playing days three decades previously. They had paired up in management at Hartlepools in 1965 and had experimented with trial separations, but still, magnet-like, they were drawn to one another by a compulsion, a chemistry and a mutual understanding of what was needed to create a successful football team. Yet as much as they talked and nattered about the game, their winning formula presumably did not include tactical awareness from set plays.

"We never practised a corner or free-kick in all the time I was there," claims Frank Clark, veteran of the 1979 European Cup final. "People don't believe me. At left-back, you normally tuck in behind your centre-backs and give them cover, but I always played a couple of yards ahead of ours. I was never sure what they [Larry Lloyd and Kenny Burns] would do next because it was left to them to call for an offside, so at any given moment they might shout 'up' without so much as looking over or giving me the nod. We just never practised that sort of defensive stuff. Then when David Needham joined us from QPR, it was obvious he'd come from a team that had been coached, Dave Sexton certainly had an influence. On his first day in training at a practice match, we got a corner and he went and stood on the near post. Robbo took the corner and, of course, with his delivery, it went straight on David's head and he popped it in. No trouble. Suddenly big Larry starts to think: 'I'll have a bit of this' and everyone is taking up positions at corners.

"Funny thing was Needham scored a goal just like that in a league game a couple of weeks later and Peter stood up and was quoted as saying the management and players had been putting a lot of hard work into set pieces! But that was Peter."

If there is a fondness in Clark's recollection, it is not a surprise. Garry Birtles called Taylor: "Quite simply the funniest man I ever met. The only bloke who could make us all laugh uncontrollably." A huge presence was missing from the Forest dressing room when he departed in May 1982, Taylor leaving with £36,000 from a testimonial game and a company car that was given to him.

IT WAS THE LURE of Derby County, where he and Clough had forged such a unique and irresistible alliance, that saw Taylor return to management in November of that same year.

Even with the benefit of hindsight it was at best a curiously ill-advised career move. He must have known how his decision would hurt Clough, but then perhaps deep down he felt that here was his chance to redress the balance and demonstrate who had been the real power behind the throne at Forest.

If Clough felt a sense of betrayal then, a 2-0 FA Cup victory inflicted by Taylor's Second Division relegation fodder over Forest in January 1983 served only to incite further friction.

But on Saturday 21 May events dictated that a seismic force with its epicentre somewhere in the Pennines would stretch those previous cracks to an insurmountable width and depth.

At the *Nottingham Evening Post*'s buildings the sports department prepared itself for a routine FA Cup final day. A few jars across Forman Street at the 'branch office' Langtry's or the Blue Bell and the final *Football Post*, the pink 'un, would be put to bed for the season and out on the city centre streets by five past five. No bother.

Then again, it was the Manchester United–Brighton and Hove Albion Cup final. And Smith must score...apparently not.

On trial as an aspiring sports journalist at the time, I can remember the face of sports editor John Lucy turning pale, puce and all shades unhealthy when a Press Association wire came tapping across the printer at the sedate office. I judged it to be a death in the family, his own even, by his expression, but instead he slumped over his desk, head in hands and murmured: "Derby have signed John Robertson!"

In a flash I reacted like an old pro and suggested a couple of pints at Langtry's to mull the matter over, but to no avail; senior figures down the corridor were already involved. Twenty minutes later, I was steering a battered old company Escort very slowly around the south Notts village of Widmerpool.

"What can I do for you, young man?" inquired Taylor when I'd finally located his home and then plucked up enough courage to knock on the door.

"We've heard you've signed John Robertson today. Can you confirm that Mr Taylor?"

"I can and I can also say I'm absolutely delighted he's signed and he'll be a great asset to Derby County."

Since I was not in the seasoned hack routine of asking killer questions then, or ever have been since, the thought of inquiring how Mr Clough might have felt did not enter my head. But then, there was already enough colour from the Clough end, most of it purple, to flesh out the story. Job almost done, Widmerpool's only red telephone box, with the A and B buttons to press, was the next port of call. Don't know how John Robertson's number was in my almost virgin contact book, but there it was, an entry under 'R' for Robbo, at nearby Plumtree. Like Taylor, he was charm itself.

"What the fucking hell do you want, McVay?" came the dulcet Glaswegian tones.

"Well it's like this. You know I'm working for the *Post* now?"

"Oh aye, course. I forgot. What's the matter?"

"I've just spoken to Peter Taylor and he says you've signed for Derby. How do you feel about that?"

"Absolutely delighted. Anything more, Davie boy?"

It was a day to be absolutely delighted, at least back at the sports desk. We'd got some valuable quotes, albeit slightly duplicated and a back page lead on Cup final day for the last *FP* of the season.

Those who subscribe to the theory of a parallel universe may have had their ranks expanded that glorious May afternoon. Somewhere along the Pennine Way, a diametrically opposite reaction, falling slightly short of spontaneous combustion, was taking place as Clough and his walking party returned to their hotel HQ after another leg of a charity ramble. Clough was based near Kirby Lonsdale, along with his entourage that included Mike Hudson, the club doctor, and Alan Hill. The group of men sat at a table with Hill, having phoned his wife Janice, aware of the news back in Nottingham.

"Sit down and I'll bring the glasses over," Clough said. He returned with a bottle of Bell's Whisky.

"Have you heard what's happened?" one of the party asked Clough.

"I have heard, son," Clough retorted and banged the bottle heavily onto the table. "And do you know what, I'll never speak to that fucking bastard again! I wouldn't cross the A52 to piss on him."

They were words and rancour that would haunt Clough to his grave. The pair were never reconciled, even though, as revealed in

Provided You Don't Kiss Me, a highly praised portrait of Clough by the *Nottingham Evening Post*'s former Forest reporter Duncan Hamilton, things might have been different if alternative sliding doors had been in place following that FA Cup defeat at the Baseball Ground.

SADLY, THE ENDING overshadowed an immense bond that had existed between the two protagonists. Kenny Burns, another former Forest player who Taylor signed for Derby, this time from Leeds United, believes that it would have endured. "When Peter was at Derby the first time and had a heart attack, Cloughie moved heaven and earth to get him sorted and get the best treatment," Burns says. "I still think that if one of them had been in real trouble and asked for help, the other would have been there like a shot. But we'll never know now."

"When we were flying out to European games and being treated like royalty, that was wonderful," Wendy says. "Both Brian and Dad shared that family touch. They made sure the families went on all the trips and they were well looked after. They were two working class lads who had not lost sight of who mattered to them. It was a heady mixture, champagne, VIP treatment, courtesy cars to the airport and hardly ever paying for anything. Even in Nottingham, you couldn't go out without someone wanting to talk, buying you a few drinks and refusing any back. It was hard to get your hand in your pocket and Dad would always say: 'Enjoy it now because it can't go on forever.' It's an overused expression, but it really was a rollercoaster ride.

"I suppose it was the scent of power as well. They had national journalists knocking on their door and waiting for up to three hours just to get a few quotes. I know my dad was not without his faults, he was not squeaky clean or anything like that, but what annoyed me was that Brian and Forest tried to write him out of the club's history."

In the final words of his autobiography, ghosted by Mike Langley, Taylor pens a forlorn hope for the future.

"It's been one long happy ending since the restoration of our partnership," he wrote in 1980 about their re-acquaintance in 1976. Both of us are aware it cannot go on forever...I hope we part on a high note and on the friendliest of terms and that football will remember us as pioneers of management – the first to see that two heads are better than one."

Taylor's return to Derby almost certainly destroyed those doubtless honest sentiments. A rift as long and as wide as the stretch of the A52 that separates Derby from Nottingham emerged; a dual carriageway that is occasionally littered with paper and junk from adjacent housing estates, dirty rubbish if not laundry aired in public on windy days by careless residents. A section of Tarmacadam renamed the Brian Clough Way. Not the Peter Taylor one. If that seems a careless omission, it can be forgiven. It was Clough's sense of the dramatic, his piercing personality that could be ambivalent, avid or antagonistic on one or all subjects, and a media presence before its time that captured the imagination and invariably created back page headlines for Forest.

If there is a shameful neglect, it is the absence of a showcase reference at the City Ground to which Taylor brought such joy and success. "In the end, Brian had changed so much from the man we all knew," says Wendy when talking about Clough and Taylor's decaying relationship. "He [Clough] had been so corrupted by fame and money and who he thought he had become that I don't think there was anything left in the friendship."

ON THE INTERNET site *YouTube*, recorded at East Midlands airport as the team returned triumphant from the European Cup final in Munich, his granddaughter Alex spots Taylor, who can be seen in perpetuity holding a rare court with the press. Dour and slightly aggressive in interviews, particularly standing 6ft 2in tall, he appears here without nerves or any trace of self-consciousness; a man of few words, but on this occasion eloquent.

And then his other granddaughter, Laura, a teacher in Kent, found out more as a staff colleague in the PE department discovered her roots and paid his own respects during a class session, bowing his head in the universal gesture of observing genius. "And that being from someone relatively young," Laura recalls. "Perhaps grandad is something of a legend after all."

John Robertson
1970-1983 & 1985-1986: 499 games, 95 goals

THERE IS A SMALL housing development to the south of Nottingham, standing as adjacent to the River Trent as does the City Ground, but a few miles east and downstream. The familiar suburban grind of commuter angst and family life striving to succeed in tandem can be seen and heard in its new-build environs that compete in the shadow of the imposing Clifton Bridge, a long span creation that daily ferries myriad transport north and south across the Trent. With just a smidgeon of thought and care, no.2 Arcadia Gardens or its equivalent on this particular development could have boasted a blue plaque, one of those indelible tributes that is an everyday reminder in everyday environs that someone special passed this way.

In this case John Robertson.

Since the location is on the periphery of Wilford, once a quaint riverside village that has expanded and made inroads into the landscape, there is good reason to demand that two such plaques be polished regularly in the region. The other would be to Albert Iremonger, the giant Notts County custodian who kept goal for the Magpies in a career spanning three decades and then kept the Ferry Inn public house that once welcomed travellers who had paid their penny and crossed from the north bank of the Trent via the Toll Bridge. A small expanse of inland water nearby is known to this day as Iremonger's Pond. A favourite of itinerant anglers, it nestles beneath shrubbery and an embankment that once sped steam trains along the now defunct Great Western Railway line. Less frequently these days, a few retired dray horses graze in the encroaching fields.

A similar rural idyll once existed where Robertson's blue plaque might have been embedded. Rather than exuding rustic charm, the sports ground that belonged to T Bailey Forman and Sons was pristine and immaculately turned out. The verdant oasis beneath the congestion and fumes of Clifton Bridge that formed a buffer between the spreading Wilford village housing, was home to two football pitches, a cricket square, a bowling green and a couple of hard surface tennis courts. As well as that there stood a cricket pavilion and football changing rooms, a philanthropic legacy of its owner, Colonel Thomas Forman, who was also proprietor of the *Nottingham Evening Post*. After the colonel died, his inheritance was sold off by his son Nicholas. And who could blame him for accepting an offer of £92.4 million for the newspaper from the *Daily Mail* group?

Despite urgings and promises from employees that they would continue to maintain the old sports ground as volunteers, his land agent, a chap called Barrington Smythe or Smythe Barrington, there was Barrington in there somewhere, vowed that the land would only return to be a sports facility 'over his dead body' even though council sources insisted that planning permission would never be granted on the location.

So after years of dereliction and neglect, the inevitable happened. Planning permission was granted and the land was sold to property speculators who promptly earmarked the green fields for a thriving community of at least 100 houses.

Somewhere in the middle, how nice it would have been to see that blue plaque installed.

Its inscription might have read: May, 1982. John Robertson, Nottingham Forest and Scotland winger, stood here.

THE TALE BEHIND that as yet non-existent plaque reveals the quintessential John Robertson and his enduring appeal to an adoring Forest public. It was indeed late May, a balmy Wednesday evening as I recall, when, on this very patch of turf, in keeping with every Wednesday night during the summer months, a motley collection of amateur players from all walks of life gathered for a game whose boundaries ranged from five to 25-a-side depending on the social diary.

Ostensibly for *Evening Post* employees, the weekly session had grown to embrace many cultures, particularly those from the hosiery and fashion industry, a strata or more below Paul Smith, namely the shop assistants and night owls who flogged expensive suits in outlets such as Birdcage on Bridlesmith Gate. No professional footballer who prided himself on his sartorial elegance could resist a trip to one of Bridlesmith Gate's boutiques where the incentive of a free silk tie came with every £100 spent on the fashion strides and shirts of the time.

How John Robertson, he of the unkempt but also unflappable looks came to be mates with Nottingham's smart set is perhaps not such a mystery. His devotion to the fashion-conscious Bryan Ferry and Roxy Music probably led him there as well as his own unique eye for that infamous laid-back exterior. At any rate, as balmy as that May evening was, nothing prepared us for the appearance of Robertson on the lush grass of the T Bailey Forman sports ground as the shadows from the matured copses that edged the playing fields began to lengthen appreciably. He was running solo that night, turning up just as the game was about to start. To put it in context, Robertson had his socks rolled down and was wearing a pair of battered old trainers which had about as much grip on the turf as Margaret Thatcher had on reality, but then the Iron Lady was busy plotting her re-election campaign by means of a conflict in a distant land. Some things never change in the political sphere.

To compound his precarious footing, most of Robbo's feathered friends from Birdcage were attired in boots with metal studs, while the opposition, mainly drawn from *Evening Post* ranks, wore plimsolls that had seen better days and action in Gallipoli and Hyson Green. If he wasn't flayed by the shrapnel from one of his own mates, Robertson was in peril from the clumsy counter attack of the journalists and print setters whose old Sunday morning side had not been known infamously as the Slashers for simply cutting copy or urinating in unlikely public places.

On a normal Wednesday, even during the football season, this might not have been the oddest appearance from a First Division and international-class winger who just two years previously had scored the only goal as Forest retained the European Cup against Kevin Keegan's

SV Hamburg in Madrid. What astounded the company most was that while the season was over for Forest and Robertson, in less than a week he would be heading north to join the Scotland squad for the World Cup finals in Spain!

It would be reasonable to assume that few players, from either team, ventured too close to Robertson. Not that he needed any assistance for our capitulation, but as he sidled past one faint-hearted tackle after another, the only thought in the minds of the majority was: "For god's sake, don't slip and clatter him!"

The prospect of such a calamity was not even a fleeting blip on the Robertson radar. Had Jock Stein, the Scotland coach, gotten wind of his star left-winger's impromptu and highly irregular fitness regime, his reaction may well have been a little less than understanding and calm. The Tartan Army may have experienced that familiar sinking feeling in Malaga and Seville later that year, knocked out at the group stages by Brazil and Russia, but they should thank their lucky stars and a shambolic bunch of rag-tag amateurs that Robertson was fit and able to participate in what was to be his last World Cup finals for his country.

IS THERE ANYONE with a football lilt in Nottingham who does not have a story about John Robertson to tell? A tale related with a smile in the voice and spring in the step?

The essence of the Scotsman is that, like many of his contemporaries in those European Cup years, he has not lost the common touch. Only, with Robertson, the elasticity of those boundaries between model professional and model supporters seemed to stretch, bend and become more than a little blurred – with an overwhelming impunity granted by his peers on either side of the terracing.

Did he like a few beers and a fag? Of course, and still does. The cinder track from the dugout to the corner flag and the adjacent dressing rooms at Villa Park was renamed Ash Avenue or Tobacco Road as the chain-smoking Robertson wended his way up and down the touchline when he was assistant to his old mate Martin O'Neill at the West Midlands venue. But whereas O'Neill was articulate, media-friendly and media-manipulative, Robertson was acutely averse to publicity, shying away from outward expression, but equally influential in the partnership's success. As a pairing, it sounds vaguely familiar.

A guest appearance on the top table at the Commodore International after his playing career was over confirmed his unease with public speaking. Anyone in Nottingham who has celebrated winning an amateur trophy from the Young Elizabethan League to the Notts Sunday Morning Division Ten will know the Commodore; anyone in Nottingham who has celebrated a night out just because they have evaded the gravy and peas from the lukewarm roast beef dinner while straining the neck to catch a glimpse of the ventriloquist's lips moving as the dummy speaks will also be on nodding terms with the Commodore. Elasticated bow ties, revolving doors and amateur boxing nights on gentlemen's evening; they might have invented the phrase glitzy kitsch with the Commodore in mind, but it had a charm of its time, a venue where young men became drunken slobs overnight and discovered the hallucinatory powers of ten pints of Whitbread Big Head bitter and its consequences the following morning. Now it has been demolished, only feeding the yearning for callow youth to return.

Its star acts ranged from George Best to Bleeding Awful and it was when the legendary Northern Ireland winger headed into town that Robertson and Larry Lloyd were asked to sit on the top table. Every wannabe-but-never-had-been amateur player in the audience that night reserved the biggest ovation for Robertson as he was introduced, nervously standing to accept the accolade, but clearly worse for wear having hit the juice early to assuage a nervous disposition. In contrast Best, who could have drunk the top table under it, the prodigious Lloyd included, was incongruously sober, a slur-free zone minded impeccably by Paddy Crerand, his Scottish former club-mate at Manchester United.

It was the night that Best revelled, for the first time but certainly not the last, in the "Where did it all go wrong, Georgie Boy?" story, but not before Robertson had mumbled a few almost inaudible words as a prelude. If Best's now infamous tale of the cash and Miss World on the bed, on its inaugural telling to the Nottingham punters, was well received, it was nothing to the acclaim that greeted Robertson's indecipherable oration. A few minutes later, Larry Lloyd arose from the two seats required for his frame and began an address, punctuated by a loud banging and clattering beyond the auditorium. The infamous 16 steps, a small stairway from the ballroom to an inner bar, had claimed another victim.

Looking around the table and with Robertson absent, probably in the downstairs toilet at the time, Lloyd announced: "The taxi's arrived for Robbo then!" Inebriated or inhaling smoke as quickly as a chimney stack at Radcliffe-on-Soar power station puffs it out, sober or sensible, Robertson remains the legend on the left wing with whom the man on the street or the terraces most identifies and empathises.

Every amateur team in the country has a John Robertson in their side, the cut of his jib and the identical lifestyle…apart from one thing. "Genius," as Alan Hill, assistant to Brian Clough and former Forest goalkeeper described it.

It was 'genius' that created that goal in that European Cup final in 1979 for Trevor Francis, the one spark of invention in a desperately dull game that pitted the tired and exhausted of Nottingham against the fresh but outclassed of Sweden; 'genius' that scored the winner in Madrid a year later; and 'genius' that bemused and belittled opposition when the little tubby boy ran into dead ends and still emerged with a goal-creating cross despite being shadowed by at least two defenders.

BUT BEFORE THE fame, Robertson suffered the stresses, strains and insecurities of a young man working away from home and not knowing what the future might hold.

It was during this period that his love affair with Bryan Ferry and the sounds of Roxy Music was rooted. His impersonations of the saggy-eyed and baggy-trousered crooner often lit up or darkened Uriah Heep, depending on allegiances and perception of points awarded for artistic merit.

For historical record, Uriah Heep was Nottingham's first wine bar and an instant hit for the in-crowd who craved sophistication in a bottle of Blue Nun. Located on the same small side street where Paul Smith opened his first boutique, like the guru designer's fashions, it was not everyone's glass of Liebfraumilch, but the frequency of its mention in this book confirms its status among professional footballers at the time. Funnily enough, Smith's empire was expanding around the same time as the cult of men's fashion tapped into a lucrative market of young professionals, footballers and otherwise, whose disposable income had suddenly increased to hitherto unprecedented levels for that age group.

If Robertson, aka Ferry, was as de rigueur as a Paul Smith shirt in Uriah Heep, his routine had been perfected in the teenage haunt of the Union, one of several rowing clubs on the south bank of the Trent already mentioned in dispatches.

O'Neill has told the story of their early friendship, young lads on a night out at the venue. "We had a bet who could pull the most girls in a season. I think Robbo won by 500 to 1. And I made up the one. But he had this way of dancing close to a girl, smooching up to her and singing *What's Your Name...Virginia Plain*? What woman could resist?!"

He remains a devotee to this day, having flown down from Glasgow during his time with O'Neill at Celtic to see a reformed Roxy Music on tour at the Nottingham Ice Arena. Whether he keeps a collection of Clint Eastwood videos is uncertain, but as well as Ferry, he did a mean rendition of extracts of *Dirty Harry* movies to keep himself and the likes of Kenny Burns amused. His other vices – smoking and a pint of best – have also been impossible to kick: a personal holy trinity that have given both support and succour, and not only to the disciple. "Robbo, you know every time I see you, I feel great," his master's voice, the great Clough, would greet Robertson on some mornings at the City Ground after a particularly taxing evening indulging in his three vices. "I know I feel bad, but you always look worse," would continue the manager.

An ability to mesmerise defenders and damsels in distress with a drop of the shoulder and a wiggle of those ample hips was spotted in those wilderness years; at least the sporting side to his talent. England manager Don Revie, clearly on this occasion just one folder short of a full dossier, noted his potential and called him up into the national team's training squad. Only to be told Robbo was in fact Scottish.

Even in those darker hours of despondency, I recall he still had time to urge on a young contemporary from across the river. Somehow he was playing right half-ish and myself left-sided of nowhere during one of those meaningless County Cup finals that extended the season, but delayed players from a beach in Spain or Skegness for a further week. By some minor miracle, I managed to beat Robertson to the ball and a final pass flew unerringly to a colleague, inducing words of encouragement from my supposed marker. "Keep that up son and they'll have to start picking you regularly."

That was around 1974 and the next time we exchanged words on the pitch came six years later. "What the fuck?! Bomber [turning to Ian Bowyer in disgust], he's just fucking kicked me. What you doing that for Davie boy? I was going to buy you a drink back at Madison's, but that's the end of that," he concluded with a smile that bordered on sincere.

The scrape down the back of the heel was unintentional at London Road, but as the Peterborough United right-back, I had already paid a heavy price in the first leg of our second round League Cup tie at the City Ground. Our tactics that particular night were simple. Stop Robertson. It shows the level of confidence our manager Peter Morris had in my defensive nous to fulfil that simple task that he asked two other players to cover around the back and front every time the ball was played out to the left wing. The faith factor was underwhelming. That one of the Posh players was a young teenager called Tony Cliss was respect enough to Robertson. Young Clissy chased and caught pigeons for a living at his rural Fenlands village, although it was over one or two yards, not 100, that Robertson exploited the weakness of others best.

Our ploy worked well for a while, but then we had forgotten about the likes of Garry Birtles and Frank Gray, who popped up with goals before Robertson, with Cliss and my other minder upfield seeking a consolation away goal, plopped in a third.

Somehow it hadn't seemed like a solid 3-0 thrashing, but then that was the Forest style under Clough; not always masterful and irresistible, but ruthless, efficient, occasionally inspirational and frequently triumphant.

NOBODY WAS MORE surprised to join Nottingham Forest than Frank Clark when the veteran full-back was given a free transfer by Newcastle United after umpteen years' service, including a testimonial, for the Geordies. That was in 1975, but the former Amateur Cup winner with Crook Town, who had been reared on a strict regime of self-discipline in the north east, pondered how the other half lived when he embarked on Forest's pre-season tour of West Germany. It was on that trip that Peter Taylor rendered his famous 'fat boy' speech to Robertson, telling him in no uncertain terms that unless he got his act together, not only would he be flying home prematurely from the tour, but that his career at Forest was over.

Judging by what he had seen during his brief time at the club, Frank Clark concurred. "When I first signed for Forest, I didn't speak to him for three months," reveals Clark. "I thought he was away with the fairies because he didn't seem to have a clue. He was always knocking about with his mate Jimmy McCann at the time and I just didn't think Robbo was being professional enough or doing himself justice. It's all a bit ironic really because it's the best thing that could have happened to me."

Although Brian Clough often referred to Clark with a reference thrown in about his pipe and slippers, the full-back was actually only 31 when he joined Forest. Clough was desperate for a left-back who could defend and a local journalist in the north east tipped him off about Clark's availability.

"Doncaster, Darlington and Hartlepool were the other clubs showing an interest, so I didn't need a lot of persuading. But when I got here I felt there were a lot of players who didn't know what being a pro was all about – and Robbo was one of them. He needed a good kick up the backside and he certainly got that from Cloughie and Taylor in West Germany. They really got stuck into him. He always had the ability, there was no doubt about that."

Once Clark, the veteran who twanged a mean guitar, and Robertson, the young pretender who envisaged himself as Bryan Ferry at least once a week, were speaking to one another, the left-wing partnership blossomed in perfect harmony. Just as off the pitch Robertson changed his diet and lifestyle at the behest of Taylor, so on it did the older, wiser head reel in and restrict Robertson's more wayward tendencies. Perched just behind him on the left side, Clark was able to manoeuvre himself and Robertson into the kind of moving pattern that was synonymous with Forest's success during a truly golden three years.

Promotion from the Second Division, nicked on the final day of the season when Wolverhampton Wanderers won at Bolton, was followed by the league title, two League Cups and two European Cups and a European Super Cup. It was astonishing by any standards, but for Forest it was akin to an incredible voyage beyond the furthest star in the galaxy.

And in many ways it was Robertson, the pioneer breaking new ground himself, who was making it all happen. "With him stuck on the left wing, well it was just perfect for me," says Clark. "He wasn't a great defender or tackler or anything like that, but I was able to drag him into the space in front of me. He learned to fill in the hole and that was part of our strength as a team that we attacked together, but got back and defended as one."

Clark admits that he was never one to dwell on the ball. "Cloughie always told Peter Shilton to kick the ball out of his hands and get the ball down their end. Then we could play a bit. I was all right defending and back pedalling, that was my strength and always had been, but, if I'm honest, I wasn't the greatest on the ball. Very, very ordinary is how I'd describe it, so that style of play suited me fine. I think it suited Viv [Anderson, the right-back] as well because he liked the ball going forward, but not thrown out from the goalkeeper."

The arrangement also found favour with Robertson. If Clark was ever in possession of the cherished orb, he had an instant and reliable outlet just a few yards away and always to his left.

"I actually think Robbo preferred to play in front of me rather than Frankie Gray [Clark's successor in the left-back berth, signed from Leeds United]. "That's no disrespect to Frankie, far from it. He was far more comfortable on the ball than me, a better player if you like, but because of that I think Robbo saw less of it. In my case, I hardly needed to look up to find him. That was always my first thought: 'Bump, there you are Robbo,' and off he went."

It was Robertson's attacking instincts, ducking and weaving, then that powerful burst over three or four yards that also acted as the best form of defence. "It was almost an insurance policy because I was never too worried about full-backs overlapping wingers coming at me all the time. I knew they would be too occupied trying to get to grips with Robbo. During that first season in the First Division, he became known for getting to the byline and getting in a cross that Peter Withe would get on the end of. If not him, Martin O'Neill or one of the other midfielders would pick up the pieces. It was uncanny, but his reputation was established and growing. Every time we went out, you could almost see the opposition banking up double on the right. They tried just about everything, even treble banking, but ultimately, the bottom line was that they couldn't stop him. They couldn't stop him getting the ball which is where their troubles began because they sure as hell couldn't stop him getting past them to that byline."

There were other qualities too. Robertson once asked Ian Storey-Moore, the golden boy winger from the 1960s, how he managed to survive given the intensity and ferocity of tackles that were flying about indiscriminately during that decade, amazed he lasted as long as he had in the game. Yet in Robertson's 1970s, the machismo element endemic in many defenders was still prevalent and the Scot had his share of physical attention, legitimate or otherwise.

"His sort of skill, where you burst past someone and deliver a cross, can't be coached or taught, it's a natural thing," says Clark. "He developed that technical skill on his own as a schoolboy. Allied with his personality he also had courage and bravery. And that's not only the bravery to take a tackle and stand up to it and get up again. Bravery comes in many ways and as most pros will tell you, accepting responsibility, having the ball in a tight area with a couple of players marking, well it takes a special player and a special sort of courage to do that.

"Robbo's trick was that he had two great feet and could cross or shoot with either foot. And then there was that ability to go up to full-backs and stop on the spot because he was so confident on the ball. Once the full-back had stopped, one way or the other, he was dead. And Robbo knew that."

Clark had reason to be grateful on various levels. He agrees that Robertson probably extended his own career and enabled him to enjoy a final farewell in Munich in 1979.

"It wasn't the greatest final, but by the time we got to play Malmo, as a squad we were knackered. They just wanted to hoof the ball down the pitch and big Lloydy just stood there and headed it back for us to attack again. They were well organised, but it took one piece of magic to unlock the game and win it for us. The cross and goal were pure Robbo."

There was the magical winner in Madrid, of course, in 1980, Robertson once more raising his game at a crucial moment and scoring from 25 yards with his supposedly dud right foot. It was the highest of highlights in a City Ground career which propelled the shuffling, tubby smoker into the great pantheon of footballing heroes. And yet an acrimonious departure beckoned in the summer of 1983 and that move to that club.

The background was Robertson craved the security of a three-year contract. He had sustained a cartilage injury in a defeat at Manchester

United in January and thereafter Forest's title hopes slipped gradually away during a February and March that witnessed nine league games played without a win. His wife was pregnant with their first child and, now aged 30, three years seemed a reasonable request. Clough's arrogance and relish for a contractual fight offered only two, however; take it or leave it. So Robertson left it and left him (Clough) in the lurch in favour of Derby County and Peter Taylor. "This time I felt I had to make a stand," the player said at the time.

As a parting shot, it must have scored a direct, painful hit smack in the middle of Clough's most vulnerable area – his ego. Ouch!

It was not as if he had not been a loyal, faithful, mostly obedient and always outstanding servant for the club – as he knew all too well. "Forest have had their money's worth out of me," he declared. Robertson even returned to the City Ground after news broke of his transfer to confront Clough and explain his motives. Perhaps fortuitously, the manager was still on his charity walk in the Pennines, letting off steam and a barrage of industrial language up and down dale no doubt. The meeting never took place.

Clough then flew to Canada for an end of season tour against Montreal and Toronto Blizzards. "I will not waste one minute, no, one second talking about Robertson," he told awaiting press before boarding his plane.

The parting of the ways finished Clough and Taylor as friends; Robertson's career faltered at the Baseball Ground where neither he nor Taylor could recapture the form or mood that had inspired Forest beyond their own potential.

But if Clough was scathing, Forest fans were prepared to forgive: even a move to Derby County. Adulation does not come much more genuine and pure than that.

Frank Clark sums it up, speaking on behalf of players and supporters alike in many ways. "Our thing was to get the ball to the fat lad on the wing. When all's said and done, he was the one player who made us all better with his contribution."

Tony Woodcock

1974-1979: 176 games, 62 goals

THE WORDS WERE music to the ear; this ear anyway. "I'll meet you in the pub at the end of the road," Tony Woodcock had advised by telephone. Who could resist such an invitation at the best of times?

He'd been working in Peckham that day, the one place you could forgive that absent-minded professional Rio Ferdinand for forgetting even if it is listed as his place of birth. I'd been chasing my tail around a country besieged by a few hefty rainfalls. When I reached south-east London, bathed in glorious early evening sunshine, it belied the flood waters that were rising around Sheffield at that moment. Still, every cloud has a silver lining. I was anticipating a pint of hefty specific gravity Belgian lager with Woodcock, while Environment Agency chiefs were anticipating a hefty bonus, specifically for defying gravity and the laws of nature by keeping middle England safe and dry amid the summer deluge of 2007.

A few miles from Peckham central, at the junction of Amelia Street and Walworth Road, the Tankard public house, smack in the middle of the Elephant and Castle, was the venue Woodcock had chosen to be interviewed. The watering hole and its environs has a certain charm and doubtless the casual visitor happily would be indulged by a company of several roguish Del Boy Trotters and his good-hearted cockney chums at their earthy local. Perhaps best to say the location was less than salubrious, as gross an understatement as estate agentese describing Milton Keynes as a cultural backwater covered in concrete. It's a lot worse than that.

As far as I was aware, none of Forest's European Cup winners had suffered financially, but blimey, the Tankard on a Monday night with *Big Brother* booming out of the requisite elevated telly seemed one domino dot and a dash of lime away from a distress signal.

THERE IS A TOUCH of irony in the preamble. Woodcock is anything but destitute or desperate. Quite the reverse.

Many have observed that football is a game of opinions and its diversity makes for part of its attraction, compulsion even. There are those who believe Woodcock was the fulcrum that swayed Nottingham Forest's rise to European success. Certainly the huge rewards that Brian Clough eventually offered him, in vain as it transpired, to remain at the club would suggest the value of this worth to the organisation. His local roots, like Garry Birtles' and Viv Anderson's, make him a natural choice as a figure to be admired, respected and envied from the terraces. But there is more to Woodcock than the perception that he was the excruciatingly shy one who knocked in the goals.

While reports of Larry Lloyd's demise were only slightly exaggerated, reports of Woodcock's bashfulness were greatly so. And now, in the Tankard on a Monday night in the Elephant and Castle, could it be that Woodcock, still intact with that annoyingly full head of blond perma-perm hair, is becoming a cult hero with a new generation of young people all over again?

It's a pleasing thought. The other night, he tells me, on some obscure satellite channel, his goals against Manchester United in Forest's championship-winning season were shown all over again. And who but Garry Birtles should ring him up?

"I was in bed and he rang to tell me they were showing some of the greatest moments from that season," Woodcock says with an enthusiasm that did not diminish during our conversation. "He said to me: 'We weren't too bad, were we?'"

Since he finished in football, Woodcock has dipped his fingers into a variety of business pies, although he was not comfortable at being labelled as a football agent when he was living in West Germany. "I was working for a big corporation and needed to get an agent's licence because I might have had to deal with players, but I wasn't an agent in any sense."

Given the modern football agent's reputation – frequently undulating in the Sleazebag Top Ten between politicians, solicitors and Peter Stringfellow – it is not difficult to understand why he distances himself so from the scavenging pack.

His latest venture derives more from altruism than avarice. Teaching young inner city schoolchildren of Peckham, Tower Hamlets and the Elephant and Castle the rudiments of business acumen in a football context is not exactly how some might imagine Woodcock preparing for life in his fifties, but the response from the underprivileged children in these parts, some of them young offenders whose horizons are limited to the tower blocks that blight the area, has inspired Woodcock – an uplift reciprocated by pupils, or at least their elders.

"They keep coming in and telling me, yes, their dad does remember me, you used to be quite famous once," he laughs. The scheme is in its embryonic stages, but already government and local authorities are taking note and Lord Harris of Peckham has been approached about expanding its remit and widening the goalposts.

MAYBE WOODCOCK'S ALTRUISM has something to do with his roots. Born in Eastwood, a distinction he shares with D.H. Lawrence, on the cusp of Nottinghamshire and Derbyshire, Woodcock was a late starter into the game – the present of a pair of football socks from his brother-in-law for his 12th birthday proving the unlikely catalyst for a career that, at its zenith, would see him elevated to Britain's highest paid football player. Unlike Lawrence, he was not the son of a miner, although his dad was a manual worker at Watnall, supervising the kilns that toasted bricks and drew up the charred air through giant chimneys, some of which remain as landmarks on the easterly side of the M1 between junctions 24 and 25.

Like Lawrence, however, Woodcock's talents enabled him to escape Eastwood, yet the affinity lingers in earnest. Earlier this year he attended the 40th anniversary of his boyhood club, Priory Celtic, a famous institution in county circles and one which presented Woodcock – and ultimately Forest – with a golden opportunity. Its founder, Jimmy Lowry, was a Catholic Scot and Celtic supporter, hence the name.

"It was a way of getting us off the streets and stopping us causing trouble if nothing else. My dad used to come and watch me play, but he didn't really know a lot about the game. In fact it was the Buckleys' dad, who came and watched one of our games. His sons Alan and Steve both played professionally and they were a strong football family.

"Their dad turned around to mine and tapped him on the shoulder and said: 'You know, there's only one lad on this pitch who is going to make a player.'

"'Who would that be then?'

"'That lad yonder.'

"And it was me, but my dad didn't have a clue."

Alan Hill, the former Forest goalkeeper working as a scout for the club, did have more of a clue and recommended Woodcock for trials. Under Dave Mackay's regime, he signed as an apprentice.

BIG BROTHER HAS GIVEN way to even more inane babblings on the Tankard telly. A clientele of truly mixed race is less than enthralled with the televisual delights, but the dulcet tones of Elton John on the jukebox only increases the banality factor to intolerable levels. Fortunately Woodcock is as focused as if a tiny shaft of light had opened up in the Manchester United back four, his eyes glinting at the space, his legs darting at uncanny pace into the channel and his brain ticking over twice as quick as that of the lumbering centre-half left trailing his posterior. Half a chance suddenly becomes a certain goal. His cultured and deadly left foot is cocked and ready to stroke the ball into the net. That was the Woodcock way during two dynamic seasons that shaped the rest of his life and Forest's destiny.

As well as bringing 19 goals in Forest's championship season and a League Cup winners' medal, 1977/78 saw Woodcock receive the Young Player of the Year accolade at the PFA awards dinner and win the first of his 42 England caps (against Northern Ireland), in an international career in which he found the net a more than respectable 16 times, a strike rate not far shy of Michael Owen's. The boy from Eastwood had become an essential and much loved and vaunted part of the Forest and England machines, despite the fact he was but 22 years of age.

On a purely social level, Woodcock always resembled the boy next door, the clean-shaven quiet one, who any girl could have taken back to their mum and dad for Sunday tea without causing offence. At least it offered contrast to Kenny Burns and Larry Lloyd.

And yet from his earliest battles at the City Ground, as much with himself as management, here clearly was a force to be reckoned with. "It was funny because when I came to sign professional Allan Brown had taken over from Dave Mackay. In those days, you got £30 a week when you signed first year pro, £35 the next season and then, like Steve Baines, you were upped to £40 a week if you were retained.

"That was how it was done. But I thought I was worth more. I thought I should have been getting £35 a week and I told Bert Johnson [the youth team coach] so. He agreed and said he would back me up and all the lads were on my side, so I stuck out for my £35 a week. At first, the club said 'no way' but after a few days, I got the contract I wanted. Don't get me wrong, I was sweating on it. Daft really, but that was my first real contractual battle. For a fiver a week."

And he won. So much for the shy retiring type.

Woodcock did not have to wait long for his debut, a 3-1 away defeat at Aston Villa on 24 April 1974. Duncan McKenzie scored the only goal and then grabbed two more at Portsmouth in what was to be his Forest swansong. But here surely, at 18 years of age, was his successor in the shape of the nimble and fleet-footed Woodcock? "I got some rave reviews and Man of the Match at Portsmouth, where we won 2-0, and I think I went away that summer believing that I'd made it. I came back unfit and unprepared really. Whatever the reasons, I just couldn't get it together or get a place in the side."

Then along came Brian Clough – and a tale of two opposites eventually attracting began. "I'd been an outcast at Forest for months, then Cloughie arrives for the FA Cup replay against Tottenham [at White Hart Lane]. I couldn't believe it when the team sheet [the squad to travel to London in January 1975] went up on the notice board. My name was on it and I thought, 'at worst, I'll get a place on the bench'. He took us down to Bisham Abbey to bond together for a couple of days. I quickly began to realise that I wasn't even going to make the bench when he started asking me to fetch the spare training balls, collect up the bibs and that sort of thing. I was putting out the cones and being a general dogsbody. Then we came back to the hotel for lunch.

"We were all sitting having our meal and Cloughie comes over. 'Young man,' he says, 'go up to my room and outside you'll see a pair of shoes. Polish them for me for the game tomorrow night then leave them inside. Here's the key to my front door.'"

The teenage Woodcock had a dilemma. Show the mettle that earned him a fiver a week with Allan Brown or capitulate to one of the most influential and dogmatic managers in English football. One of the most? Make that the most.

Fortunately Woodcock had some assistance at the dining table, and not just a directional note, pre-sat nav naturally, as to which way to pass the port and stale cobs.

"As Cloughie was talking I was looking around for allies," Woodcock says. "Here was the new manager showing who was in control and I didn't have a chance. I didn't want to seem like a go-fer, but should I stand up and say 'no' or what? The only one who raised his head and looked around was George Lyall. He nodded and seemed to say, 'go on son, just do it'. And that's what I did.

"I always remember Jimmy Gordon [the trainer] coming up to me. 'Don't worry son,' he told me. 'He did this with Gordon McQueen at Leeds. And he was a good player.'"

Although the trainer perhaps did not mean it quite so cuttingly, it still left Woodcock tainted as Clough's shoe-shine boy with a future destined to fall short of the inelegant Scottish centre-half's. A life in domestic service, rising to butler status, may have beckoned as a career. Some weeks later, Clough bumped into Woodcock, whose disappearance from the first team radar compared with a kamikaze pilot on his first flying lesson above the Pacific Ocean, in the City Ground kit drying room.

"How are you, young man? I haven't seen you in a while," greeted Clough.

"And so it went on," Woodcock recalls.

"He kept playing me on the left wing, which I didn't really like, but then that gave him his chance to have a go at me from the dugout. I was doing all right, but all the time I was just waiting for him to have a pop and shout: 'Woodcock, get yourself over here,' etc. I was frightened to death of him, as most of the players were, but I hated it. So eventually I plucked up enough courage to tackle Cloughie. He was walking across the car park one morning and I ran over.

"'Boss, can I have a word?'

"'Course, son.'

"'Well, it's just that I hate playing on the wing and you seem to have a go at me every time I get the ball. I can't play when you keep shouting at me.'

"'Well, I thought it might motivate you.'

"'It's just the opposite. I'm a bag of nerves.'"

Clough paused for a moment to consider the implications of the young man's words, the deep wound that he might have been inflicting on his psyche and the consequences that it might have had on his fledgling career. 'Well, you can't win them all,' he noted glibly and glided off to his Mercedes leaving his inquisitor standing alone on the City Ground tarmac.

"Did he know what he was doing? Was it all part of a plan? I just don't know," reflects Woodcock, who could have been nicknamed Hank Marvin such was the shadow figure he was becoming at Forest. "The question I asked over the years was: 'Did Cloughie know what he was doing?' Because the next time I saw him face-to-face was in his office. I'd been doing reasonably well, playing on the left, midfield and centre-forward. So I went in and asked him if I could play in a holding role, between the attack and midfield.

"'You know what that tells me about you?' he said. 'You're too lazy to play in midfield and you're not brave enough to play up front.' And with that I was out of his office again."

Thus twice rebuffed, Robert the Bruce may have empathised with Tony the Woodcock's recurring optimism when he next entered Clough's office. "Once again I'd been doing pretty well in the reserves and the [Nottingham] *Evening Post* had been talking up my chances of getting in the first team. So we played away at Newcastle on the Saturday and when I got on the team bus John Sheridan [the reserve team coach] stopped me and asked what that was on my face. I'd grown some stubble and a bit of a beard, but what the hell, I liked it.

"'It's going to get back to him, you know that,' John told me, but I didn't mind because I went up there and scored a great volley, one of those that just flew in from nothing.

"So on Sunday, I got a phone call from the manager: be in his office at nine o'clock sharp on Monday morning. In those days that meant two buses to get to Trent Bridge from where I was living, not a Porsche-driven journey into the car park. When I got in the office, Cloughie asked me how I felt. I said I felt really good about myself, the way I was playing and told him about the goal. 'I'm not talking about the bloody game, I'm talking about that fact that you weren't shaved. I don't care if you score a hat-trick, you'll never play for me again if you don't shave that off.' And that was me out of his office yet again…"

It could have been the end of a less than beautiful friendship there and then. Woodcock found himself on loan to Lincoln City, managed by Graham Taylor, and Doncaster Rovers, with Stan Anderson in charge. As part of the learning curve, the periods away from the City Ground were as pivotal as they were instructional. "Graham Taylor was years ahead of his time. He used to take us out onto the pitch and ask us to stand in our positions, feel the surface and think about what you might do if the ball came to you. He held mini Olympics where the winners would get a Mars bar. Running, hurdling, all kinds of things. Then there might be two tied on points at the end of the day. 'We'll sort it out tomorrow with a tie-break,' he'd announce and we all spent the night thinking what event would decide it…stamina, strength or skill? Then he'd get us in the dressing room the following day and get out a game of Kerplunk and the last two from the previous day would play that until someone lost!

"It was daft fun, but it made a big impression on a young lad like me. There were some characters at the club then; Percy Freeman, Dennis Booth, Sam Ellis, some really seasoned old pros. I scored in a practice match from the left wing one morning and told Graham Taylor that I really fancied playing centre-forward. So he started me there in the next practice match and, without being unkind to big Sam, I was a bit younger and sharper and scored a hat-trick against him with some ease.

"Taylor announced the team on Friday, saying that there was only one change to the side that was playing Brentford and that I was playing centre-forward. Suddenly, a voice booms from the back of the dressing room. It was Sam Ellis: 'There you are, son. I've played you into the team.'"

Absence did not make the heart grow particularly fonder for Woodcock. Lincoln were flying high in the Fourth Division, in the midst of a promotion surge that would reap a record goals and points haul for the club as crowds approaching 20,000 generated an atmosphere that the Forest reserves in the Central League could never equal.

In between his stays at Belle Vue and Sincil Bank, Woodcock, now slightly more confident and aware of his own worth, even asked Clough to play him up front.

"Why should I, young man?"

"Because I'll score goals for you."

"Good answer, young man."

But still the enigmatic manager walked off, to leave a bemused Woodcock pondering his next move.

AS IT HAPPENED, the Anglo-Scottish Cup, aptly, given Woodcock's Bruce-like stoicism and determination to try, try again, supplied the chance he had been harking after. His partnership with Peter Withe was an instant success, and became one that guided Forest out of the Second Division by the skin of their teeth and Bolton's final-day defeat at home to Wolverhampton Wanderers.

There was no looking back.

Woodcock scored his first goal at the highest level in the domestic game against Wolves in a 3-2 victory at Molineux on 10 September 1977. He remembers it well. The following day he married his childhood sweetheart Carol, having asked Clough if he could have Monday off.

"It was the week after Arsenal had beat us 3-0 at Highbury, our first defeat and Kenny Burns had been sent off, so I didn't know how Cloughie would react. We were all in awe of him then, just didn't know which way he might go. He said it would be no problem. 'Leave it with me,' he said. And I did. He had a mate in Jersey who had a hotel and Cloughie paid for us for have a few days there, flight and all, for our honeymoon."

THE LEAGUE TITLE, the League Cup and a European Cup; it all came so fast and furious for Woodcock, one of the reasons he felt compelled to leave Forest just a month short of his 24th birthday.

Yet he treasures two moments most of all. "When I was growing up, Manchester United – Law, Best and Charlton – they were the ones who I supported. So when I played for Forest reserves at Old Trafford, it was such a special occasion for me. I was playing left-back and I had one of those games. Everything I touched came off, I must have made three goals by overlapping alone. No kidding. Even the referee grabbed me by the arm after the game and asked me to sign his notebook. 'I've just seen a future England international tonight,' he told me.

"I ran off the pitch as quick as I could, got showered and jogged up the terracing at the Stretford End. I just stood there alone and imagined what it must be like watching all those great players down the years. It was an eerie feeling, but I never forgot it. Then I got the chance to play their first team [at Old Trafford, 17 December 1977]."

The festive period is always crucial for clubs chasing honours or avoiding ignominy, but this was especially so for Forest. Larry Lloyd had broken his toe the week before in a win over his former club Coventry City and David Needham, signed from QPR, was making his debut at centre-half. The following week, defending champions Liverpool would be paying a visit to the City Ground eager to prove a point to the upstart runaway leaders.

"I remember Ian Bowyer sitting in the dressing room and telling us all that if you were going to do something, make a name for yourself, then this was the place to do it. We won 4-0, thrashed United and I think I suddenly realised that I had arrived. As had the team. I wasn't credited with one of the goals, but I claimed it anyway. I remembered standing at the back of the Stretford End after that reserve game and thinking that I'd come a long way since then.

"We weren't big names at Forest, but we made our mark on that Saturday afternoon. I think people began to take us seriously after that." Being named PFA Young Player of the Year by his peers that season would seem to vindicate the opinion.

If the escalation from Second Division obscurity was befitting of the Clough–Taylor pairing, it also suited Woodcock. His reputation as a goalscorer and creator was established, as was his England career that was being forged, albeit under Ron Greenwood's cautious and outmoded stewardship. As Forest chased an improbable treble of a second consecutive league title and League Cup plus the European crown in 1979, the clamour to sign the forward whose contract expired in the summer reached incredibly intense levels.

"There were no such things as agents in England at the time," Woodcock recalls. "In fact later on I joined one of the first, Jonathan Holmes at SFX, but in 1979, they were largely based only in Europe. You wouldn't believe some of the things they got up to, either. I used to go and stay in hotels with Forest or flying off from Heathrow and I'd get the porter or luggage handlers coming up to me and thrust a note in my hand. 'Mr so-and-so would like you to ring him,' and then he'd be away into the crowd. Proper cloak and dagger stuff. Honestly it was like gangsters."

Real Madrid, Juventus, Barcelona and Inter Milan were among the suitors, but it was the German Bundesliga that could claim the most powerful financial muscle in Europe in 1979, having enticed Kevin Keegan to Hamburg from Liverpool two years previously. With Clough reluctant to offer Woodcock a new deal, a series of covert meetings with officials of FC Cologne put the Germans in pole position to snatch the 23-year-old England forward away.

"I was a working class lad not really used to dealing with these sort of people and to be honest I had several bouts of cold feet. But I also knew that if you were a local lad then you wouldn't earn the same amount of money as somebody who had been bought in. I wanted to know how much I was worth to someone else. Forest was all I'd known and Cloughie was a sort of security blanket. He would be there for my protection. I must admit I felt a bit nervous."

In the end, Clough and Taylor, the masters of mind games and wars of attrition, finally made their move. Too late. "They took me to a hotel room," recalls Woodcock. "And said there was a contract for £1,000 a week on the table. [The average professional in the First Division would be earning £200 a week at the time.] I told Cloughie that I had already promised Cologne that I would sign for them and I could not go back on my word."

Too late – and too little. Cologne were offering twice that amount, despite paying £500,000 for the England international. And that weekly wage was nothing to the riches he found in boot deals and shirt sponsorships. For the first time in his life, the working class lad from Eastwood was earning more off the field as an icon than his footballing talents merited on it. His arrival in Germany sparked publicity that might even turn Victoria Beckham an envious shade of green. Fans turned out in their droves for autograph sessions, while on the negative side, the media even hinted that he might be gay.

"'Welcome to the German press,' I thought at the time. Mind you, it hadn't helped when Kevin Keegan was asked if I would have a problem speaking German at press conferences. He told the German press that I didn't speak much English at the best of times. Thanks for that, Kevin. We did become friends, though. Every time we played one another, the press would build it up as the Mighty Mouse, which was Kevin, and myself, who was the quiet, still type. 'Fire versus Water' it was billed."

WOODCOCK RETURNED TO the domestic game after playing in England's failure in the 1982 World Cup finals, engineered by hapless management and coaching rather than the players, it has to be said. Arsenal paid the same £500,000 fee as Cologne had parted with to tempt Forest to sell one of their most prized assets, making Woodcock Britain's highest paid player at the time. Unleashed from the rigid man-to-man marking that the German sides deployed on forwards in those days, he revelled in his return to English football. "I couldn't believe the time and space I was getting. The English lads thought they were getting tight, but that was nothing like the tight I'd known in Germany. Two or three yards meant the freedom of the park."

In fact the only close marking that Woodcock endured came from the paparazzi. Rumours of an affair with a London-based businesswoman meant that even his effective turn of pace, now diminished by injury and time anyway, could not execute an effective escape from the prying camera lenses. His marriage over, he returned to Cologne where he married a German girl because she reminded him of his former lover in London. Unsurprisingly, it did not last.

Happily, there has been reconciliation all round and what he calls 'a patchwork family' including sons and daughters, can share holidays and memories without pain.

Over two decades after the affair that caused something of a scandal at Arsenal, he has also been reunited with partner Susan, with whom he shares a house and business interests from their home in Berkshire.

IN RETROSPECT, intriguingly, like many who left the Forest fold, Woodcock would never again scale the heights, at least in terms of trophies, that were reached at the City Ground. It had been Clough's arrival that had started an enduring saga of opposing wills, psychological mind games or just plain good fortune depending on your point of view, whereby both protagonists, player and manager, finally achieved their disparate, yet collective ends. Clough, financially secure from his Leeds bounty, yearned for the success denied him at Elland Road and prematurely terminated at Derby by his own ego and folly. Woodcock, like any working class youngster who envied George Best and played his formative football on a council park, wanted fame and fortune. And not necessarily in that order.

In the Tankard, the music has long since died and the night, once so young, is fading fast into a gripping blur of more *Big Brother* or peroxide cretin, inducing viewers to ring up and gamble on the turn of a mammary gland. Surely the mean streets of Brixton and Toxteth were never so desolate and without hope of salvation as a Monday night parked in front of Channels 3 and 4.

"We had so much, so young at Forest, it was unbelievable," Woodcock says, remembering 1978 and '79 without spoiling those halcyon Forest years by recalling the latter as the one in which Margaret Thatcher came to power. "But for me, it was important to get away and achieve something else. I learned a new language and I have travelled the world in style and seen some great sights thanks to football and Forest. And, thanks to leaving at the right time, I've been able to earn money that has given me and my family the chance to do things which I could only dream about otherwise."

The young charges he had been coaxing and cajoling that day may take comfort from that. In Hyson Green, St Ann's and the Meadows, they might also ponder his story. Who knows?

Football has left Woodcock as rich in recollections as he is fiscally solvent; money and memories he has taken willingly and with good grace. His greater legacy may yet be what he can give back to a few young pretenders and offenders.

Viv Anderson
1974-1984: 425 games, 22 goals

THE NIGHT WAS young and so were the two occupants of the car travelling north in the Park, one of Nottingham's most prestigious regions of real estate. Privacy was one of the benefits of owning a Park property, but it came at a price. Just getting from A to B in the place meant navigating tiny irritants that came in the shape of traffic islands linking each concentric circle of the estate to another. There were other tiny irritants, but since most of those tended to hang out at the Park squash club or tennis courts, residents in general were free to wander in relative safety during waking hours without the need to unleash a can of pest repellent.

The car in question was a Ford Corsair, a green hunk of a vehicle that any tank commander would have welcomed into the regiment and put the fear of Adolf into any Panzer division. Its 1966 vintage disguised its true age because its armour plating and 0-60 ratio measured in calendar months suggested it may have been involved in the Normandy landings. Certainly it shipped in water and was partial to a bit of sand when travelling close to the Skegness coastline.

As I fiddled around one roundabout after another in the early evening winter darkness, it was impossible to tell how my passenger was coping. Viv Anderson and I could recall our schooldays at Fairham Comprehensive together on the short journey from the city centre to my flat in the Park to replenish liquid supplies for another aimless bash in Nottingham later that night. If it's true that your life does flash before you in the face of death then Viv was probably at his junior school stage as we lurched around one roundabout and tight corner to another.

Trouble was the car had been bought off Vick the mechanic whose premises were near Central Avenue in West Bridgford. Vick was a charming Scot and friend of compatriot Ian Scanlon, a Notts County left-winger and forward and later potent goalscorer for the Magpies. His mate Vick had supplied plenty of cars and repairs to players on both sides of the Trent and this latest Corsair was another one of his admirable fleet of second-hand motors. It was a bit of a 'bodge job' to say the least. Most of the dash and steering wheel was original and some of the bodywork likely manufactured at a Ford factory, but the gearbox and control stick seemed to have been purchased at an auction to raise funds for victims shortly after the SS *Lusitania* went down off the coast of Ireland.

Vick's premises and workshop, a passing tribute to the art deco style that has survived in just a few corners of West Bridgford, have long been demolished. A faceless, sterile bank, what else, with more cash machines than staff has replaced it, but across the road, the Co-operative funeral parlour can still report a healthy trade in corpses in an industry which, like financial institutions, seems to thrive on the lifeblood being drained out of human beings. Never sure whether the back end of the Corsair was in tune with the front and uncertain as to whether it would obediently follow its leader around the corners, even Viv may have been turning pale as the old rust bucket clanked and clunked its way through the Park. "You know Dave, I envy you," he said. "I wish I had the flat and the car. Things are really going well for you."

I AM NOT SURE where it all went wrong for Viv Anderson – rangy full-back in the all-conquering Forest European Cup-winning team, England international and former Arsenal and Manchester United star – but some light years later as he sat in a brand new black Mercedes, owner of swanky houses in Nottingham and London and the envy of black, white and any red-blooded males aspiring to sporting success, I reminded him of the conversation.

"Naaa, can't remember that mate. Must have been pissed, the pair of us."

Our latest rendezvous takes place in the offices of his travel and corporate business enterprise just off Altrincham's main street. It's an interview punctuated by the odd phone call, but mainly the rattle of Anderson's laughter echoing around the top floor over a mug of coffee and digestive biscuit. It will be a familiar sound to Forest fans and ordinary folk in Nottingham who witnessed the lad from Clifton Estate fulfil his ambitions and, privately maybe, also lived their own dreams in vicarious manner from the Trent End terraces.

The Forest trophy cabinet alone reveals the extent of the team's phenomenal success from 1978 to '81, built on the brilliance of individuals melded into a team unit, prompted by the likes of Anderson's roaming runs from right-back, but there was more to their popularity than just silverware and a regular outing for a tin of Brasso. Forest were one of the last sides who not only talked and walked among their public, the public also related to them. None more so than Anderson, one of three local finds who developed through the youth leagues of Nottinghamshire then the City Ground apprentice system. Tony Woodcock followed a similar path, while Garry Birtles entered the professional game later on. A gregarious spirit from a solid family background, Anderson embraced success almost nonchalantly. His darkest hours, apart from the riveting car journey from hell in a rickety Ford Corsair, were slightly different. The disappointment of being rejected by Manchester United as a kid could not compare with a dislocated knee injury he sustained in the Forest reserves having just forced his way into the first team. "I was back in the reserves playing Liverpool when I overlapped down the right wing and Alec Lindsay just came across and clattered me, around knee high. When I got up, I could see the knee had come out of its socket so I put it back in and went off to the dressing room. Fortunately we had the top bone surgeon in the country at the game, Dr Jackson, and he had me up in the hospital and operated on that night. It probably saved my career.

"Funny thing was he used to tour all around the world giving lectures to medical students. He used to start his lectures by holding up an X-ray. It was mine, the knee stapled together just after the operation. And he'd say: 'Do you know, this person is still playing top class football even today!'"

If Anderson was laid up for three months, it probably did not curtail his social activities. Not that they included the enormous binge sessions which were all the rage in some quarters of the Nottingham football fraternity. Nor did he get heavily involved later on when he joined the infamous drinking club that was supposedly Manchester United FC in the late 1980s.

Anderson, like many of his contemporaries, felt at home with the craic of the Nottingham city pubs like the Flying Horse, the emerging wine bars such as Uriah Heep, an integral part of the Forest success story, and, as a young, unattached male, sampling the chicken in a basket to discover if it could really taste any worse at Scamps, a flourishing nightclub in Wollaton Street that had them banging on the doors to get in despite its culinary perils and a steep flight of concrete stairs at its entrance that would have deterred a pack of Erik Bloodaxe's sex-starved, bloodthirsty and famished Vikings intent on rape, pillage and a leg of roast monk.

"The drinking thing at United was a myth anyway," Anderson says. "There is no way that Paul McGrath, Bryan Robson or Norman Whiteside could have consumed the amount they were supposed to have done on a Friday night then performed at that level the following day. Not in front of 65,000 people every other fortnight, it's just not possible.

"I liked to go out with the lads in Nottingham and we always seemed to meet in Uriah Heep for a glass of wine and some lunch on a Wednesday. The married lads would go off and pick up the kids and meet their wives and I suppose myself, Woody [Tony Woodcock] and Robbo would carry on and go out on the town. But on a Friday? Never; hardly ever Thursday come to that. It just didn't happen.

"Of course there were some lads who could appear a bit aloof. Shilts [Peter Shilton] used to like to go gambling on his own, then he'd appear down Madison's [nightclub] alone and have a bottle of champagne in the corner. But the lads slaughtered him. 'Any chance of a glass then, Pete?' and to be fair he responded. Trevor [Francis] could have been the same, but it was soon knocked out by the gaffer. I don't think there was a bad apple among us and that says a lot.

"We went for a tour of Australia for three and a half weeks, can you imagine that, all of us confined together. You have to get on fairly well for that to run smoothly. It's amazing but when I was at Middlesbrough [assistant manager to Bryan Robson after a spell as player-coach and still the oldest Middlesbrough player to pull on a shirt at 39] you had to force the players to go away on a bonding session.

"If there'd been a few bad results or something needed sorting, we'd ask them if they fancied a break. Well the foreign players all wanted to go home to their country and the other lads all said they didn't fancy it and had other things to do. Unreal. One season at Forest we were over in Majorca 13 times. Cloughie couldn't get enough of it. He had his place over there. Some Fridays he'd call in the groundsman and order him to water the pitch. Then he'd get a local referee to inspect it.

"'Can't bloody play on that, can we?'"

"'No, you're right Mr Clough. We'd better get it called off.'"

"And so off he went and the Forest squad followed for one of their famous 'bonding' breaks in the sun."

ANDERSON'S FIRST ENCOUNTER with new manager Brian Clough, which saw him substituted in the FA Cup tie with Tottenham Hotspur suffering from cramp, is common knowledge to the Forest faithful. His name wasn't in the party for the replay, Clough's first victory as Forest manager on 8 January 1975, which led a young Anderson to rethink his career options. Even later, when he was dropped for being too taciturn ("I thought I'd better liven myself up a bit after that") Clough clearly had sufficient faith in Anderson's laconic style and effortless rhythm that took him beyond defenders, gliding down the right to support and create for the front pairing and midfield.

He says it's only now he can reflect on the whirl that catapulted him and his colleagues into the realms of fantasy and records that are likely never to be emulated. For instance, what side promoted from the Championship today would look beyond surviving in the Premiership, let alone winning it, then knocking off the European Cup for the next couple of years just for fun?

Amidst all of this came his first full cap for England, against Czechoslovakia on 29 November 1978, edging out West Bromwich Albion's Laurie Cunningham as the first black player to be picked for the senior side, a selection that bestowed upon him and his family a spotlight that Anderson did not seek and a subsequent status that he discusses candidly.

Racial tensions were never far from the news, given the social unrest in Britain and in Nottingham. The late 1950s riots in St Ann's, when gangs of teddy boys clashed with West Indian immigrants, mirrored unrest in Notting Hill and other London suburbs. It also invited a stigma to the area, bordered by Hyson Green and then Radford, which has blighted it ever since. Early 1970s Nottingham was improving, but with a second generation of Caribbeans and an influx of Asians, it was scarcely an equal opportunity utopia inspired by racial harmony.

In football terms, young black players were making rapid progress among the professional ranks. In Nottingham, not only Anderson but Tristan Benjamin and Pedro Richards, a Spaniard by nature but Meadows schoolboy in tutoring, were also establishing themselves at Notts County. In fact many thought that Richards, educated at Roland Green along with Forest player Bert Bowery, to be the more promising prospect of the two talents, although his resistance to authority and a refusal to join an England Under-21 training camp did not enhance his cause.

In the event, Anderson matured to England player on merit, but the pair remained good friends. Richards' death just before Christmas Day 2001 shocked the local community and it was Anderson, through corporate contacts, who helped with what has become a commemorative annual golf day to raise funds for his children. Poles apart in mentality and attitude, the pair were well suited in some ways. Richards spoke fluent Spanish and pidgin English and carried himself as a well-groomed Spaniard of Basque origin. Anderson was born and bred in England and carried himself just as stylishly as an emerging professional sportsman and hero of the people. The colour of their skin was for others to discuss and contemplate its meaning.

"I didn't want the role model thing," says Anderson. "But I suppose it comes with the territory. I always saw myself as just a black lad playing in my local team. But others saw it differently. Still, it never ceases to amaze me even today that people recognise me because of it. In London, they'll stop me in the street and talk. I've been doing work for the FA abroad that took me to an orphanage in Malawi. As soon as I stepped off the plane, a chap came up and said: 'Hey, aren't you Anderson, the black player for England?' So I suppose I can live with it, especially as things have changed so much.

"It's disappointing to hear of racism rearing itself again in some of the Baltic countries, but I can't understand how Spain has come into the equation. With Forest I played there so many times and there was never a problem. Maybe because I wasn't a front player like, say, Emile Heskey, who attracts more attention. I don't know."

Recognition was something Anderson the rangy full-back could not avoid during his Forest days. Except perhaps on one fateful early evening in the summer of 1981. As fatigued commuters wended their weary way down Clumber Street, a thoroughfare linking Nottingham's two main shopping centres and once described as the busiest in Europe, imagine their surprise to see a group of young men walking on all fours with their trousers down to their ankles desperately clinging onto the pavement in case the world revolved a little too quickly or their heads started spinning out of control.

Remember, even though the following story took place more than a quarter of a century ago, some of the protagonists would, while standing in one of Nottingham's fashionable boutiques, bet £100 to guess correctly the sex of the next customer through the door. And then, as an added bonus, a further £100 to predict the exact shade of their hair. "Sheer boredom," as Rachid Harkouk, the Notts County and Algerian player, once told me. "If I'd been playing today and earned what they are earning, I wouldn't have lasted ten minutes never mind ten years."

Now read on.

"It was a close season and a few of us including Peter Wells [former Forest goalkeeper], Rachid Harkouk, and Brian Kilcline [notorious drinking partners at Notts County] had been locked in a pub at lunchtime, it was just down from the Market Square," Anderson recalls, heaving with laughter at the thought. "So what did we do? Well, we played Kerplunk and then Connect 4, I think. We were getting bored and it was opening time again, so we had a bet. We all had to drop our trousers and make a run for it down Clumber Street to the Victoria Centre and see who was the first one to fall down.

"You can see all these people heading home from work looking down at our backsides. 'Isn't that so and so?' And they were probably right."

Perhaps not the best example of how the players identified with punters, but at least there were no concrete bunkers, underground tunnels or heavyweight bouncers to ferry players to their cars after a game as is the case at Old Trafford.

"There's not the contact anymore and I can't blame the players for not wanting to get out too much. I've been up here for the best part of 20 years and I've seen Roy Keane out socially about three times. There was a nightclub around the corner from here [in Altrincham] and Wayne Rooney went in one night, starts talking to a girl, all harmless. Next day his photo is on the front page of the newspaper, taken by someone with a mobile phone. You don't need that.

"I went to an event at Old Trafford recently and saw Rio [Ferdinand] there. He said to me, I wish I was playing during your time because they can't move or go out anywhere at night for fear of someone reporting something bad."

THOSE WHO SEEK to find a hidden corner in the Anderson psyche will be disappointed. Locating the Loch Ness monster could prove a more fruitful and rewarding lifetime endeavour. "I just loved to play football, to me that's what it was all about," he says without a trace of cynicism. Even though life could be tough on Clifton Estate, once the largest housing conurbation in Europe, and at Fairham Comprehensive, a school that once attracted national newspaper headlines for its rioting pupils, there is no hidden agenda or plea from the wrong side of the track from Anderson.

Anyone trying to scratch beneath the surface in the hope of locating anger would be consumed by his normality and an affability that has spanned the decades. Revellers in his formative years at Forest will recall Anderson, even later at his peak, pounding the streets of Nottingham with a select band of friends that included former Forest team-mate Bert Bowery and Viv's brother Donald.

Every year Bowery and some of that inner circle reunite in Amsterdam, Prague or even Dubai where Anderson shares business interests with European Cup-winning team-mate Tony Woodcock. Affirmation that Anderson does not forget his roots easily. Stretching a hand out to catch a 68 bus to and from Clifton for training every day assists the memory of origins. Cleaning the first team dressing room after training as an apprentice is another indelible benchmark. He eventually bought a Hillman Hunter, gold in colour, but it was Woodcock, a portent of things to come, who stole the show with a Mini Cooper S. "A real babe magnet. We used to queue up to see if he'd give us a lift up town in it after training." In many ways those roots kept Anderson at Forest, not quite outstaying his welcome, but probably lingering longer than any of the European Cup-winning side. "It's amazing, but within a few years the entire team had broken up.

Woody and Frank Clark had gone, but then I remember Clarky saying after Munich that it was all downhill from now, and in a way he was right. How could it get better?"

Familiarity did not so much breed contempt, but it did erode the relationship between Clough and Anderson. "I was the last one of the team to leave, I suppose because I was a local lad, loved playing week in and out and it was easy being with my mates. I was comfortable and liked my lifestyle. Some lads came in, Justin Fashanu, Ian Wallace and Peter Ward and you look at who they were replacing... But I didn't think too much about it. Most of the lads who came were OK, but in comparison... [he even cites Raimondo Ponte and Hans Jurgen Rober, the latter having visited the Dubai Centre of Excellence he runs with Woodcock]. It was in my last season [1984], things started to turn sour. There was that famous story of us going to Glasgow and Cloughie pulling up at David Hay's pub and putting a round of drinks on him for all our lads. [Hay was the Celtic manager against whom Forest were playing in the second leg of the UEFA Cup at Hampden Park the following night].

To he honest, things were deteriorating by then. We beat Celtic at their place 2-1, the first time they'd lost in a European competition at their ground, then got cheated out of the semi-final against Anderlecht by a bent referee who'd taken a £30,000 bribe. But we hadn't been paid a penny in bonuses until then and after we lost, we were told there would be none. Cloughie had always looked after us up to that point and we'd taken him at his word, but I lost some respect for him after that if I'm honest. I could easily have stayed for another year, it was my testimonial coming up and I was getting married. But then Arsenal came in and it was time to go. The bonus issue was the straw that broke the camel's back."

IT WAS THE END of an era, literally, for Forest and Anderson. He moved on to Highbury, where the team was always compared, unfavourably, to the Double-winning side of 1971. Don Howe's regimental fitness fanaticism and tactically-led regime contrasted markedly with the Clough and Taylor doctrine of sangria and Cala Millor therapy. Even when George Graham took over, only a League Cup winners' medal, a mere trifle in his Forest collection, was secured during his last season before Alex Ferguson ensured Anderson and

Brian McClair were his first acquisitions as Manchester United manager.

"If it was bad at Arsenal, it was worse there. At Forest we'd only had a Duncan McKenzie or Ian Storey-Moore for comparison, never an entire team. They talked of the Arsenal 1-0s at Highbury, while United said: 'If you score, we'll get five,' bearing in mind they hadn't won the title for 20 years, which was probably why. You had Best, Law and Charlton on your back, so believe me you had to perform.

"That was the difference there. If you went down to Southampton and got beat it was a disaster. That's why some players, and I don't mean any disrespect, like Le Tissier will stay at a club like Southampton. It's better to be a big fish in a little pond because you can play shite for six games down there and people will forgive you when you have a decent game.

"At Manchester United, Liverpool, Chelsea or Arsenal, if you have six shite games, you don't get to see it again. You're out the door, end of story."

In a divine retribution, though not one he would admit to, he and the Robertsons, O'Neills, Withes et al have left their own indelible legacy on Forest as much as Clough and Taylor. While no manager since, including even the valiant Frank Clark, can compare to the Clough–Taylor era, it is also fairly certain that no Forest team can be mentioned in the same breath as the class of 1978-81. Deep down, there must be a degree of satisfaction in the knowledge that a triumph such as theirs is unique and out of reach to future generations. As Anderson says: "We all know it and can see it, the rich are getting richer and money talks. Having said that, it's how you spend it. You just have to look at David Platt at Forest. He wasted £18 million and for what? But then Fergie has made his mistakes. But when you are talking about £30 million packages for a player these days, it's almost unreal."

If mention of Platt is a further twisting of the knife for the Forest diehards, at least Anderson can still tell some classic stories to partially heal an open wound. His tale of being stranded at Peter Taylor's snow-swept Widmerpool home by Clough when he and Mark Proctor refused to move on loan to Derby County, then managed by Taylor, is legend. The pair walked miles over fields to hail a taxi from a Keyworth pub with an outing in the A team the following morning as reward for their reluctance.

He's about to tell me another anecdote about Clough calling him out of his warm-up bath to replace him with a stand-in full-back half an hour before kick-off when his phone rings. His ex-wife Debbie is in Paris with their son having just descended the Eiffel Tower. There's that laugh again. Even in divorce, fuelled by lurid Sunday tabloid stories, the pair have remained friends.

The conversation turns to characters in the Forest dressing room. Ian 'Bomber' Bowyer's dry witty sarcasm and Larry Lloyd, heavy metal in humour. And Kenny Burns, who has been telling me his wild man image was a tad unjust. "Kenny? Unjust? Let me tell you, when I was single I lived at Clifton Grove, not far from my mum and dad's place at Clifton, and he'd come and pick me up in the morning, 9.30 sharp. I'd meet him at the end of the road near some traffic lights and he'd have the engine running and his little baby strapped into a seat in the back. Next to him on the dash would be a stopwatch.

"'Morning Kenny.'

"'Aye morning.'

"Then he'd click the stopwatch and whoosh, we'd be off."

Anderson falls back in his swivel chair and pulls a pressurised gravity face as taut as those of some veteran London hacks trying to perfect yet another tricky re-entry manoeuvre into Terry Venables' posterior.

"It didn't take long before we were pulling up at the nursery just around the corner from the ground. He'd stop the watch and look at it and then mutter '30 seconds out'.

"Unjust? Kenny was as mad as a hatter. I remember his missus, Louise, telling me how they'd been driving along a busy dual carriageway when some bloke carved him up. Kenny went potty and chased him down this road with his wife shouting and screaming: 'No Kenny, oh no don't.' Anyway he cuts this bloke up and storms out of the car just as this bloke is desperately trying to wind his window up. I mean if it had happened today, he would have been onto the papers and everything. That was Kenny, though.

"Me and Woody used to pin him down in his hotel room on away trips and tell him: 'So you think you're hard then.' We'd give him a slap and you could see the red mist rising. 'Go on Woody, give him another slap.' Whack, Woody would hit him across the face and then

I'd give him one for good luck, but we both looked behind to make sure the bedroom door was ajar. It was our escape route. 'Right, one more each,' and he'd be cursing and cussing and then we got the hell out of the room as fast as we could move."

And then one last reminiscence.

"You remember Terry Curran?" (Who couldn't and what a great feed-line? The gypsy-like flying winger from Donnie made his debut when Les Bradd's 89th minute header defeated Forest at the City Ground to keep Notts County top of the Second Division in August 1975.)

"He'd had enough of Cloughie and Forest, totally fed up and wanted away. So he came into training all fired up and told us he was going to hand in a transfer request he'd written the night before. We all nodded and told him, if that's what he wanted to do, then do it. Next thing, he's knocking on Peter Taylor's door because Cloughie was away that morning. He stormed in and confronted Pete who was a bit startled behind his desk.

"'Yes Terry?'

"'I've had enough of you two. I'm in and out of the fucking team, so you know what you can do. You can stick your fucking team up your arse.'

"And with that he throws the envelope at Pete's head and off he marches. He's got only as far as the main gates by the car park when Pete dashes out of his office and opens the glass door at reception. 'Hey, Terry, TERRY!', Pete's shouting from the glass door across the car park. 'What do you want me to do with this? Pay it?' He'd only gone and handed him the wrong envelope and given him his electric bill."

THE INTERVIEW IS concluding now. There has been talk of Forest moving from the City Ground and relocating to a site near Clifton, a bold plan of grandiose proportions. New ground, new access routes, but same old team. Still, there could be an Anderson Stand in the offing to commemorate his adjacent roots. And even an Anderson Shelter by the touchline to protect the manager from hurled abuse when things go wrong. Who knows, there might be a bench named after Peter Taylor!

"Do you remember when we played centre-half together for Fairham?" Anderson is now ushering me out of his building.

"Yep," I reply. "They still had a bloody picture of you up on the wall outside the head's office the last time I went there. Strangely not one of me…"

"I always had to cover for you anyway!" Cue cackle of laughter fading as the front of his premises shuts.

If there is someone out there with a bad word for Anderson, I'm still searching. And still the question lingers. "So Viv, where did it all go wrong?"

Garry Birtles

1976-1980 & 1982-1986: 278 games, 96 goals

FRANK CLARK WAS blessed with his avuncular mood as the team coach pulled away from Hillsborough. Never mind Sunday, bloody Sunday, here was another Saturday afternoon in the stiffs and even the most die-hard of Owls fans would surely decide that they'd rather be in Tesco with the missus if it was Wednesday, bloody Wednesday reserves. Thus the proverbial ten men and a dog saw Forest reserves and their Sheffield Wednesday peers in an afternoon of toil that was best quickly forgotten.

For Clark, seasoned veteran of Newcastle United, it was simply another brief and compulsory chapter in the rich, yet occasionally impoverished, tapestry of the game. He had experienced the highs of winning the Inter Cities Fairs Cup with Newcastle and reaching a Wembley FA Cup final, although the Geordies' somewhat devious and irregular route to the Empire Stadium in 1974 still raises the hackles on the back and scalp of older Forest supporters.

No matter. Clark had been to Wembley before that as an FA Amateur Cup winner with the famously formidable Crook Town side of the 1950s and early 1960s. His time in the game was far from over, both as a player and manager, as Forest supporters can testify, but in the late summer of 1976, Clark's playing career was in limbo. He had not yet acquired the dreaded label of 'utility' player, implying a jack of all trades but master of none and certainly not a man fit to be picked ahead of others in any given position. With his own future uncertain, however, the old lag could still spot a distress signal from distraught youth feeling the pangs of an unrequited love.

As the bus departed Hillsborough following the unremarkable match, one of its passengers sat with his head tucked into his chest, staring bleakly into the abyss that is disillusionment; an act otherwise known as contemplating one's navel. This was the first game of the 1976/77 season and for Garry Birtles, at least, career prospects were at a low ebb.

"How's it going then, son?" Clark asked the deflated youngster.

"Not brilliant."

Birtles was infamously compared unfavourably to a half-time cup of Bovril by Brian Clough. It had been Peter Taylor's faith in the Long Eaton United centre-forward that had earned him a contract at the City Ground – but little else.

"It's not going to come overnight, son."

"I know that, Frank, but I'm thinking of packing it all in. I'm going back to laying carpets," whinged Birtles.

"There's no magic wand to make this thing happen. You've got to wait your chance and keep applying yourself."

The platitudes of an older professional may have drifted above Birtles' gloom that day, probably deepened as the bus sped on its way through Sheffield during the daylight hours, but at least it demonstrated the belief in the fledgling centre-forward that both Clark and Taylor shared. Even so, the lad who had supported Forest as a youngster, watched them with his dad Ray from the terraces, and signed a petition in favour of naming Brian Clough as the new manager, felt rejected by the club he cherished.

Maybe crushed would be too strong a word. But the carpet fitter who previously would have crawled across several miles of glass-encrusted lino previously grazed by a herd of incontinent Guernsey cows just for a trial with his beloved Reds was now willing to make the return journey on hands and knees just to escape.

"I used to pop to the job centres in Chilwell and Beeston and see if there were any carpet fitters needed," Birtles recalls. "It was that bad at times. At least I knew how to lay floors and knew there was a future in it for me. I was comfortable with that."

If anything reaffirms why Birtles is among those readily named by supporters as one of their heroes, it is that glimpse of human weakness, the humility and self-doubt inherent in us all (politicians and *Big Brother* applicants apart, of course) that has endeared him to the Trent End and indeed the Nottingham public for over three decades.

IF THOSE MOMENTS staring glaze-eyed into job centre windows was a nadir, the darkness before the dawn, then the sun rising on his debut in March 1977 was scarcely the shining light Garry Birtles was seeking on the road to Loftus Road, Turf Moor and other unlikely shrines of the beautiful game.

There was a conversion of sorts; Birtles, the nimble, lean front runner had been turned into an attacking left-sided midfielder as Forest coaching staff recognised his stamina and predatory talents and attempted to nurture them in a deeper position by building up the player's body strength.

"I hated every minute of it," says Birtles.

A 2-0 home defeat of Hull City vindicated that assessment. An encouraging two points maintained Forest's push for promotion from the Second Division that season, but did nothing to suggest that this was a turning point for the player, nor indeed an earth-shattering debut.

Worse, if that was possible, was to follow.

His only other sighting that season had been in a friendly at Grantham Town's windy and open-ended London Road ground, as a substitute. Following facing Hull, he returned to the Lincolnshire outpost to start a game.

If that could be considered progress, there were several giant strides backwards around the corner. Tony Woodcock and Peter Withe forged the front-running partnership that made the initial inroads into First Division defences that soon evolved into six-lane motorways as the championship title was lifted with incredible ease and grace. Two pre-season friendlies in West Germany and a couple of run-outs in testimonial games for Henry Newton and Les Bradd in April was the sum total of Birtles' contribution in that momentous year.

Certainly nobody had pretended it was going to be easy after Forest had paid Long Eaton £2,000 for Birtles on Taylor's recommendation. His arrival had raised some eyebrows, almost as high as the scaffolding which appeared to support his hair, but then all crimes against fashion and sartorial elegance, even the self-inflicted ones, were pardoned in an official amnesty about a decade ago. Mercifully.

Ironically it was Ian Storey-Moore, then with Manchester United, who had heard about Birtles after an impressive showing against Burton Albion and recommended him to the Old Trafford scouting hierarchy. The whisper became a thunderclap of an alarm bell as Taylor and Clough railed at the prospect of a young lad from Long Eaton being hijacked by Manchester United. Clough's damning initial verdict on Birtles and the Bovril came at Enderby Town, but it was that left foot shimmy, the instinctive drag back that Taylor saw during his first trial match for Forest against Coventry City reserves that subsequently earned him a contract.

"I got a right bollocking in the dressing room [at Highfield Road] for playing Patience before the game, but then I was just an amateur, didn't know any better. I remember Sean Haslegrave scored our goal, but I knew nothing about Peter sitting in the stands in his flat cap. But then nobody else did either."

A split second of potential, a moment in time that shaped Birtles' and Forest's destiny, a mere bagatelle of skill. He had been offered terms by Mansfield Town, on £110 a week, and Lincoln City and Leeds United were monitoring his progress. No mention of Manchester United at this stage, but it was always Forest that he hoped would eventually show an interest. When they did, he was more than happy to sign for £60 a week.

In his last amateur game, for Sunday morning side Long Eaton Rovers, Birtles changed in the less than salubrious environs on the Victoria Embankment, where strong liniment doused the fumes of stale alcohol and the attempts of last night's chicken vindaloo to evacuate the premises and bowels of its occupants. Valuables were never left in the old wooden pavilion.

The contrast to his final professional game for Forest at the Bernabeu just five years later could not have been more vivid.

"I always remember we played Clumber K and B, an all black side, good team, and drew 1-1, but it wasn't the best of games for me. But it was always Forest I wanted to join. I grew up with Forest, seeing them get beat by Valencia in the Inter Cities Fairs Cup and then the likes of the Baker, Storey-Moore team. I saw them thrash Manchester United

4-1 at the City Ground with a Chris Crowe hat-trick and that against Best, Law and Charlton. It was a great side, Hennessey, Barnwell, Hindley, Wignall, Newton, you could go on. Money wasn't the issue when they asked me to sign."

Money, though, was the issue; as far as Forest were concerned anyway. That and an unfortunate barren run for Steve Elliott, that presented Birtles with an opportunity that has rarely been grasped so dramatically on the bigger stage. Withe, so prolific in the title-winning season, had asked for a pay rise; no more than £10 a week, far from excessive, if anything a humble request given his prowess for being in the right place at the right time in the penalty area, more often than not after a Robertson dummy, two-yard dash and cross from the left. But this was Clough and Taylor with whom Withe was dealing and they had decided to accept an offer from Newcastle United for their centre-forward.

That brought in Steve Elliott, a promising youngster who had plundered goals with ease for the reserves in the Central League. He was expected to make the step up without too much difficulty and thus fill the ample boots of Withe. Uncannily, however, Elliott and Forest suffered the sort of goals drought that is manna from heaven for end of the pier comedians who can juxtapose the words 'brothel' and 'score' in a sentence guaranteed to raise a titter from Skegness to Scarborough.

Forest's sequence of results read like the form figures of some of the nags I wager on. An unblemished string of duck eggs, eight in all, which at least meant the opposition would have been equally incompetent given a free pass in a bordello.

True, four 0-0 draws in the league and League Cup were followed by ten goals in two matches, six coming in a benefit game for long-serving Mansfield Town full-back Sandy Pate, then four against Oldham Athletic in the second leg of their cup tie. But poor Elliott was unable to register in either of these games. He had seen shots and headers rebound off all sections of the woodwork and every conceivable part of a defender's anatomy, but management felt it was time for a change.

And what a change.

In the space of seven days Birtles enjoyed a winning debut against Arsenal, an experience he shared with 16-year-old Gary Mills, and a fighting draw at Manchester United in front of a crowd of 55,000.

Oh, and in between there was that European Cup debut against Liverpool. Anyone at the City Ground that balmy September evening surely cannot forget the Forest performance, the start of a momentum that grew into an irresistible force which lasted for two unforgettable seasons on the continent.

I know it was balmy because I remember sitting outside the Trip To Jerusalem, the oldest pub in Blighty by all accounts, downing a few pints on the cobbled stones to the front of the place. For most who came to quaff at Ye Olde Trippe later that night, the talk was of the defending champions being beaten 2-0 and Birtles' goal, a routine chance in its execution, but remarkable in the context of the novice who finished with the nerveless aplomb of a veteran. And then Colin Barrett's volley after Birtles' shot had been palmed away, the crucial second that induced Birtles to respond to Phil Thompson's first half taunt that a one-goal lead would be insufficient to defend at Anfield in the second leg.

"Will two be enough, then?" Birtles inquired of the centre-back later to be linked with supersonic passenger aircraft travel via his elongated nose as Barrett's shot thumped into the back of the net.

"I was well out of order," says Birtles of old 'Concorde snout'. "Thompson was an established England international and I was playing in my first European game. But I couldn't help myself at that moment in time."

Nearly a century on, with the laws relaxed only late in the 20th century, you can only think that the current binge drinking culture among youth is an inherent throwback to the days when their parents glanced nervously at the clock in case a rogue landlord called time without ringing the bell and so depriving clients of an extra slug of bitter. At the Trip on September 13, the drinks flowed in unbridled and universal celebration, however. Well almost universal.

As a Notts County player, and one in decline at that, there was more than a touch of envy at Forest's rapid rise to fame across the River Trent. The balance of power had shifted irrevocably to the south bank, without doubt, and not even several pints of strong Belgian lager could erase that from the memory, much though it was being decimated in other areas of recollection.

And yet, there was a yet. Because at Meadow Lane, we had known Robertson, O'Neill and Woodcock, as they say nowadays, before they were famous. They were good eggs and I knew Viv Anderson to be among that basket, as well as Birtles from his days in amateur football. Yes, there was envy. But for most of the County players who had grown up, or at least attempted to mature in tandem with the Forest contingent at the City Ground, there was also sneaking admiration, a pleasure in their achievement tinged with inevitable jealousy but above all a satisfaction in the knowledge that the ordinary good guys had succeeded.

Best of all, on 13 September, they had smacked the Scousers in a place where it hurts most – just above the Cavern Club and slightly beneath the Merseybeat, a very tender fragile spot called ego.

Could it have happened to a better person than Birtles, the insecure carpet layer from Chilwell, who once thought about chucking it all in?

"Whatever else happened to me at Forest, I didn't change as a person. Why should I? I was the same lad who laid carpets and my friends were still the same good mates as I'd always known. I still see some of them today. You don't forget your roots and I never have. I remember my dad Ray getting me to control a tennis ball in the back garden as a kid. When I was in the dressing room at Long Eaton United, I used to do the same thing as a warm-up. He ferried me everywhere and I owe him a lot, but you never stop having that rapport with fans. Why should you?"

AS THE GRADIENT OF Birtles' career inclined steeply to the top, part of his ritual was a Saturday night meal at Grange Farm, one up from a Berni Inn, yet still a venue where waitresses were known to faint if wine orders exceeded Blue Nun and diners asked for anything but T-bone steak, well done.

This is not a patronising reflection; that was the way it was in the 1970s and Birtles was part of that decade that witnessed fans mixing freely with players and a swanky night out for the majority meant a three-course meal, with ice cream dessert, at the Sawyers Arms or the Shard at Tollerton. It was not quite the Tommy Lawton, Tommy Capel days of walking down Arkwright Street together before kick-off and discussing tactics, but the Cadland, his local pub in Chilwell, was where Birtles and some Forest players would retire of a Saturday night or Sunday lunchtime and dissect the finer points of the Reds' latest triumph.

The local heroes were among other distractions in a predominantly male domain notably smattered with members of the opposite sex, whose cleavage and conversation was more exposed and basic than the Rochdale back four. A lathering of hairspray, that was decimating the ozone layer years ahead of its time, only added to the ambience. Fair to say the Cadland's clientele failed to reflect the dowdy nature of a suburb whose main claim to fame was the army barracks and bus depot down the road.

"They were fantastic times, I was managing Long Eaton Rovers on a Sunday morning and I was surrounded by people who I could call genuine mates," Birtles recalled. "As a family we'd go down the Cadland on Christmas Day with other couples and their kids. There was no reason to leave that sort of environment behind."

Although Birtles was not a Forest apprentice like Tony Woodcock and Viv Anderson, he had graduated from the Notts Youth League and Clifton All Whites, the club that also uncovered Forest's Jermaine Jenas and Peter Wells (one was black, the other ginger) and Notts County's Michael Johnson, among many others. Strangely, and, as Richard Littlejohn might exclaim: 'You couldn't make it up', the club was told to change its name in the mid-1990s because it alluded to racially offensive undertones. For the record as one who played for the famous All Whites, its name derives from the colour of its kit, its integrity from the hordes of multi-racial players it has and still does encourage to play the game since its inception in 1963. None of which, of course, deterred politically correct local government cretins from meddling in an attempt to justify their existence and richly deserved final pay packages.

Chances were that most aspiring young players had come across one of the trio in those formative years, increasing the empathy so that they could relate to and connect with their phenomenal football success.

Not that Birtles needed anyone to keep his feet on the ground other than the maestro.

"On my first day at the club I was down the bottom end, the away team dressing room where the reserves changed, sitting on one of the tables tying up my boots. The room was full. Suddenly Cloughie poked his head round the door, he'd come from the directors' room from the other end of the corridor. 'Hey son, get off my fucking table,' he said and his voice bounced off all the walls.

"He wanted to show he was in charge. And he did. I was shit scared of him."

He was not alone. Birtles tells how grown men used to run through rucks of nettles at the club's rustic training ground at Holme Road, a whim of the gaffer's if he felt the side had underperformed at the weekend. 'Now take them back through them again, John,' he'd ask in that condescending, patronising tone of his captain John McGovern. And, of course, they obeyed to a man, despite the obvious pain threshold and unseen pitfalls of divots in the shrub land.

The good times more than compensated for nettle rash, though.

Two goals scored against Southampton and Peter Wells in a 3-2 victory in the League Cup final in 1979 helped secure the trophy for the second consecutive year. The previous one, celebrations had been put on hold after a goalless draw with Liverpool at Wembley. Even so, a party planned at the Rancliffe Arms in Bunny, Alan Hill's watering hole, for later that night did not, like Forest, conform to tradition.

"We thought the party would be cancelled, but BC [Clough] said it was all right," recalls Hill. "At 11 o'clock I'd managed to get most of the punters out, but locals and fans got wind of it and nearly 3,000 were waiting outside the pub after closing time. We'd only drawn, but the party still went ahead. And just about every player and their partners turned up. I remember Frank Clark playing guitar late into the night."

Despite that less than harmonious recollection, that shindig was symbolic of the Forest *esprit de corps*, one which Birtles readily embraced. His own natural ability endeared him to his peers and Birtles, as a Sky Sports or *Nottingham Evening Post* pundit today, does not hesitate to promote and praise a team that was undervalued in its halcyon period.

"You had the likes of Robbo [John Robertson], who was a genius. He was like the rest of us with his upbringing and he took plenty of stick from Peter [Taylor] for his chip pan habits. I remember when he used to turn up for training with a fag on, driving an old clapped-out Fiesta and with his jeans ripped and nothing on top. Brilliant. You couldn't get away with it now, but he could because he was a genius.

"I've heard players like Bryan Robson, Jimmy Case or Frank Stapleton call him lucky. There was nothing lucky about Robbo. He just was a cut above. And then Trevor Brooking and other internationals used to pipe up and say they could never play for a manager like Cloughie. Excuse me, but how many European Cup and championship medals did he win under Ron Greenwood?

"The social life was great, but then so were our results. We'd play in Europe and get back to East Midlands in our blue blazers, grey trousers and ties and to a man, we'd head up to Madison's [the most popular disco/nightclub in town]."

Special times, as Birtles and his contemporaries often point out. The sort impossible to replicate in any top flight team winning European or domestic honours today.

Yet if the goal against Liverpool was a defining moment for Birtles, another arrived of equal significance as the player and Forest defended the trophy they had claimed against Malmo in May 1979. A year later, on 28 May 1980 in the Bernabeu Stadium, was to be Birtles' moment of truth. As Forest prepared for the historic European Cup final with Hamburg in Madrid the first team squad had set up base camp far away from the glamour of the Spanish capital.

"We were staying in some dilapidated old place about an hour's drive into the mountains outside Madrid," Birtles recalls. "Apparently it was once a monastery, but it was a real run-down place, miles from anywhere. It used to be haunted which made the whole thing that more spooky. In fact the family who ran it did bear a passing resemblance to the Addams family. It was typical of him [Clough]. That was his management style, along with Peter Taylor. We even trained on what was a roundabout in the road, admittedly in a region that was not densely populated. But there we were, on the eve of one of the biggest games in our lives and the history of the club and we were kicking balls around on a traffic island."

An odd location for the likes of Kenny Burns and Larry Lloyd, surely destined to locate the monks' wine cellar – if Clough had not already beaten them to it.

At home, Aston Villa had lifted the championship, while West Bromwich Albion secured fourth position, two rungs above Southampton and three ahead of Forest. Yet if the East Midlands' finest had floundered by their own standards in the league, in Europe it had been business as usual for Clough's eclectic team.

"We just had a mentality that we thought we could not be beaten in the competition. In the third round we lost to a good Dynamo Berlin team at the City Ground in the first leg and everyone thought that was it. But the players in the team were magnificent and in Peter Shilton we had the best goalkeeper in the world at the time. Trevor Francis got two in Berlin and Robbo scored from the penalty spot and we were through."

Francis, whose header had secured the European Cup 12 months previously, also figured prominently in the semi-final defeat of Ajax, scoring one in the 2-0 home leg victory before Forest survived a battering, according to Birtles, in Amsterdam, progressing to the final despite losing 1-0 to the Dutch champions. However, the £1 million man suffered a recurrence of an Achilles tendon injury and missed the final, leaving Birtles to lead the line alongside Gary Mills, just turned 18 and an unlikely replacement for Francis, but a selection befitting the maverick management duo.

"We started off 4-4-2, but after about 15 minutes the gaffer and Taylor realised that they were ploughing through us too easily, so he switched to five in midfield to stem the flow. Remember that Hamburg were flying then with Kevin Keegan in attack and players of the quality of Mannie Kaltz and Felix Magath. The season before we were favourites to beat Malmo, but on this occasion, we were definitely underdogs."

Forest were certainly inferior on the substitutes' bench, which seated only four players instead of the regulation five. Stan Bowles, the talented but unpredictable former QPR forward with a weakness for four-legged friends and turf accountants, was miffed to learn that he was not in the starting line-up and refused to travel with the squad.

"I think he just threw his toys out of the pram," recalls Birtles. "But if left us with four on the bench."

However, the hasty reshuffle to a 4-5-1 system brought the best out of Birtles who responded with arguably his most significant contribution in a Forest shirt. He worked tirelessly in splendid isolation, shielding the ball, holding up play in between a relentless pursuit of lost causes. He was also involved in the winning goal, falling to the ground as he played a one-two with John Robertson before the Scotland winger guided his shot unerringly in off the far post.

"Keegan was getting frustrated. I remember he tried to kick the corner flag as I headed off to hold up the ball and kill some time as the game dragged on. It was even better than Malmo because we had gone out and proved everyone wrong again. There are not many teams who have won the European Cup in successive years and considering where we came from, it was a fantastic achievement. That's why I am so upset by the shambolic lot who have let the club slide to where it is today."

CLOUGH, AT HIS MISCHIEVOUS best, ordered his squad back to the 'monastery' in the hills following the victory while wives and girlfriends remained in Madrid to celebrate.

"A few of the lads like Larry, Martin [O'Neill] and Robbo called a taxi and joined up with their partners. To be honest I was so knackered, I just fell into bed and slept all night."

It was the performance of a lifetime from Birtles and Forest. The team that had heralded the new age of expected silverware was gradually dissolving, either by consent and old age when Frank Clark departed to Wearside and Sunderland in management, or naked ambition to achieve more when Tony Woodcock left for the old Wehrmacht in Cologne as one of the highest-paid forwards in Europe.

Birtles, too, had caught the eye.

"He was a great athlete, could run all day. A smashing technique and left peg and one of those who could hold the ball up. Cloughie loved that. He didn't want his forwards flicking it on and losing possession. He wanted someone where the ball would stick to his feet and bring others in to the game. He played murder if his forwards flicked it on."

The assessment of Frank Clark conjures up Birtles at his best in Madrid that night, his best being something for which Manchester United were prepared to pay £1.25 million.

Sadly, like many a Clough/Taylor protégé before and since, it went pear-shaped away from the City Ground and Birtles snatched at the chance of returning to Forest on half the salary two years after his transfer to Old Trafford in October 1980. Notts County followed in 1987, one of several glittering new signings made by John Barnwell in a thwarted attempt to raise the Magpies back to the Second Division. Somewhere down the line after that, Birtles experienced financial hardships that are inconceivable for players of his status today. It is a period of his life he keeps secret, although he admits he was grateful for the PFA's help during some of his darkest hours.

A few years ago, while moving to a new house, Birtles sold his first European Cup winners' medal from Munich to Phil Soar, then the Forest chief executive. The price? £3,500, the sort of figure the Beckhams might have lavished on one of Brooklyn's Christmas presents.

"I needed the money at the time to buy some furniture and stuff," Birtles says. "I have regrets about it, but then it was necessary at the time. I hope one day Phil will allow me to buy it back off him."

Like Woodcock and Anderson, Birtles married a local girl and long-standing sweetheart. Like the pair of them, the marriage ended in divorce. Happily for all three, their ex-wives are friends and their children are, well, just as adoring as ever one suspects, which indicates a maturity and love of the family imbued in all decent folk.

If Birtles can reflect how lucky he has been, then so too can Forest fans, who should rejoice that the carpet fitter did not return prematurely to his original profession on a whim and with a whimper that dismal morning in Sheffield. Had he done so, how then would he and they have missed out on this splendidly illuminating anecdote?

During an interview at the City Ground last season, Nathan Tyson interrupted the question time and paused for a moment. Grabbing a nearby match day programme, he confronted a bearded chap of middle age years who was idling in the background.

"Could I have your autograph?" Tyson asked. "It's not for me. It's for me dad. He collects them."

The novel role reversal of reluctant autograph hunter reveals much about Tyson and the family man who bucks the perception of wayward young professionals with too much time and far too much money on their hands.

His target was Birtles, a somewhat famous incumbent of the No.9 shirt that Tyson was sporting in 2006/07. The veteran was happy to oblige. He signed the book 'Garry Birtles'. That's who he is. Always has been. Not prone to change.

His family, those close and those still stood in a time warp on the City Ground terraces, would be proud of him. And so would his dad.

Kenny Burns

1977-1981: 196 games, 15 goals

BY ANY STRETCH of life's expectations, it is supposed to be one of the happiest days of your life. Instead, the afternoon that Kenny Burns finally made it to the register office, on time and sober, and made a decent woman of the girl who became his second wife, turned out to be an unmitigated disaster.

As wedding days went, this one, back in February 1979, would have provided countless hours of material for the gurning grumblings of Les Dawson and a variety of deadpan northern comics on *The Comedians* happy to relate their tales of desperate woe and the misery of others to cheer up punters drooling over pints of tepid Tetley, bottles of Babycham and flat lemonade and a beef pie, mushy peas and mash supper.

"Marrying her was the worst decision I ever made in my life," recalls Burns with a facial expression that would have graced Egremont when the annual World Gurning Championships come to the Cumbrian town. "That and signing for Leeds United."

If the second part of that statement and its ominous undertones are a terrible indictment of the Yorkshire club, how bad was the marriage! It evokes Tommy Lawton's reflection on leaving Chelsea and London to sign for Notts County in 1947. "It was the worst day of my life," he recalled. "I should have stayed in London and left the wife, but I got it completely the wrong way round."

There is more to the dark chapter than just a failed and ultimately acrimonious split with Louise, who many thought was the calming influence that transformed Burns from wild man of Birmingham to mild man, relatively speaking, of Nottingham.

Little did he know that another union was going to cause upset, this one blessed not by the local registrar, but a far higher authority, namely that of Brian Clough and Peter Taylor.

Just a few days previously, Burns believed he had pulled off a masterstroke by dodging a mid-season trip to Abu Dhabi, one of the many journeys that Clough's nomads undertook, anywhere from Altrincham to Zanzibar, during the course of a campaign. The games were usually testimonials or for charity, with fringe benefits for the Forest hierarchy naturally.

"Gaffer, can I miss the trip?"

"Why's that Kenneth?"

"I think I'm going to marry the lassie."

"That's good, Kenneth. No problem. In fact, I might come along if you're going to invite me."

It was not exactly the response that Burns wanted, but the reception at his Toton home following the civil ceremony saw celebrations in style, especially by those stood behind the bar he'd had built in his conservatory. "Pete [Taylor] was there drinking champagne and eating prawns most of the day and we were all getting in the party swing," Burns recalls. "Then suddenly in walks Cloughie and I thought: 'Thanks for making the effort, gaffer.' He was dressed in that green tracksuit top, navy tracksuit bottoms and some battered old white trainers. He had come with Barbara [his wife], a lovely lady who was always immaculately turned out. And he brought his gardener!"

In fact Dave the gardener, like many of the Clough entourage over the years, was present merely as a chauffeur. Barbara did not drive and Clough's chances of being under the legal limit, at any time of the day or night, were negligible at best. "So he comes in and kisses the bride and everybody," continues Burns. "Then after about half an hour, he summons me to the kitchen. 'Kenneth, me and Peter would like a word with you in private.'"

Actually, there was more than one word, but the two that mattered were a sobering antidote to the heady cocktail of bubbly and prawns. "Trevor Francis. You know me and Peter are going to sign him."

"No, I didn't."

"Well we are. This week. And we wanted to know how you feel about that."

Two words also sprang to Burns' mind. "Oh fuck!" But instead of blurting out the limited vocabulary to the management duo, Burns mustered a brave face.

"No problem at all."

But, of course, there was a problem. A huge one. And his name was Trevor Francis.

He and Burns had been team-mates at St. Andrew's, but if Francis was acclaimed as the Boy Wonder of Birmingham City, Burns certainly was anything but his caped crusader buddy, Batman.

"Let's just say he knew his wines and I knew my beers," Burns says. "In fact they wouldn't serve beers in the sort of establishments he went in. I suppose we were two young boys at the time. He was on a fortune and I was on £35 a week. Was I jealous? Of course I fucking was."

The animosity between the two was rooted in their disparate backgrounds. Francis; shining middle class product imbued with a precious talent. Burns; a young lad from the rough edges of Glasgow, who honed his skills between jumper goalposts five or six hours a day with endless bottles of ginger pop or lemonade as thirst quenchers. At Birmingham, Burns felt he was doing the donkey work up front, creating the goals for Francis that earned him his much vaunted status both as fans' hero and, ultimately, million pound man.

"We had a chairman called Clifford Combes at Birmingham, a real gentleman. The gaffer [Clough] told me once that he almost signed for Birmingham to be their manager because of the chairman. He was the nicest chairman he'd ever met in football. He used to come back from his place in the Bahamas and always sit next to me on the team coach and offer me friendly advice. 'Next time you see the whites of the goalkeeper's eye, Kenny, you have a go,' he'd tell me. 'Don't always be making them for someone else."

Clough and Taylor were as good as their word and completed the signing of Francis on Friday, 9 February 1979. With Jimmy Hill's Coventry City dropping out of the bidding at £900,000, Forest raised the bar and became the first British club to pay £1 million for a player.

Burns was chuffed to bits.

"When he came to Forest, I was the one who had to show him around the dressing room and introduce him to the lads," Kenny recalls, but his facial expression suggests he might have preferred a trip to Abu Dhabi or even a re-run of his wedding day instead of those meet and greet duties.

"I suppose with the boy wonder, he had the silver spoon in his mouth and I came from the back streets of Glasgow. Maybe that's why the Forest supporters related more to me and some of the other lads. We were just an extension of themselves, really. There were a lot of lads on the terraces who were good at a job – mechanic, plumber, electrician – but I couldn't do what they could do. I think we played a style of football that was the way they would have played it on the parks. It was fun and enjoyable – and we won quite a lot as well!"

Although Burns maintains the two of them never came to blows – scarcely a contest, obviously – he kept his eye in and maintained a sharpness for physical contact with occasional target practice at Francis during training. "He came to the right place in terms of getting special treatment. He would have expected that, but the gaffer gave him none and neither did any of the other lads. I saw somewhere recently that Trevor was going on about his early days at Forest, how he wanted to make himself useful at half-time and poured us all a cup of tea. My arse. He did that because the gaffer would have told him to do it if he hadn't. That was the rule for substitutes. The players sat down at half-time and the subs poured the tea and carried the cups over. If they didn't do it, they soon did!"

ALTHOUGH IT'S FAIR to say that it was rather more intense and focused on the £1 million man, Francis was not alone in attracting Burns' contempt. Anything that moved in an opponent's shirt discovered the nastier side of his nature, one that's well disguised these days as a raconteur who can entertain and enthuse in equal measure either as an after-dinner speaker or at the 19th hole of his second favourite sporting arena, the golf course.

The Burns that stepped out onto a football pitch was a different animal; big on preventive action, small on talk, unless it was mouthing off to the officials, the enemy or even his own players. He claims most of his disciplinary problems stemmed from chastising pocket battleship Gordon Taylor, a Birmingham team-mate and naturally enough an out-an-out left-winger given his subsequent union leanings and fat cat salary to match, for failing to deliver crosses into the box where Burns maintained he could outjump anyone.

"Gordon had his shorts and sleeves rolled up and was like that bloody little road runner. Beep, beep, he was off. But he never got his head up and crossed the ball. That's when I'd start on him and the ref would tell me to button it. But I couldn't."

Burns' temper was legendary right from his formative steps in the game. Three dismissals in four games ('I think I had flu for the other game') for Glasgow Amateurs, clearly a misnomer in terms of GBH proficiency, an impressively consistent sequence of bad behaviour that ended his hopes of signing for Rangers in his formative years before Birmingham City scout Don Gorman recommended him for trials.

It was during those try-out games that his defensive prowess, a latent asset that had remained largely dormant until he signed for Forest, first emerged. "I was up front against their youth team, but all the lad playing alongside me wanted to do was dribble. I thought: 'I've had enough of this' and told them I was going to play centre-half. I did all right, kept the boy wonder – who happened to be one T. Francis – quiet and they offered me terms."

After making the Blues' first team and becoming a regular in the First Division, Burns pays tribute to his days in the Boys' Brigade and Hill Wood Boys' Club, that turned out the likes of Alex McLeish and Andy Gray, and his landlady in Birmingham, 'Aunt Daisy', who beefed him up with her regular helpings of meat and two veg at her digs. Despite these calming influences, word of his 'wild ways' had spread to Clough whose reluctance to sign the 'shit-stirring bastard' is as famous as Taylor's secret surveillance mission to Perry Barr dog track in Birmingham to spy on Burns and Paul Hendrie. "I wasn't surprised Pete went along, he liked a flutter himself! But I always liked the dogs, I grew up with them back in Scotland; we didn't exactly breed them but we kept a few there and we went to flapping tracks all the time. But I never bet more than a tenner or £20 at the most."

Burns was on holiday with Louise, the woman to whom he would be betrothed in Stapleford, when news came that Taylor had persuaded Clough that the gambling man would be all right for their growing team. "Willie Bell [Birmingham coach] rang me up and said:

'We've agreed a fee for you. Your mate Brian Clough will be phoning you.' Did I know Brian Clough? Yes, but not as a mate. I didn't get it. Years later, I saw Willie at a testimonial dinner and he said that a good source of his told him that I had been tapped up by Clough. Apparently his source was never wrong. But I told Willie, on this occasion, he was."

Clough phoned the holidaying Burns. "Ring me after you hit the tarmac in England."

Burns obeyed and met with Clough and Taylor in the Four Counties pub in Tamworth and after two days of negotiations involving tea and sandwiches with the Clough family, sweet peas and flowers at Bardill's garden centre, Burns signed. As a centre-forward.

"Cloughie never once mentioned to me that I was going to play centre-half," says Burns. "The deal was done on Sunday, a fee of £140,000. I can remember to this day that he warned me that he might sell me for a profit some day, sooner rather than later if needs be. I turned round and told him that he could do that if he was fed up with winning trophies. It brought a look from him. He must have thought I was a right so and so, but he didn't say much back. In fact on Monday morning I reported in for the usual pre-season photos, individual shots and the like. He welcomed me to the ground… then I didn't see him for a fortnight.

"We went on a tour of West Germany and it was Jimmy Gordon who took us training. One day he got out the bibs. 'Right, the following lot bib up. Shilton, Anderson, Barrett, McGovern, Lloyd, Burns; O'Neill, Bowyer, Withe, Woodcock and Robertson.' So I thought: 'Right, I must be playing centre-half.' And away I went at the back."

What followed was an astonishing transformation of both man and professional footballer by any benchmark.

Had the words of his former Birmingham team-mate Roger Hynd finally sunk in?

"Aggression is nothing unless it is controlled," Hynd told Burns once. Even with the red mist positively blinding and Hynd championing Trevor Francis' cause, the hot-headed Burns must have thought at least twice about arguing with one of the most dedicated of professional footballers, a non-drinking zealot but a brute of a centre-half whose physique was a cross between Hulk Hogan and Betty Stove. That's big and broad and fearsome. And all man.

Playing quoits with a 16-pound iron ring tossed the length of a cricket pitch into a clay square as a child growing up in a Scottish mining village probably explains some of the muscles that rippled beneath the blue jersey of that former Glasgow Rangers and Crystal Palace defender. Maybe his advice did not fall on deaf ears after all. By the end of that first season, Forest were champions, and Burns was at the Café Royal in May 1978 to be presented with the Sportswriters' Player of the Year statuette, although he cherishes the Forest Supporters' award with equal pride. A few weeks later he flew off to Argentina as one of the Scotland World Cup squad, although trying to evoke memories of Ally MacLeod's Tartan Army in South America that summer is an ill-advised manoeuvre in this present company. "I don't think Brian or Pete could have envisaged how it would all turn out when he bought me and put me at the back with big Larry. But it all gelled from that first game at Everton when we won 3-1. Ipswich came along when we were top [in October] and Mick Mills [their England full-back and captain] said we were a bunch of has-beens and nobodies." Forest won 4-0 and Peter Withe, who might have fitted into either of those categories, scored all four.

Burns continued to play the stylish sweeper alongside Larry Lloyd's imposing frame, although occasionally he was ushered into midfield, famously at Elland Road in the first leg of the League Cup semi-final. "It was the quickest midfield in the country with me, John McGovern and John O'Hare! There wasn't a decent sprint between us, but like all of Cloughie's tactics, it bore fruit."

A semi-final rout of waning Leeds, 7-3 on aggregate, thrust Forest within sight of their first significant trophy under Clough and Taylor, notwithstanding the Anglo-Scottish Cup won against Orient the previous season. Chris Woods defied his age and inexperience as well as Liverpool in the Wembley final, standing in for the cup-tied Peter Shilton and keeping a clean sheet in a 0-0 draw. Back at Old Trafford for the replay, another amongst the many fabled tales of Burns' dodgy dentures unfolded to compete with being yanked out to terrorise Kevin Keegan in the Bernabeu tunnel in Madrid or being crushed to smithereens by a boisterous Martin O'Neill in Innsbruck. There used to be a popular song concerning a child's dearest wish for Christmas being the present of two front teeth. The saga of Kenny Burns' itinerant falsies have now overtaken it in repetition only with a few fillings and cavities added or pulled as appropriate. "John McGovern had been injured at Wembley and Larry had tossed the coin in extra time as the senior player. But before kick-off at Old Trafford, the gaffer throws me the ball and tells me to lead them out. I always took my false teeth out in the dressing room, wrapped them in tissue and gave them to one of the reserves to put on the bench.

"At the final whistle, after John O'Hare had been tripped up in the box and we'd won thanks to the penalty, I asked one of the lads to go and get them, but they were nowhere to be found. In all the celebrations they'd gone missing, so there was me lifting the first piece of silverware that we'd won under Cloughie and Taylor with a huge gap at the top of my mouth. I was never the most handsome, but I would have liked to have had them in for that one."

THE HISTORIC SIGNIFICANCE of that trophy is not lost on Burns. It was a stupendous season, but he still had his altercations with authority and Clough. Not least those £50 fines delivered with silent intent in envelopes marked by the red tree of the Forest emblem: one for trying to loft a crossfield ball over Manchester City's Dennis Tueart was a painful blow to the pocket.

"I remember it because Shilts had rolled the ball out to me on the edge of the penalty area. I was so bloody shocked because I'd never seen him come that far off his line before. I thought: 'I'll hoof this one over to Robbo, we always tried to find him on the left first,' but Tueart got a head on it, thankfully not enough to get it on target because Shilts was stranded. After the fine, every time I got the ball I gave it to big Larry. 'Here, you have the fucking thing. I can't afford another £50 fine!'"

Another envelope came the now fondly adored titan's way when ITV cameras caught him head-butting Arsenal's Richie Powling in a defensive wall during a 3-0 defeat at Highbury. Burns maintained, still does, he only sneezed and the Gunners lad caught a cold, but Clough thought otherwise.

How could you believe a bloke, no matter how many times he cries atishoo, who cites one of his finest moments as the night Kevin Keegan turned tail and disappeared up his own perm in Madrid? Retaining the European Cup against SV Hamburg was the pinnacle of that three-year axis that hoisted Forest above Liverpool as the premier side in

England and on the continent. The story owes much to the fearsome Burns–Lloyd partnership.

"I like to think we got stuck in," Burns says with unwitting understatement. "That's why we appealed to the man on the terraces. We had a thing in the team that Cloughie instilled in us, that was, if one of us got done by somebody, one of the others would do him back, because the referee would be waiting for the player who was hurt to retaliate. Sometimes Clough would shout from the touchline: 'Kenneth' and point to his shin. Then I'd get stuck in and have one of the other side and he'd look over with a nod and a big thumbs-up.

"There weren't many in our side who could do it. John McGovern could tackle, but not hurt them, Frank Clark used to block the winger and Viv [Anderson] was just awkward with his long legs. There was me and Larry and Ian Bowyer who'd dig in when it was necessary. You need that sort of backbone in any successful side. I remember seeing Paul Hart's side when they reached the play-offs [Championship, 2003]. They had some good lads, but they played what I'd call academy football, very neat and precise, but as soon as someone put the boot in or they came up against a physical side, they couldn't handle it. They didn't have anyone who could give it back, they just didn't know what to do."

That naïvety did not apply to the unholy trinity of Burns, Lloyd and Bowyer, although in the case of Burns and Bowyer, the pair could play too – and more than just a bit – while Lloyd was outwardly the stopper, struggling to release what he felt was the Colin Todd ball player inside. Or maybe Sweeney Todd was nearer the mark.

"I like players when they are remembered in pairs, like Todd and McFarland and Andy Gray and John Richards at Wolves, they were a good pairing. I think that's a good sign and Larry and me were the same; a good pairing. We covered for each other and every time he went for a header I expected him to miss it and he did the same for me. But I didn't give a shit who it was on the other side. If the chance came to get in a tackle or mix it, then no matter who or how big the name, we'd let him know we were there. And that applied to big Joe Jordan, who in fairness was one of those centre-forwards who could give as good as he took."

THE BEAUTY OF THAT Forest side, a recurring theme whenever one of the squad talks, is the riotous assembly of diversity that moulded into a winning unit. Burns moved from East Leake to Toton and discovered his own corner of tranquillity called the Copsey Club, a snooker and drinking venue not far from Long Eaton dog track. "Robbo was into his Martini and lemonade with an umbrella, then, so he shot down Uriah Heep's with his mates. Fair enough, although these days he's a pint of best bitter man. But we all socialised together. Coming back from games at night we'd all shoot down to Madison's and God knows we had a few drinks and then drove home. That's how it was then, no use pretending any other way.

"We had plenty of days off. Pete and Cloughie made sure of that. Sometimes after a Saturday match the gaffer made it clear that if he caught anyone in the ground training before Thursday he'd fine them. But you only have to work in an office or anywhere to know if you get a few days off you come back with a spring in your step and raring to go. It's only natural. Now and again, we'd go golfing on a Wednesday, but even the lads who had never held a golf club in their lives, Viv, Tony Woodcock, Robbo, they'd come to the course after we'd finished and sit around with some sandwiches and drinks and take the Mickey out of each other."

Friday was squash day for Clough, when he would summon Garry Birtles or John McGovern to play him and get a lather of a sweat on with the rest of the squad awaiting his presence in the committee room.

"He'd come in and say 'same again tomorrow, keep the ball'. It was our cue to go to McKay's café on Muster's Road. Twenty chip cobs, sixteen coffees, ten with milk, that sort of thing. Of course, Robbo stopped there a bit longer than most of us!"

The West Bridgford café has become part of the players' folklore in cementing team spirit, just as across the Trent, a bacon and sausage bap after training in the café on the corner of Iremonger Road next to Meadow Lane fostered camaraderie among Notts County footballers. That, and a few late night lock-ins at obliging city centre pubs like the Spread Eagle, owned by Pete Quilty, a self-styled Singing Landlord and County fan whose voice was best kept locked in one of the beer fridges at his Wollaton Street watering hole.

Adjacent to the courtyard that housed the Isabella nightclub, before Madison's stole its thunder, it was eerily empty before the 10.30pm pub closing time, only to be engulfed by Forest and Notts players after hours in search of a decent pint at a reasonable price before daft nightclub prices took their toll. Added to that the City Fire Brigade HQ over the road, and between 11pm–1am, the crowd could be best described as lively and entertaining.

While Burns had arrived as Madison's displaced Isabella's and Babel as the place to be seen gyrating around a handbag on the dance floor, Forest assumed the focus of attention for Nottingham's increasingly sophisticated, or perhaps wealthier, social scene. And yet that ingrained working class stock, which bonded Burns to his faithful in the stands, would not be moved.

"We all liked a drink, some more than others and yes Larry was notorious as well as myself. But we were never Big Time Charlies. Yes, eventually we got some Toyota-sponsored cars, coupés in black and silver, but we paid £500 a man for the privilege and I've a pretty good idea where the money went to [Clough being one plausible suspect. Like Milo Minderbinder, the accidental capitalist in *Catch-22*, what's good for the company, is good for you. But more especially for Milo].

"But I remember Ian Bowyer winning our first sponsored car, an Austin Princess 2.2. It was like a bloody bus; ten ton in weight because of its engine. That wasn't glamorous. In fact one day we were playing at home and as usual went to Trattoria Conti on Trent Bridge for a pasta and then off to the Albany Hotel for a kip before the game. Ian Bowyer was giving us a lift up there in his brown Ford Capri GXL and I started to fiddle with his upholstery.

"'What you doing, get your hands off that,' Bomber said, turning to me in the passenger seat and getting irate. Suddenly we piled into the back of a Roller. Whack. Bomber drove straight off, didn't even stop. It was going to cost him £50 for a new indicator panel, but he wasn't going to get involved.

"'What's the matter?' I asked him as he pulled up outside the hotel car park. It was as I was getting out that I noticed his tax disc: a Shipstone's Brown Ales beer mat. Oh. Don't think the current Premiership champions would have similar problems, would they?"

Burns, like most former professionals, recognises the obscenity of financial reward bestowed on top class footballers today without being resentful. He earned £70 a week at Birmingham, a salary doubled when he joined Forest. At the end of that unforgettable first season, Burns thought he deserved more. "So I went to the gaffer's office and he was sitting there reading the paper. I'd already reckoned that I should ask for £350 a week and be happy with £300. I knocked on the door and went in. 'Yes Kenneth?'

"'It's like this gaffer, I think, after all I've done this season, I should get a rise.'

"'Really, how much Kenneth?' Clough replied, without moving so much as the thumb that was keeping the morning newspaper in place between us.

"'£350 quid a week.'

"'OK.'"

And out walked Burns thinking: "Yes, I've done you, you bastard." Then, after a moment's hesitation, he reassessed the situation. "You bastard. You've done me."

Burns says a similar situation occurred the following season following the first European Cup victory.

"'How much, Kenneth?'

"'£850 a week.' (Happy to take £745.)

"'OK.' (Not a twiddle of the thumbs or movement of the newspaper.)

"'Got him this time. Hold on, he's fucking screwed me again.'

"I remember John McGovern told me when he was speaking to Denis Law how he used to knock on Matt Busby's door and ask for a rise. Always, he said, he came out of the manager's office having accepted a drop in wages. That's how I felt with Cloughie, even though I knew I was getting more."

During the course of his contract, before he opted for the ill-fated move to Leeds where Allan Clarke was his well-meaning but equally ill-fated manager, about to be replaced by Eddie Gray, Burns had earned £5,000 for helping win Forest's first European Cup. Persuading Clough to be an easy touch with bonuses was a far trickier matter. "We wouldn't have earned a penny if we had not won in Munich, that was the way he operated. By the same token, having won the championship the previous season, we found that most teams were on £100 a point, so we asked if we could be on the same. 'Not a fucking chance,' came the reply. 'Why should I pay you lot £100 a point if you're going to get relegated and fail?'

"But what he did do was increase it to £100 a point in the top six and double that in the top three. He also said he'd pay us £1,000 a point after we'd reached 53 points [two points for a win] because normally that would put you in with a shout of winning the title. As it happens we had no chance of catching Liverpool by then, but we won three and drew one of our last four games which saw us second [ahead of West Bromwich Albion by a point]. So that earned us £7,000 in four matches which wasn't a bad little end of season bonus."

BURNS' CENTRAL BLOCKADE with Larry Lloyd still engenders painful or happy memories depending on your standpoint. There was a dichotomy to Lloyd, as I knew him as manager of Notts County whilst reporting for the *Nottingham Evening Post*. He could spit a dummy out of his pram from 50 paces or turn a pint of Home Ales flat with a sulky face at the drop of his name, but, having been on the receiving end of one of his 'reducers' during a charity game at Meadow Lane, he was someone best to know as friend rather than enemy.

Burns tells stories of how Tony Woodcock and Viv Anderson would regularly play-fight on away trips, jumping out of wardrobes and cupboards in the style of Burt Kwouk, aka Cato, the Japanese manservant setting about Peter Sellers in the *Pink Panther* films. But then came a trip to AEK Athens, when the hotel was perched on the edge of the Mediterranean. "We were all geared up for a bit of sunbathing when Jimmy Gordon came in and said we should get our training kit on for the beach. The gaffer [Clough] was there and he said: 'We're going to have a game of rugby.'

"'At last: a proper man's game,' Lloydy said. So first thing he got the ball to his hands and started running, one of the lads tripped him up. Suddenly there were 16 players on top of him putting the boot in, elbows, knuckles, the lot. He got a battering. When he got up, he was looking for a bit of revenge, but nobody owned up. 'It must have been him, Larry.' 'No, I think it was him over there.' We didn't take prisoners: no matter how big.

"But then that was Larry. I remember when David Needham joined us from QPR, well, he'd walk around a beetle rather than stand on it. But actually he fitted in well. The 'Pig Farmer' we called him because he was always turning up in dirty wellies. He loved his country life. Dave was signed to cover for Larry, who'd broken his big toe. Larry's greeting to Dave went something like this. 'Uh, hello, you're here to replace me. Well, don't worry, I'm fucking going to have my place back as soon as I'm fit.' And nice to meet you Larry!

"But then the one thing I would say about Larry is that he was never two-faced. I mean who would want another one like that? Not even him."

The irreverent banter cannot disguise a mutual respect, however, even if Burns was clearly the epitome of hard man and ball player, while his partner had only perfected half of that combination.

BURNS LAMENTS HIS departure from Forest and admits he went to Leeds for the money and a big pay day without considering his future. "I thought the team was breaking up, but I wish I'd stayed. I didn't see the likes of Des Walker coming through and Stuart Pearce on the horizon. It was a huge mistake.

"Allan Clarke [the Leeds manager] was a massive Clough fan, but the trouble was the players were crap. Leeds were shite and I fell out with Manny Cousins [the Leeds chairman who had hired and fired Clough during his infamous 44 days at the club a decade earlier]. I ended up playing for Pete [Taylor] at Derby, but the side wasn't good enough by then."

Unlike John Robertson, there was no final fling for Burns at the Forest.

"I'm glad Robbo got to go back there. It was good for him and the gaffer. Mind you, by then he'd got so slow that he was dropping his shoulder, but couldn't get back up in time to dodge the full-back!"

His one-liners are in fact a joyous celebration rather than a degradation of the Forest phenomenon in which he played a critical and crucially crunching part. He was the lad who fractured his right leg tackling on the streets of north west Glasgow, played in goal with a plaster cast and practised kicking with his left leg. Not only could he pass the ball with both feet with unerring accuracy, he could land a blow on an opponent's shin with an equally potent punt of the limbs.

"I used to look at the great Leeds team, Bremner, Giles, Hunter and all," Burns says. "They were players who could look after themselves, but play when they needed to. I like to think I was like that. I could play a bit, but if the chance came to hurt someone, then I'd do it, whatever part of the pitch it was on."

And he proved to be usefully ambidextrous in times of need as well. Back to that European Cup final in Madrid where Mr K. Keegan replaced Mr T. Francis as public enemy No.1.

"They had this lad at right-back called Manny Kaltz and he didn't half like getting forward. Robbo didn't fancy playing the entire game at left-back. Anyway, he got forward early on and it was the only time Keegan got the run on me. He'd done me good and proper, so as he spun and turned away I put my arm out, straight, like cricketers do today, and shouted: 'Viv, he's yours.'

"Next thing Keegan's flat out on the floor and getting up. 'You bastard' (there's a high pitched squeak in the Burns rendition of the Scunny bubblehead). 'You fucking bastard.'

"Apparently I'd caught him right in the Adam's apple and he was not best pleased. I apologised to him, but he was having none of it. Well some people are like that aren't they? That's the sort of person he was, a sarky little bastard."

You can take the boy out of Glasgow, sure enough...

Stuart Pearce

1985-1997: 522 games, 88 goals

BEING SENT TO Coventry was never quite so bad as some people made out. For a generation of pre-pubescent boys, it meant a day out in the city where Talbot cars, in fact any motorised vehicle that came off the production line there for two decades, was another rust-ridden nail, quite literally, in the coffin of the British motor manufacturing industry.

But the numbingly tedious war of attrition between management and the trades unions that punctuated working life during the 1960s and 1970s did not concern the busloads of pupils who travelled to the West Midlands. Here was a chance not to see the enduring glory of religion epitomised in the preserved ruins of the old cathedral flattened by the Luftwaffe during their unrelenting blitzkrieg of the city during the Second World War; here instead was an opportunity to escape Stalag 17, otherwise known as school and its ring of fences, and buy a postcard of some fading deity or another as proof of temporary liberation from the classroom regime.

A day out at Highfield Road for grown-ups was not always embraced with similar enthusiasm. The stadium best resembled one of those Shipstone's or Home Ales estate pubs built to encourage their clientele. And who wouldn't be driven to drink by florid upholstery and patterned wallpaper undermined by sea green or navy blue carpets? If seasickness didn't overwhelm customers, the tenth pint of Shippos was certain to do the trick.

Inside Highfield Road, if the chintzy décor wasn't bad enough, the sky blue playing kit that turned chocolate brown on away days turned anyone who caught sight of it turning a bilious shade of green before being arrested by the fashion police. Perhaps that's why Alan Hill, in his capacity as Forest chief scout, decided to travel incognito to see relegation-haunted Coventry City play one night as the 1985 season drew to a close. Anonymity and disguise were the essential ingredients of the technique preferred by Peter Taylor when sizing up potential acquisitions, but Hill raised the tactic to a new level that evening.

After the First Division game, mingling outside among the terraced houses and tiny cobbled back streets that hemmed in Highfield Road, Hill wore his sheepskin collar high above his neck with a flat cap pulled down as far as it might descend. The players were drifting away to the car park when Hill made his move. "Excuse me mister, could I have your autograph?" he said, stopping one of the Coventry players in his tracks and thrusting out pen and paper.

The empty pages in the autograph book may have revealed a lapsed collector or a middle-aged man who was taking up a new hobby. It was neither. "Mr Clough and the chief scout would like to know if you would like to play for Nottingham Forest," Hill said.

"I don't know who the hell you are, but I'd love to."

"Then put your phone number here, son. And ask your mate Butterworth if he fancies it too."

Had he been caught or reported then, Hill might have faced a *sine die* action by the FA, but as it happened, the camouflaged hoax autograph hunter had just taken the first tentative steps in bringing an iconic figure to the City Ground.

Brian Clough dialled the number (pre-mobile phones, of course) the following day and confirmed to the voice at the other end that he would be signing him. And his mate Ian Butterworth.

CLOUGH'S SEARCH FOR a natural left-back since Frankie Gray's return to Leeds United had been largely fruitless, with Ian Bowyer and Kenny Swain filling the vacancy as manfully as could be expected. But the arrival of Stuart Pearce for £240,000 from the Sky Blues heralded a new era of Wembley triumphs for Forest, albeit in some ill-advisedly named and dodgily contested competitions apart from the League Cup.

Pearce, though, became the acceptably snarling face of Forest's brief renaissance, the bulldozing bulldog of a full-back swathed in the flag of St George. He would be the motivator, the captain, the leader and he would do it all from the front, with teeth gnashing and mop of straight, blond hair flailing, shorts rolled up fearsomely high on the legs and short sleeves showing just enough muscle and tattoo to frighten the bejesus out of quivering opponents.

While the Trent End hailed him as one of their own, his image spawned a thousand imitators masquerading as England fans; cretins who felt it their duty to inflict themselves on cultured and civilised mainland Europe, itself a squalid enough experience for the indigenous population who also had to suffer their urine, foul-mouthed expletives and excrement as part of a depressingly familiar ritual of visitation rights.

Pearce's cult status, while later embraced by more moderate England fans, belongs at the City Ground.

This was their 'Psycho'. Not the deranged nutter banging his head against a gendarme's baton, but the stoic, inscrutable skipper who led by example, scored the goals that mattered and clattered the prima donnas that didn't.

"Not for one minute did I believe it was a nutcase nickname," Pearce said. "More a pet name – and it worked both ways. When I came out on the pitch, there was a rapport. All crowds have their favourites and it's usually someone they can see rooting for their football club. I couldn't help the way I tackled. That was part of my game. If I had stopped doing it, I wouldn't have been in the side."

Here was the former part-timer and sparky with Wealdstone who advertised his own services, with a contact telephone number, in the Forest programme; the player who raised the St George flag in his garden daily and appreciated his good fortune at being made a Forest captain and an England defender. If there was such a thing as a first class compartment for working class heroes, Pearce would fit snugly into it.

An uneasy relationship and distance that he cultivated with the press only enhanced his standing amongst supporters.

"I didn't think just because I was a professional footballer that I should have to give interviews after the game," he said. "If there wasn't enough to write about 90 minutes of football then something was wrong. They [the journalists] had seen the game – they have opinions. Let them write about it. It's not necessary to have my opinions as well."

If only Pearce knew how many journalists would agree with that sentiment rather than the dictum from newspaper offices, both national and local, that insists on slavishly regurgitating vapid players' quotes and the puerile platitudes of management.

EVEN IF HE WANTED to talk after his Forest debut, against Luton Town at Kenilworth Road on 17 August 1985, a distinction he shared with Butterworth and Neil Webb, it is likely he was too gobsmacked to get his words out. Following the 1-1 draw and the fiasco of the Forest team coach being blocked in by a parked car, Clough stormed off the bus and demanded the car keys before driving it out of the ground and parking it on an adjacent street. It was only when he had calmed down that he realised the folly of his actions and the car was returned to its original parking bay.

If he was too in awe of the manager then, Pearce's later dealings with a Clough deteriorating in health and judgement, set him aside in the Forest dressing room. He may have been the one who introduced punk, Madness and ghetto blasters to the home team changing room, but he also brought a calming influence and open liaison between players and management at the club.

From Hill to Frank Clark who later managed him, the backroom staff agree that he was the one player ultimately who could hold his own with Clough, probably because he had earned that respect. He rarely warmed up before a game; his love of loud music was enough motivation, although if he asked Clough to play his own kind of music for the pre-match anthem, the manager was always lambasted for his choice (again) of Frank Sinatra.

Other former players are not so charitable about their captain who briefly would be their manager. "He knew the value of a pound," was how one euphemistically demeaned him for being careful with his money, but generous with his services when cash incentives were on the table. In his defence, a lucrative offer to play in Japan during the twilight of his career was declined.

On the eve of the FA Cup final against Tottenham Hotspur, certainly Pearce, like any other professional at the time, reaped the financial rewards of the build-up to the showcase event. An envelope with £1,000 cash for one article for the *Nottingham Evening Post* was the going rate in 1991. He even resorted to asking one of the *Post* reporters to place an advert in the paper for the items for sale column because he knew staff would get 10 per cent discount on a £6 insertion.

Does that frugality derive from his background, though? An employee of Brent Council then elevated to superstar status simply counting his blessings and money. Is that so wrong?

"When I left school I had no qualifications to speak of," recalls Pearce. "I tried to join the police force and the army, but the police turned me down and the army said I wasn't interested enough in joining them. So I got a job stacking in a warehouse and testing radios and TVs. It was my sister who told me to go and get some electrical skills and I joined the council on an apprenticeship."

He had turned down Hull City and a drop in wages before he agreed to join Coventry aged 21 in 1983. His elevation to England's World Cup squad at Italia 90 and Forest leadership was as rapid as it was spectacular, punctuated with those stunning left-foot shots from dead balls, open play and all angles. His free-kick in the 1991 FA Cup final against Spurs would have been a fitting effort to secure the famous old trophy for Clough; sadly the referee's leniency with Paul Gascoigne and Des Walker's late howler dealt a cruel blow to the manager and his last chance of winning that elusive pot had slipped away forever.

Less than four years later it was Pearce, lurking but frustrated like a caged rhino, who popped up in the six-yard area at London Road. Among the muck and nettles and with boots flying, his head went down and the captain converted a centre that put Forest back in the game at relegated Peterborough United; 2-0 down had become 2-1 before two more goals from Stan Collymore claimed a 3-2 win and instant promotion back to the Premiership.

These are just some of the heroics that Forest fans recall of Pearce; that and regular visits to Wembley for a plethora of minor trophies, but two that counted, the League Cup being secured two years in succession in 1989 and 1990, evoking the Clough–Taylor era a decade previously.

Pearce, Forest scarf around neck, would be at the head of affairs, holding aloft silverware as he would, figuratively speaking, hold aloft the scalp of another 'fancy dan', as my old County boss Jimmy Sirrel used to call them. Invariably these would be another winger heading for Row B or the dirt running track enclosing the pitch. Since it was more often than not Pat Nevin, Pearce didn't even bother to count the Chelsea scarlet pimpernel as a genuine 'bag', preferring just to check the pocket he kept the Scotsman in or the advertising board he was hiding behind during the course of a game.

Nevin's revenge was a fitting one. He found it far easier to retaliate against his nemesis in a newspaper column, safely snuggled hundreds of miles away at home replete with drooping bottom lip and suitably menacingly flared nostrils.

The fact that Pearce did not forget his roots was another factor in how Forest fans and players alike warmed to him. His father Dennis was a postman whose shifts worked in his favour in being able to see his young son play in Saturday morning school games [older readers will recall that golden but long forgotten era when teachers worked half a day at the weekend to justify the 42 weeks' holiday they suffered marking books for the remainder of the year].

His dad also cleaned his boots and was a mild disciplinarian. Although he never considered himself a father figure at the club, his previous life in the world outside the cocoon that is football, virtually impenetrable today, did place him a unique position.

"You could always tell the lads in the game who had come from part-time, the way they spoke and their mannerisms. It was difficult for young lads then. They broke into the team before they were hardly out of their teens. They were going down nightclubs and girls were throwing themselves at them and God knows what else. Of course, it is all very flattering, but it was also a false sort of thing. Non-leaguers like myself had lived a bit of life and struggled a bit more. I think we appreciated what we had, the time we had in the game and how quickly it could be taken away. I kept my feet on the ground because I only had to look around and see people struggling to pay their mortgage [two years after he signed for Forest, Britain suffered a stock market crash in October 1987, known as Black Monday. Among its repercussions, that lasted for almost a decade, were exceptionally high interest rates, an unprecedented amount of homeowners lumbered with negative equity that led to thousands of repossessions].

"Don't get me wrong, I was never a father figure, but if I thought that I could help a young lad by giving him a piece of advice, I did, whether it was about his game or about hanging around snooker halls in the afternoon [before 'dogging', 'roasting' or other activities associated with canines and Sunday lunch became popular with professional footballers, one of their biggest vices was to idle away the day spotting pinks and sinking a few reds in the corner pocket at a local snooker emporium. Heady days of youth indeed].

"I would have done that for anyone. That was Stuart Pearce the person, though. Not the captain of a football team.

"People used to come up to me in a restaurant in Nottingham, but when I was away from football, I didn't want to talk about it. They might have gone away thinking I was a miserable old git, but that's the way I was and am. If they wanted to pester me at the ground, at my place of work, then that was fine."

Pearce was never a 'miserable old git' to his admirers; he was the electrician who once worked for a living, like the mere mortals on the terraces. His appetite and enthusiasm for the game, harnessed along with a bludgeoning left peg, set him apart from the working class lads who stood and sang his praises yet he was the embodiment of all their aspirations. Pearce's success made that ambition appear less than a fantasy or illusion, more tangible and almost within touching distance. As his stock rose so remarkably, he frequented a world apart from his biggest fans yet he remained close as if a kindred spirit to those who worshipped him.

Among those is Danny Mouncer, an avid Forest fan of mid-20s vintage and well known among the club's many and varied website chatrooms, official and otherwise. He recalls his one and only meeting with his great hero as a tongue-tied teenager in a city centre hairdressing salon. "It was shortly after Pearcey broke his leg for the first time for West Ham United. His wife, Liz, had just finished having her hair cut and was approaching the exit. Being a gentleman, I held open the door, oblivious to the fact my hero was just about to hobble around the corner on his crutches. I almost closed the door on him by accident to which he gave me a mini scowl as if I had done it on purpose. Those who know me understand that I'm not often speechless, but I was for those ten seconds. I would have given him a piggyback down those stairs if he had asked!"

LIKE MANY OF HIS generation, Mouncer was born too late to see Storey-Moore and Baker in their City Ground pomp mesmerising the Trent End. Their birth dates also deprived them of the Clough–Taylor era and those staggering European nights when the unlikeliest of dreams and ambitions, for fans and players alike, were fulfilled. Their compensation, particularly in desperately thin times for the former European champions, was to have seen Pearce at his glowering, galvanising best. His every sinew seemed to embody the needs of every genuine football fan, those who prefer a pint and a pie as opposed to prawns and a pretentious Pinot Grigio.

Pearce appeared to have an inherent talent to intimidate crowds and opponents in equal measure. How often did a searing run down the left wing raise spirits? As Mouncer recalled it: "The old Trent End roof would rattle to the roar of Pearce approaching with arms aloft, fists clenched and captain's armband securely attached to his right bicep. You would look around at fully-grown men gripped with passion, ready for that particular moment. It was as if they had worked all week just to watch and savour Psycho's rallying cry. They probably had.

Forest have always had a large unfriendly rivalry with neighbours Derby County. Rams fans hate Forest and vice versa. Bigwigs at Nottingham Forest usually avoid the issues with Derby to prevent causing tension in the run-up to matches. One Guinness-loving ex-manager (Joe Kinnear) even summed up Derby County versus Nottingham Forest as 'just another game'. Pearce once described how he could never work for Derby County in any capacity. That sums up what this man meant in the eyes of Reds supporters. A sense of 'one of the lads', 'one of us' if you like. His long-running feud with Derby right-winger Ted McMinn was a highlight from a fan's perspective. More often than not, McMinn was usually being sent ten feet into the air or into the advertising hoardings every time they met.

Pearce was simply something else. A complete one-off. An amazing part of the club's history.

That lasting impression is a legacy that both young and old Forest fans can cherish and naturally Clough must take some of the credit. Pearce was perhaps always destined for the national team and the fame he eventually earned. When Coventry manager Bobby Gould paid non-leaguers Wealdstone what was then a king's ransom of £30,000 for a part-time player in 1983, the Sky Blues' manager sensed that here was someone a bit special.

Clough's knack was to elevate good players to be very good or almost great ones; in some cases exceptionally great like John Robertson. Pearce was already halfway up the ladder, not on the lower rungs, when Clough grabbed him by the scruff of the neck. Both manager and player can be grateful for their expeditious rendezvous in life, just as Sir David Beckham and Alex Ferguson (sorry, the knighthood should be the other way around despite the publicly Posh perception) should be equally enriched and heartened for their simultaneous development and mutual success at Old Trafford. Pearce, like Beckham in his heyday, really was the heartbeat of the team, reversing fortunes by sheer endeavour, a willingness to tackle lost causes and, of course, the occasional sublimely rapacious free-kick that defied the laws of motion, more often than not when the natural course of a game seemed to be running away from Forest.

Above all, Stuart Pearce led by example.

If the 'boy done good', don't mention it in any cockney tones to Pearce. His regular captain's column in the *Nottingham Evening Post* was often witty and informative, but he took exception that the hierarchy at the newspaper injected his Wealdstone twang into the copy. Years later, in his management days at Manchester City, his distrust and general avoidance of journalists whenever possible was cemented when a leading national newspaper columnist quoted him in the same manner.

IN THE MANNER OF most true heroes, Pearce has had his fair share of disappointment to deal with, and the way in which he did so only served to enrich his legend. There was, of course, the Italia 90 semi-final penalty shoot-out failure. A pizza ad helped the nation mourn, but the denouement would be that ejaculation of emotion when, six years later, Wembley Stadium witnessed the redemption of a left-back who had become their favourite son as he welted a penalty past Spain goalkeeper Zubizaretta and let loose a primeval yell, matched by those tumbling from the ageing stands.

Disappointments at Forest ranged from two relegations, one as caretaker-manager, to defeat in the 1991 FA Cup final, despite that howitzer of a free-kick. But the sublime football that Clough's side played, which made the Forest of the mid-to-late 1980s the team for the neutral, belied Pearce's image as a hard nut, as Psycho. His left foot boasted as much culture as Brian Sewell, and as much haughtiness, too, as the ball was regularly despatched at breakneck speed accurately into the net. His movement and running saw Pearce become a deadly weapon in Forest's attack. He notched 88 goals for Forest in 522 games over 12 seasons. Yes, he was a dead-ball specialist, but he could also lash a moving ball on the run as well as any striker, and when it fell to Pearce on the edge of the area, opposing fans' hearts would leap into mouths.

TOWARDS THE END of the 2006/07 season and through the summer break, his time was understandably somewhat consumed with his imminent and entirely expected dismissal as Manchester City manager, daughter Chelsea's stuffed horse lucky mascot notwithstanding. In a similar vein, his appointment in charge of the England Under-21s surprised no-one. An ability to communicate with a squad let alone co-ordinate one comprising millionaires, Johnny Foreigners who employ people to employ sparkies to change the plug on their hair dryer when the fuse blows, was perhaps not the job description that most appealed to Pearce at the City of Manchester Stadium. He subsequently admitted he was effectively caretaking again, keeping the seat warm for a more illustrious name who would be allowed free rein with the purse strings. There was yet more Pearce dignity and humour in the way in which he dealt with the situation which had seen him touted for the England job just nine months previously and then become a dead man walking under new owner Thaksin Shinawatra.

His best inspirational lines at Forest were running up and down the pre-match line-up of Reds players before the UEFA Cup game with Bayern Munich urging each one to 'remember you're an Englishman'. Energetic patriotism to be sure verging on a Basil Fawlty level of Teutonophobia, but certainly sentiments lost on Dutch team-mate Bryan Roy.

So has Pearce now found a niche in attempting to galvanise and inspire England's youngsters to greater heights and to accept responsibility in an age when culpability is a dirty word and owning up to a mistake the most damning and disastrous career move in politics, sport and any other business you care to mention? For all his detractors, and there are some surprising candidates willing to step forward here,

Pearce could never be accused of shirking his own responsibilities. He took pride in the shirt, whether it was Garibaldi red or emblazoned with three lions. Surely he is the perfect role model for the cream of young English footballers today.

Some years ago, Pearce escaped when he evacuated his driving seat to avoid being squashed like an orange carton by one of the council's finest rubbish collection vehicles as it toppled onto his car. An ignominious cause of death on the certificate, no doubt. Flattened by faulty bin cart. But surely a death worse than the fate that awaits the likes of Joey Barton. Who knows? If it's true that past life flashes before someone staring death in the face, Pearce, after that near-death experience, might have felt there was more to come, an existence unfulfilled when it comes to his managerial career.

If he has work still to be done, it is perhaps an ultimate goal. To nurture young talent that one day may be good enough to oust the foreign legions from the Premiership and eventually emulate the achievement of the boys of 1966.

It's a tall order. But if Pearce is equal to it, Forest fans will not be surprised in the least.

Stan Collymore

1993-1995: 77 games, 50 goals

WHEN THE DAY OF judgement arrives for Stan Collymore there may be those on high who have to consider the facts and review the evidence regarding his fitness to enter into sacred ground – to spend his afterlife wandering among the exalted company of Tommy Lawton, Tom Finney, Stanley Matthews, Bobby Moore and a wealth of revered sporting talent and athletic prowess in football's Hall of Fame.

If so, he may well find the verdict delivered thus, in the damning fashion that Fletch, one of Ronnie Barker's most joyous comedy creations, was sent down to Slade prison every week in *Porridge*.

'Stanley Victor Collymore,' the right honourable Judge Barker would proclaim, 'you have pleaded guilty to the charges brought by this court, and it is now my duty to pass sentence. You are an habitual liar, who accepts arrested development, fire extinguishers and dogging ceremonies as an occupational hazard, and presumably accepts discovery, punishment and the company of egocentric weathergirls in the same casual manner. We therefore feel constrained to commit you to the maximum term allowed for these offences – you will go to Merseyside for two years, from there be taken to Villa Park where you will be detained at Her Majesty's pleasure in solitary confinement before spending the rest of your sentence at Leicester open prison (La Manga branch open 24 hours summer weekdays for gambling and drinking), and a further few months in a Bradford psychiatric ward run by guv'nor Geoffrey Richmond.

And may God have mercy on your soul. Now take him away.'

Should Collymore's ultimate fate dictate that he must spend eternity in a groundhog day scenario of his own botched career, would he be able to change the course of events and reform his life? The answer is a simple no.

Would Forest fans have had it any other way?

Again, the answer is probably in the negative.

FOR TWO YEARS after he signed as one of Frank Clark's first acquisitions at the City Ground in 1993, Collymore riveted, roused and left all who came to see him perform in raptures. Opponents and jaundiced hacks alike. Ian Edwards was not among that latter ensemble, more a young reporter who had been handed the potential poisoned chalice of covering Forest for the *Nottingham Evening Post* in 1988. Although two League Cup victories awaited, this was a club in partial decline that masked the very private, but sadly sometimes very public, vertical slope that Brian Clough was sliding down at a rate of knots.

They proved to be formative, educational and invaluable years for Edwards, but post-Clough, the arrival of Collymore was the catalyst for a new era that should have been the springboard for a glittering career. "In some ways we were sort of kindred spirits," recalls Edwards, who moved on to report Yorkshire football for the *Daily Mirror* and now fronts a sports agency business in the Midlands. "He was from Cannock, as I was, and his mother, on whom he doted, lived around the corner from my parents. I remember when he came that he was like the proverbial breath of fresh air. We did a series on his life story and we talked for hours over a tape recorder.

"The thing was he was eloquent, plausible and came across very lucidly. He spoke in sentences and words that, well, professional footballers just didn't use. He was an intelligent lad. There was a football writers' bash in Birmingham that I was invited to and he said he'd pick me up at junction 11 of the motorway. I mean, you just don't get that sort of thing happening today with your average superstar."

That eloquence and charm was good news for Forest fans. Those traits are anathema to Neil Warnock, but it is a frightening thought that the then manager of Notts County had first refusal on Collymore. Phil Robinson, a Stafford-born lad and County player under Warnock at the time and now manager of Stafford Rangers, explains why. "I knew Stan had been released by Wolves in 1990 and had seen him play at Stafford a couple of times. He'd been recommended, so I asked Neil Warnock if he'd have a look at him. I used to bring him over every day for a fortnight for training at Meadow Lane; always remember a nightmare journey along the A453 past the power station into Nottingham. It came down to the final day for Stan, I think it was a practice game and Neil was playing up front with him. Stan just refused to do any running and Neil was becoming increasingly frustrated. He showed him how to chase down defenders, close them down and then turned around to him. 'That's how you do it son, now can you try it?'

"Stan replied [Black Country accent to the lilt of Benny of Crossroads Miss Doiyan required here]: 'But gaffer, oize sticking ball in the back o'net when it cums moy way. Wot else does yu want?'"

Not to give Collymore a contract, apparently.

Warnock's sharp eye for talent saw him relegated with County that season, but Collymore found salvation when Colin Murphy offered him sanctuary at Southend United, a blessed relief after the chastening voyage of discovery sharing a dressing room with Ian 'Awighty Wrighty' Wright at Crystal Palace for almost two years. Some say the experience, enough to edge any potential lemming with a tentative grip on the will to live over the cliff top, could have been a cause for his later depression. Certainly, it applies to thousands who have had the brief encounter by media since.

CLOUGH HAD ALREADY made inquiries about Collymore as Forest lumbered towards relegation from the Premiership in 1993, but it was Frank Clark who succeeded in signing him – and nurturing the talent and personality that was beyond Warnock – early in his City Ground managerial days.

"I'd known about Stan from my days at Leyton Orient," says Clark. "I used to get around London quite a lot then watching reserve games in the Football Combination as it was. Most of the lads came from

First Division sides; Tottenham, Arsenal, Chelsea or Palace, and they wanted to stay in London, but there was no way Orient could match any of their wage demands. We just didn't have the money. Stan, I knew, had had a difficult time at Palace. There was a dressing room that included Mark Bright and Ian Wright and he'd come from Cannock and Stafford Rangers, so he took an awful lot of stick. He got slaughtered, which is normal for dressing rooms, but Stan couldn't cope with it really and who could blame him?"

Clough had kept an eye on Collymore and also Colin Cooper, a promising centre-back with Millwall, but the Forest board refused Clough the funds that might have saved the club from relegation. Ironically, it was the get-out-of-Forest-relatively-free card that Roy Keane's advisers had inserted in his contract that enabled Clark to complete the deals after which Clough had hankered.

"Roy had a clause saying he had to be sold for a certain fee, £3.75 million, if Forest were relegated," says Clark. "So we knew we couldn't keep him and in the market at the time, he was a bargain price. The player got ten per cent, so it was a matter of getting the deal done really. We made a bid for Cooper which was accepted and we [Clark and Alan Hill, his assistant] were down in Lancaster Gate tying up the loose ends with the Millwall secretary. No sooner was the ink dry on the contract than Alan said: 'Come on, let's get Collymore now.' We'd got the best part of £4 million to spend and had just shelled out £1.5 million on Colin, but Alan was more of an impulsive person than me. 'Let's get the deal done and sorted,' he told me. Normally I needed to chew things over and think about it, but on this occasion, I was glad I didn't."

Clark had had dealings with Vic Jobson, the Southend owner, who was generally reviled by his own supporters and by Clark's admission 'a tricky customer to deal with'. "I made the call from Lancaster Gate because I'd known Vic before and had spoken to him. I understood why people didn't like dealing with him, but I said, 'Look Vic, no messing, how much do you want for Collymore?'

"'Two million pounds.'

"'OK. We've got a deal.'

"Jobson agreed and then said that Stan was returning from holiday the next day with his girlfriend. He told us that Stan didn't have an agent at that time, but there was one trying to get hold of him,

Ambrose Mendy, a boxing promoter, because he knew a deal was imminent. So me and Alan stayed the night in London and next day set off for Croydon because we knew that's where his girlfriend lived."

In the days before sat nav and mobile phones, it was a real chase against time with Clark and Hill on a glorified motorised treasure hunt with only limited clues in south London. In the end, they discovered first prize at a neat little semi in the capital's borough. "We offered him terms in the front room and Stan was glad to sign. We sorted it out there and then."

Ominously, controversy blighted Collymore's initial days at Forest and he did not appear in Forest's opening games. Rumours abounded that his jaw had been broken in a night club fracas in Southend on the eve of the first match of the season, away to Southend. He was then unavailable for selection due to 'illness'. The nickname Stan Collywobbles swiftly followed. It was an inauspicious start which hardly augured for cult status being bestowed any time soon. With Keane departed and Nigel Clough gone in similar circumstances to Liverpool, Clark's attempts to restore Forest to the Premiership were beginning to resemble *Dad's Army* on manoeuvres in Walmington-on-Sea.

It was not until 26 September that the real Stan Collymore stepped forward. Edwards remembers it well. "It was a Sunday game against Bolton Wanderers at Burnden Park, a televised match. I was sitting in the press box next to John Lawson [formerly a Forest correspondent for the *Post* and later Clough confidant during his time as joint owner of a local news agency]. It was a bit of a nothing game and John turned around to me and said: 'Not being funny, but why have they bought this lad? What does he do because I haven't seen anything yet.'

"A few seconds later, Stan picks up the ball halfway in the Bolton half with his back to goal. He's got two men up his arse. He spins them both, sprints off to goal, drops a shoulder and within eight strides, he's pinged one into the top corner.

"'Ah, that's probably what he does then, is it?!' John said."

Forest lost 4-3, their third successive defeat and their fourth in their first eight matches. Good times were just around the corner, though. "We played up at Sunderland in November and Stan took a throw-in from Des Lyttle, who must have been just outside his own penalty area on the touchline," Edwards purrs at the memory. "Stan turned one man, then another and opened up and burst past about three defenders then hit it from 30 yards, again into the top corner. Even the north east press corps stood up as one to applaud it.

"We just sat there and said sheepishly: 'Hey, don't worry. He does that every week.' But it was true! That season, you could become blasé about him. Ask any Forest fan from that era and they'll tell you the same story. He was the most exciting centre-forward I'd ever seen in my life and I'm sure he was the most exciting one any Forest fan had seen."

BUT, OF COURSE, WITH Stan Collymore there was baggage. Always baggage. Enough excess to keep Ryanair and Easyjet in clover for several months. Baggage that even Spanish luggage handlers on a three-day work-to-rule week being paid quadruple time for placing the right bag on the wrong carousel and totally wrong aeroplane wouldn't touch with their momma's paella. It was that heavy and potentially combustible.

His refusal to move into the Nottingham area from his Cannock home caused some resentment. Dressing rooms are simply microcosms of the world and general offices wherein petty jealousy and resentment lurk. Collymore's penchant for travelling only to away games on the team coach and being driven back with a mate to Birmingham or a London night spot, only fuelled the flames of disaffection that here was someone afforded special privileges.

What some players failed to comprehend was that it was not because Collymore believed himself to be above others or aloof. He was perceived as being good for the team and results by Clark and his captain Stuart Pearce. Collymore's arrogance as such was not born of his own ego, simply that he was a loner unable to control his own emotions and impulses, often oblivious to their consequences. That he was frequently the epicentre of several seismic tremors left him as bemused by the ensuing furore as he was impervious to it. None of which excuses or can vindicate the instigator.

"I can tell you a story that sums up Stan," offers Clark. "I used to be quite sensible and not treat players like little kids, but at the end of each month, I would have a drawer full of envelopes for Stan. They were unpaid fines that I was going to give him, but Liam O'Kane [first team coach] would always say: 'Don't do it. Let the lads sort it out. He'll win us games.' And, of course, he did.

"Either Pearce or Colin Cooper would always stick up for him. They reported back to me about Stan, but they just said: 'Let him get on with it. Don't rock the boat,' because while he was doing his stuff, nobody wanted to upset Stan. He was the exception to the rule every time."

His propensity for deceit was as astounding as his goalscoring exploits. Listening to Forest staff, it seems that Collymore had more grandmothers than Wayne Rooney on a long weekend in Amsterdam. "He told us once that he couldn't make training because his grandma had died," Alan Hill recalls. "So the club sent a sympathy card and some flowers to his mum, who promptly rang up and told us that his grandma had been dead for three years! It was usually on a Monday morning. There was a bad accident on the A38 and he couldn't get in. We checked up and there had been none. Then there was a night in Norway on a pre-season trip. We'd organised a night out at the races, those pony and trap style races that are popular in Scandinavia and on the continent. We waited on the team coach but there was no Stan. Liam [O'Kane] went to his room and came back a few moments later.

"'Says he's not coming.'

"'Why's that then?'

"'It's cruelty to animals.'

"So we went without him, although typically it turned out he'd been pulling a woman at some nightclub the night before and invited her back to his hotel room. It was endless really. Frank had all those envelopes with fines, but while Stan was doing it on the pitch, we just left him to it.

"A prime example was a game away to West Bromwich Albion in that promotion season. It was a Sunday match and we stayed away overnight and Frank, myself and Liam went for an Italian meal in the hotel. We knew Stan had popped out, visiting friends in the West Midlands and all that, but by ten o'clock he hadn't returned. So we set up a vigil and as it happened, Stan came back at half past six Sunday morning. The three of us had a meeting and we decided that we should leave him out of the side, but Liam was adamant. He was convinced he would do well and score a hat-trick, bearing in mind it was a lunchtime kick-off. So we played him on my hunch.

"He didn't manage a hat-trick, but Stan scored two, one a gem when he beat about four of their defenders and put it away. We won

2-0. For me, he was the best centre-forward in Europe in his time with Forest. His vision and touch was just something else for his physique."

Collymore's predatory prowess was also pretty impressive, especially as his stock in trade rarely included the simple or routine finish that is the trademark of the game's truly prolific goalscorers. Jimmy Greaves, Denis Law and Alan Shearer were all capable of the spectacular, Law in particular, but that tended to be the exception to the rule of an instinct that saw them drift into the right area at precisely the right time.

With Collymore, his technique allowed for diversity; his 'right area', the vulnerable zones for opponents, ranged from anything between the six-yard box and his own penalty area. The angles from which he scored were as acute and obscure as his inner psyche.

Such was his dramatic impact on Clark's promotion chasing side that his *pièce de résistance* perhaps cannot be defined during the 1993/94 reclamation of the Premiership status Forest had been deprived of the previous season. But two goals at London Road as that restoration was confirmed on 30 April will always be recalled by those that were there. Despite injury and suspensions, Collymore scored 24 goals that season, a country mile ahead of Colin Cooper and Scot Gemmill, who managed nine each. Maybe the divide between the First Division and the Premiership was not the gulf bordering on a chasm that financial expediency and the greed of the Premiership hierarchy has created today. Even so, Collymore's exploits in the top strata were worthy of attention. He eclipsed his previous season's First Division tally of 19 goals, by scoring 22 in 1994/95.

WITH FAME, THOUGH, came the lure of fortune. And the inevitable Collymore brainstormer. The deterioration of goodwill and bonhomie within the dressing room was gradual, but irreversible. His reputation on the field inflated in tandem with his antics off it. The steady rise appeared to match the favours and benefits he was receiving from an indulgent management, only too aware of Collymore's ability to influence a game as the club steered an unerring course to a top three finish.

It was to be the season that Jack Walker's millions finally would pay dividends as Blackburn Rovers snatched the Premiership title from Manchester United and reversed the positions of the previous season. Forest could not replicate the virtually unrepeatable feat of Brian Clough's 1977 side, winning promotion from the Second Division and then claiming the championship title (strange how the modern game has inflated wages yet devalued titles that are alien in old currency).

Yet their effort in claiming third position stands the test of time given subsequent history. Collymore, allied with the fleet-footed Dutchman Bryan Roy, punctured defences at ease and left the likes of Liverpool and Leeds United, then a powerful force in English football before their chairman Peter Ridsdale started feeding goldfish and his and David O'Leary's egos. *Quelle dommage* as the French might say.

But as the Forest juggernaut thundered irrepressibly along, to the delight of their supporters, one trucker's mood was about to turn dark. Around 12 January 1995 in fact.

Speculation abounded that Collymore was the chosen transfer target of Manchester United manager Alex Ferguson (pre-knighthood days). Canny Alex was happy to discuss such matters with the media (pre-accusations of flagrant nepotism with allegedly less than virtuous agent son). Even *Fantasy Football League*, the programme that so ridiculed Collymore's team-mate Jason Lee, relayed a sketch whereby Ferguson phoned Frank Clark only to discover the Forest manager was suffering from the flu and unable to take a call about his centre-forward's availability and impending transfer to Old Trafford.

The *Evening Post* ran a back page story on that Thursday, a gut feeling from within the industry, that Collymore was the man to whom Ferguson would turn to galvanise not only their Premiership season, which was foundering on the twin Ewood Park SAS strike force of Sutton and Shearer, but also the long-term future of the famous club.

As the *Post* hit the streets, around 11am in the days before new, more enlightened ownership decreed that it would be published in the enemy territory of Derby, the rest of the country was aware that Andy Cole, the Hyson Green Boys' Club lad, was the main man for Fergie. As it happened, his £7 million move from Newcastle United (Keith Gillespie as a £1 million makeweight), managed by Kevin Keegan, heralded an irreversible shift in fortunes for both clubs. For Collymore, the signals were fearfully similar.

It hadn't helped that both Cole and Collymore belonged to a football agency which was the domain of Paul Stretford, a man damaged in many eyes by involvement in the Wayne Rooney transfer saga, but a significant power broker in the increasingly influential and odious world of agents at the time. Did Collymore the client feel betrayed by his Mr ten per cent? Had he been, in the vernacular, shafted? He might have thought with some justification: 'Why should Cole, a graceless specimen both on and off the pitch, be chosen above the multi-talented and sublimely gifted me?'

It is pure guesswork to surmise that financial gain was involved in Cole's transfer. Perhaps it was just good judgement on the part of Ferguson. But it's a salient point to raise. They call it sliding doors or the more appropriate 'what if' syndrome.

Was the phone call ever made to Clark? Answer: yes. Did Fergie want Collymore? Without doubt. Could the greatest manager of the modern era have turned Collymore's career around? The jury is out on that one, but one thing is for certain, he would have made a better fist of it than the Spice Boys of Anfield and the insipid Roy Evans.

MEANWHILE BACK AT the City Ground, the meltdown had already begun.

Ian Edwards observed Collymore's eventual isolation, a self-imposed exile, that would lead to Merseyside and a British record transfer fee of £8.5 million. "He gave a press conference in the Jubilee Club, talking to all the national newspapers, about how he was misunderstood, how his colleagues didn't appreciate him." The following day, the *Evening Post*, then a respected broadsheet of some repute, featured the story, highlighting Collymore's gripes in bullet points and detailing his reasons for bemoaning his lot. It was the end of Edwards' mutual trust with the player that had enjoyed such a happy beginning.

"He seemed to think that I had singled him out, but in fact it was nothing that had not appeared in the national newspapers the day before. I tried to reason with him and took in a load of cuttings that were in praise of him, but he was having none of it."

Happily the pair are now on speaking terms, but for Collymore his absurd outburst ended an already fragile relationship with colleagues. Stuart Pearce, the Forest captain, led by example. Whenever Stan scored a goal, and in that Premiership season it wasn't long before one came along, he often dashed off to the byline or visiting Forest fans ploughing a lonesome trail. Spurning traditional routines, nobody bothered to follow him to join the celebrations. Why should they? After all, they didn't pass to him, didn't understand him. In short, his team-mates were not worthy of his magisterial presence in the same shirt. At least that's the way Collymore's churlishly petulant and public rant had come across.

An exasperated Clark watched on, delighted with his team's progress, but dismayed by the damage that Collymore was inflicting on himself and on the dressing room. "He had been quoted as saying that some of the players were not good enough to be playing with him," Clark recalls. "Not surprisingly they ignored him when he scored a goal. I remember we played Sheffield Wednesday [at Hillsborough on 1 April 1995] and put in the best performance I think I've ever seen from a team I have managed. Collymore and Bryan Roy scored two apiece, but they seldom talked to each other and Lars Bohinen couldn't stand either of them. It was a difficult enough dressing room, but that day everything just clicked and we won 7-1. I told them afterwards: 'Look, you might not like each other and not talk to one another, but this is the sort of thing you are capable of on your day.'"

It was Forest's fifth consecutive win and part of a 13-game unbeaten sequence until the end of the season that lifted them to third place, enough to ensure a berth in the Champions League these days.

"Stan always gave the impression of being aloof," says Clark wearing his hat now as vice chairman of the League Managers' Association. "But there was a lot of shyness involved. I knew that. He'd had a difficult upbringing in Cannock. He was neither white nor black with a white mother and a black father and he'd come with a wild reputation having been kicked out of several clubs including Wolverhampton Wanderers.

"He didn't have any real discipline from his father [who left his mother and allegedly beat her up according to Collymore's memoirs] and I think it's difficult for lads with that sort of background to come into a game which is male dominated and requires a different sort of discipline. Des Walker had the same sort of problems at Tottenham Hotspur; there was no authoritarian figure in their lives and I sometimes wonder whether or not football doesn't make enough allowances for these sort of youngsters. Football is a results industry and perhaps it loses more talented players because it makes judgements rather than try to understand. Without a male father figure at home, it can be very, very difficult."

Clark reflects with a fondness derived from the success Collymore's extraordinary skills bestowed upon Forest at the time. Ian Edwards is equally lavish and balanced in his praise. "Generally speaking a manager's ego knows no bounds and you only have to look at those who lined up to try and tame Stan after Forest. But Liverpool didn't pay a British record fee for him just to curb his ways. Everyone who followed, from John Gregory to Martin O'Neill, saw the ability in him. Obviously he had issues, but his talent, on a good day, far outweighed those.

When he went to Liverpool, apart from the goals he scored, how many did he make for Robbie Fowler in that first season? Could Alan Shearer, England's best centre-forward at the time, drag the ball left and right and cross it the way Stan did with either foot? And yet the story goes that Jamie Redknapp eventually apologised to his Liverpool team-mates because it was he who persuaded Stan to sign at Anfield. He caused that much trouble. But then going there with Fowler and McManaman running the show, you could see that Stan wouldn't be able to fit in as one of the boys.

"People say he was a wasted talent like Gazza [Paul Gascoigne]. But I disagree," argues Edwards. "It was worse than that. At least Gazza won England caps, an FA Cup medal and spent some time in Italy at his peak. Stan did nothing like it and won nothing. He won't want anyone's sympathy, that's for sure. But I would defend him against those who say he believed his own hype. In my opinion he wasn't conceited. He knew he was good, but he wasn't really into all that hype stuff.

"I think he was clearly a tormented soul. When he left, I was ghosting a Stuart Pearce captain's column for the *Post*. I'd been on at him for ages to do one on Stan and it was only the week after he left the club for Liverpool that Pearcey accepted. He told me then that Stan Collymore had more ability in the top half of his little finger than he had in his own body, holding the digit up before me. But he won't win more than the two England caps he'd gained with Forest because of the way he is." [In fact Collymore won a third, playing for Aston Villa, against mighty Moldova in 1998.]

IT WAS AT Villa Park where the darkness descended over Collymore, fittingly so given the darkness that descended from a bottle over Villa manager John Gregory's barnet on a regular basis. Gregory dismissed his 'depression' that required frequent trips to the Priory Clinic as remedy. "I'd be depressed on £30,000 a week," countered Gregory sarcastically, and in fairness, the old barrow/ butcher boy had a point.

Stan's life descended into further farce; he was accused of slapping around one of England coach Sven-Göran Eriksson's later lays (hard to put a name to the face, there were so many) and became embroiled in the inanities of reality television before admitting to an activity that required participants to observe people having sex in public toilets.

In autumn 2006 he attended a football forum as a panellist in a local Nottingham night spot, tickets being sold at £19 a head. "I didn't pay that much to see him play. And he was good then," rebuffed a fan who preferred anonymity in his absence from the event.

IF HISTORY JUDGES Collymore less than kindly, at least he has a champion of his Forest heyday in the manager who in effect transformed his career. A fan with an analytical eye that can penetrate the thickest of skins nevertheless.

"Maybe I should have been harsher on him, I don't know. But I can honestly say he was the most naturally talented player I have ever worked with," Frank Clark insists unambiguously. "There was a game in particular at West Brom when we were under the cosh and he picked up the ball in his own half from a throw-in and ran the whole length of the pitch. Nobody touched him or the ball until their goalkeeper picked the ball out of the net. He must have beaten six or seven players on the way [this was the famous game before which Collymore had been out in the early hours of the morning beforehand].

"Then near the end of the season, we played away at Derby County in midweek, both of us going for promotion. I played Stan on his own up front as I always did then with five in midfield, Bohinen, Scot Gemmill, [Steve] Stoney, Ian Woan and Dave Phillips sitting in the middle.

"Stan was never one for hassling defenders and we accepted that. I told him to let them drift wide and go into a channel. But somehow he must have realised the significance of the occasion, Derby, promotion at stake, in the thick of the action, the whole lot. We were 2-0 up, but not comfortable and suddenly for half an hour, he was doing doggies across the width of the Baseball Ground pitch. From one side to the other, chasing defenders in possession like a madman. I knew then that he COULD do it if he wanted. But he had to want it."

In 77 games, Collymore had scored 49 goals. He'd cost £2.5 million, but Forest were about to turn that into a £6 million profit.

"There was nobody at the City Ground who could get them out of the seats like Stan. It was only too late that we reacted to try and get him to stay. He'd been getting ripped off in commercial deals and by this time Stretford [his agent] was ahead of the game in getting Stan a move. It was our first year in the Premiership and we'd qualified for the UEFA Cup," remembers Clark. "Stan was entitled to a new contract, but he'd already had his head turned by the England set-up and the Liverpool lads and nights out in London. I told him that we would match anything another club offered and that I was planning to build the side around him and that Pearcey wanted him to stay and was happy to play that way if he would stay at the City Ground. I told him that he wouldn't get the same treatment he'd received at the City Ground at Anfield. It was a different world up there. But the lad was set on the move.

"You look at the Drogbas of this world and I'd put Stan up there with him on a physical level and far better technically. He didn't need any backlift, some of his shots were just explosive. And he was a superb athlete, he had everything. But, of course, Drogba, Henry, the foreign players, have all introduced a new regime. They look after themselves.

"Yes, Stan had psychological problems, there is no doubt about that. He was a bright boy, above average intelligence, but when Terry Venables called him up for the England squad, he just didn't know what to make of him. I suppose now, he can say he's a wealthy lad and he scored some wonderful goals and gave the fans some wonderful memories, all of which is true. But it's romantic rubbish if a professional footballer with his talent has not got a cupboard full of medals and caps. You have to blow it and underachieve to finish up like that.

"I'm sure Stan would disagree. And that's a shame. But what I would say, from my personal point of view, is that, for all his aggravation, he was worth it."

And how.

Jason Lee

1994-1997: 49 games, 15 goals

IT WAS A MOMENT of insanity that Jason Lee was contemplating. Some might have called it madness; an apposite description given the nature of the beast inside the Nottingham Forest dressing room.

There was a distinct swagger to Lee's gait as he entered the City Ground car park, as if Real Madrid had lost one their galacticos to Forest in a price-bidding war with Inter Milan. In fact, he had just arrived from the land of whelks and jellied eels stalls that represent a fair portion of Southend United's claim to fame. Alighting from his convertible Wrangler Jeep, the £200,000 acquisition was immersed in masses of dreadlock hair running wild up top, while a pair of stone-washed, torn and tatty jeans suggested he had not stopped off at a Savile Row tailor on the journey from Essex. Meanwhile, in the hallowed sanctum of the Forest first team dressing room, a portable sound centre, 'ghettoblaster' in the slang of the day, was pounding out a tune familiar to the inmates.

Suggs, known to his parents as Graham McPherson, was leading the singing on another Madness number. The favoured theme music of Stuart Pearce held sway, unchallenged, as was the norm for both the wishes and tenacious tackling of the inspirational captain.

Barely had the strolling Lee located his kit peg when he calmly walked over to the music machine and ejected the Madness tape, replacing it with something more akin to his roots and his 22 years of age; a brave, some might say foolhardy, act.

Given its potential for conflict at the outset, it was the start of a remarkably good-natured friendship between the England full-back and the fledgling centre-forward, whose career has accumulated football clubs in the manner of 1970s and '80s goalkeeping legend John Burridge.

"I saw the BMWs in the car park and knew that there were some top class players at the club and that Pearcey was a Forest legend," says Lee. "He was still playing for England and was an icon with the fans, but I was a young lad trying to prove myself and I always thought you have to earn respect, not just expect it because you are older and have won this and done that."

Lee's philosophy is well said. Despite enduring a torrid, torturous exposure by television that ridiculed his talent and, worse, tried to taint his professional reputation, Lee retained a dignified yet determined silence that seems beyond the capacity of not only his peers but even those in high office who were educated to know better.

He could never claim, nor would he, to be an outstanding Forest player, but his contribution was commendable, his loyalty and effort unquestioned. For that, and for his perseverance during those deeply troubled times, Forest fans took him to their hearts. Trying to make good for his family, friends and his employers, railing against unfair criticism and struggling occasionally with overwhelming odds and a loss of confidence; who, without the benefit of silver spoon birthright or regal privilege, could not identify with that?

His, indeed, is the cult of the common man.

LEE, BOUGHT BY FRANK CLARK as temporary cover for the injured Stan Collymore, discovered the daunting nature of that mission had been compounded when he became the brunt of a cruelly relentless, but nevertheless originally mildly amusing to the neutral, one-line gag perpetrated by David Baddiel and Frank Skinner on their *Fantasy Football League* television show.

The Premiership was still in its formative years then, its packaging and marketing concept yet to be formulated, its riches yet to grow beyond even its own comprehension, let alone that of the man on the terraces (yes, terraces still).

If Lee's sudden elevation was his big break, his misfortune was to be the victim of the celebrity cult whose self-serving and rampant ego was already manifesting itself in television's mindlessly drivelling backwaters. Baddiel and Skinner, talented showmen and 'a couple of bright lads with a university education' as Frank Clark, the Forest manager then, described them, readily exploited the growing stature of footballers through a broadcasting media with which they were in tune and already established and comfortable. It was a dubious pursuit of hirsute avant garde that the comic duo seized upon, Lee's dreadlocks harnessed on top of his head in a bun-style that was reminiscent, at least in the *Fantasy Football* scheme of things, to a pineapple.

Suddenly schoolkids around the country were singing:

> He's got a pineapple on his head
> He's got a pineapple on his head

They were to be followed by grown men, at every ground that Forest visited, chortling the same words over, and over, and over again.

At a stroke, the spoof sketch made Lee probably the most instantly recognisable footballer in the country. Plying his trade on the top rung of the domestic game, he had become one of the Premiership's leading media stars, albeit not in a fashion of his choosing. What should have been a one-off lampoon actually became a long-running gag, with footage of Lee spurning a sitter scarcely enhancing his credibility as a predator among the Premiership ranks. Even Clark was cast as Mr Potato Head in the recurring sketches.

As in the case of *The Mousetrap*, the audience was familiar with the venue, saw all the gags and red herrings coming long before even the cast and knew without a shadow of a doubt that the butler did it, yet was strangely drawn back to witness events unfold.

Spoof soon turned to ridicule. Unfortunately for Lee, while his Forest form dipped and his chances were being spurned in musical montages thanks to the new innovation of cameras being at every top flight football match, the essentially tacky environment of *Fantasy Football* and its presentation turned his regular unsolicited turn into something akin to a repeat series of *On the Buses* with Blakey, the butt of what passed for a joke in that comedic farce from the 1970s.

Bumping into the pair in a dark alley to reciprocate the humour, or at least put his side of the story, crossed Lee's mind more than once as the show's popularity grew in tandem with the striker's dreadlocks. "They asked me quite a few times to go on the show, but I refused," he says. "I thought the best way to answer any critics was to keep silent and keep playing, trying to improve and get my place back in the first team. That's all I'd known all my life, it was the only way I could handle things. What other option did I have? I didn't see that I had any other choice. I'd been given a great chance at Forest by Frank Clark and I didn't want to throw my career away just because somebody wanted to have a laugh at my expense. I'd learnt from my early days in the game that there is always someone who wants to knock you down, have a go at you. If you don't learn to deal with that very quickly, you might as well get out of the game because you won't survive."

Survival is a familiar concept to Lee. He was hewn from a tough Forest Gate childhood in the heart of London's East End and despite an apprenticeship with Charlton Athletic, his path has not been one strewn with cushy numbers or glowing acclaim.

It was during that same season of 1994, when Lee joined Forest, that some lunatic fringe in the local city council decided to cover the Market Square in sand for a fun-laden few weeks that would be branded Nottingham-on-Sea. The Kiss-Me-Quick hats were shipped in from Skegness, but at least some expense was spared – the nodding donkeys obviously already resided in the Council House. (Over a decade later the same strain of lunatics redesigned the Market Square, known for years as Slab Square because of its very slabby appearance, by digging up the entire environs at a cost of millions of pounds of taxpayers' money with a view to transforming Nottingham's pivotal focus. And what style did the innovative new vista that emerged take? Er, slabs. Very expensive ones. How brilliant is that?)

Lee found the relocation from Southend-on-Sea to Nottingham-sur-Mer less than intimidating, as his dramatic entrance to the City Ground training regime confirmed. "It was just such a fantastic opportunity. I remember when Steve Thompson took me to Lincoln City [in 1991] and I was playing in a pre-season friendly against them at Sincil Bank. I couldn't believe that Forest had brought over 4,000 fans to see them that night, and this was in the last years of the Clough era. I thought then that this was a big club and if ever I wanted to improve and move on in football, this was the sort of club I needed to be playing for. So you can imagine when they asked me, I didn't even hesitate. I knew I was coming as a replacement for Stan [Collymore] because he'd been injured, although me and Stan never crossed at Southend.

"Barry Fry, who signed me at Southend, knew his stuff and the players from the lower leagues, so it was a great education for me playing around 100 games or so at Roots Hall. Forest were trying to bounce back into the Premiership at the first attempt and were having a bit of a wobble about March time with Stan out when I came."

Lee would be part of the successful squad that eventually claimed second place and promotion behind Crystal Palace, a 3-2 win at relegated Peterborough confirming their ascension. Collymore scored a couple and Pearce the other, the catalyst for unbridled celebration at the London Road ground swelled by a huge Forest following.

Danny Kirkman was one of hundreds who felt compelled to join in the fun – until, that is, he was flattened by one of the hordes of red shirts that invaded the pitch after the final whistle. As one of many Forest followers weaned on hard times in the early 1970s but nurtured by the dramatic impact of the Clough/Taylor years, fans who still melt into dewy-eyed romantics when reminiscing about triumphs in Manchester, Munich and Madrid, even though the clarity of latter events on many of those long journeys and nights become ever more shrouded in a fog – or more appropriately flagons – of strong Bavarian lager or chilled San Miguel, Kirkman had taken to the turf in wild celebration of a return to the big time.

Despite that barge to the floor, Kirkman cherishes the moment promotion was regained at London Road among his most precious Forest memories. In keeping with his like-minded friends on the terraces, he also recognises Lee's contribution. "Jason was never the greatest player, we all knew that," he says. "But there was something about him that the fans really liked. Call it a never-say-die attitude or a willingness to shed blood if necessary. They appreciated what he was trying to do and that was before the *Fantasy Football* thing. After that, they were even more behind him. Not many players got a bigger hand or cheer when they came off the bench or were substituted. The crowd warmed to him and I think he really appreciated that himself."

Lee admits now that the feeling was reciprocated. Certainly a crucial goal at The Valley endeared him to supporters turning twitchy after a four game sequence that included two edgy draws and a defeat at Portsmouth during the promotion run-in with Millwall and Leicester hot on Forest's heels. Lee's second goal for the club, the only one of the game to defeat Charlton in early April, allayed fears of an unrelenting stutter, steadied a few nerves and kept the automatic promotion push, avoiding the dreaded play-offs, on course.

STAN COLLYMORE WAS simply irresistible during the 1993/94 promotion finale, as indeed he was throughout the following season in the top flight. "We played a funny sort of system but it worked," remembers Lee. "Frank relied on just one man up front, a strong powerful figure and the way Stan was playing, it had to be him. I remember then that next season my appearances were restricted, but by then I had gained a bit of a reputation as a supersub, coming on and either scoring or assisting with a crucial goal here and there. It was a great season for Forest and a brilliant one for me."

Forest finished third in their first season back in the top flight with Lee making just five starts as Collymore, partnered up front by Dutchman Bryan Roy, a summer signing from Foggia, totalled 40 goals between them.

Even though Collymore departed to Liverpool for a club record £8.5 million at the end of the season, the smart money was on new signings Kevin Campbell, from Arsenal, or Concordesque-conked Andrea Silenzi, from Torino, leading the line alongside Roy and Lee's chances appeared to diminish even further. Robert Rosario, another big target man bought by Clark from Norwich City just before Lee, had toiled in vain to make an impact and was also surplus to requirements at the City Ground, so it was clear that Lee must either cut it with his more illustrious colleagues – or cut out.

"They were interesting times because, although Forest did not have the wealth or pulling power of Arsenal or Manchester United, they were determined to put themselves on the map. Lars Bohinen had been quality in midfield and with Bryan Roy still at the club, nobody seemed to think that I would get so much as a look-in. I think I surprised quite a few people though [he started 27 matches and was substitute in 13 in 1995/96 as Forest won every game in which he scored]. I had walked into the club not worrying about reputations and I knew I had to work my socks off to get into the team and then stay there. The incentives were all there for me. I was still the lad who came from the rough end of the East End and now was in the English Premiership at grounds I'd never dreamt about playing at. Every week was another adventure for me and I didn't want it to stop."

An uplifting UEFA Cup run that accounted for Malmo, Auxerre and Olympique Lyonnais, compounded that sense of adventure and a dream-like journey into the unknown for Lee. This was Forest's first flirtation with the European circuit since the infamous semi-final defeat by Anderlecht in 1984 when Spanish referee Guruceta Muro, bribed by Constant Vanden Stock, the Belgian club's president, helped Anderlecht retrieve, then overturn a 2-0 first leg deficit. Forest had, legitimately, qualified twice by winning the League Cup in 1989 and 1990, but it was not until 1990 that the five-year ban imposed on English clubs following the barbaric behaviour of Liverpool fans at Heysel Stadium in May 1985 was lifted.

Clark's Forest made an impressive re-entry onto the European stage and, with other teams faltering, they were the last English representatives in Europe and the only ones to extend their participation until after Christmas, where, in the quarter-finals, they were drawn against the formidable Germans Bayern Munich.

"It was an amazing experience, just to be on the same pitch as Bayern and their superstars at the Olympic Stadium in Munich, it really was," says Lee. Having beaten Malmo in the first round, there was a sense of kismet about the competition this time as Clark trooped his players back to the scene of Forest's greatest triumph, their first European Cup final success over the defensively obsessed Swedes and what was to be the current manager's last game in a Garibaldi red shirt. Initially, the omens seemed to be in Forest's favour in Bavaria once more with another night of celebrations on the continent on the cards.

Mehmet Scholl and Jürgen Klinsmann scored for Bayern, but it was Steve Chettle's effort, a precious away goal in Germany, that seemed to augur well for the second leg.

On 19 March, four days after the Ides that Caesar so casually failed to beware, Forest were not so much stabbed in the back as the victims of a full frontal assault, led by the irresistible Klinsmann, recapturing the sort of form that had bestowed upon him the Player of the Year award the previous season, voted by the football writers, following his exploits in north London with Tottenham Hotspur. Klinsmann claimed two, and Jean-Pierre Papin, Thomas Strunz and Christian Ziege one each as Bayern cantered to a 5-1 win (Steve Stone for Forest) and a commanding 7-2 aggregate win.

Lee and Forest need not have been too downhearted. Bayern removed Barcelona in the semi-finals and thrashed Bordeaux 5-1 in a two-legged final to become only the fourth side to have secured all three European trophies.

THAT SEASON LEE scored eight Premiership goals, the same as Roy and five more than Campbell. Nevertheless, his distinctive hairstyle and occasional lapses in front of goal had been magnified into parody by Baddiel and Skinner, even though Forest finished a worthy ninth in the table. "They used to ridicule all sorts of people. I know they used to have a go at Andy Cole, but the haircut thing didn't make me into a bad player. Indifferent form would do that and I didn't think I was doing that bad. That's when I think the Forest fans took to me. They knew I hadn't cost a fortune and that I was not a big time Charlie, but I was trying to do my level best.

"To their surprise I'd managed to keep some of the bigger names out of the side. Even so, one of the worst things was that I felt it was embarrassing for Frank Clark. He'd bought me from Southend and put me in the team, giving me that opportunity. I wasn't playing badly, but now we were getting a lot of publicity for all the wrong reasons. And yet Frank always stuck by me, he never lost faith in me. There were other factors at the time as well. I wasn't married, but was going out with the girl who would be my wife and all my other family were incensed with what was happening on that show. I didn't want them fighting my battles, but they felt for me and I knew I would come through it.

"It was a privilege to play pro football, especially at somewhere like Forest, and I was always grateful for whatever talent I'd been given to enable me to do that. I was determined that the show and how I was portrayed would not get the better of me. Why should it? Some people suggested that I change my hairstyle, but even if I wanted to, and I probably did by then to be honest, I couldn't. It would have seemed like I was giving in to the two of them and the pressure, which I certainly was not. I wanted to stick two fingers up to them by keeping it."

Even if there was a glimmer of light at the end of the players' tunnel for Lee, and there was a saccharine-laden act of revenge that would be served less than tepid about to come his way, the centre-forward could not have foreseen that the good times, all be them admittedly brief, were about to come to an end for Clark and Forest. Wales forward Dean Saunders and Nicola Jerkan, the Croatian defender, joined the club in what seemed a positive attempt to restore European football to the City Ground during the summer respite. Set against that optimism, internal politics, always on the agenda at Forest, was ripping the club apart and sending it ultimately on a path of self destruction from which it has never recovered.

With the carrot of a £15,000 bonus dangled before the 207 committee members whose share was a nominal £1, greed and the green-eyed monster of envy emerged from its corner where it had lurked for many years. Eventually the club sold its soul to a bunch of soulless asset strippers without the slightest concern or interest in its welfare or affairs. In pursuing that course, casualties came and went, Clark being one as chairman Fred Reacher and the board stalled on vital player investment as the vultures hovered over the City Ground inspecting debit and credit accounts and the minutiae that represents the number-crunching, paper-clip counting fraternity, but surgically removes the heart and soul of any organisation that previously has dared to encourage vitality and individual spirit.

It was prevarication on a scale only eclipsed by Nero and his fiddle. Perversely just as Rome burned to Nero's plucking, so the Forest fire was extinguished as Reacher and his boardroom chums waited impotently to be stuffed by the incoming consortium.

Clark was dismissed in December, much to his relief perhaps, as an indecisive board dithered on team funding and the side toiled at the foot of the Premiership. Manchester City beckoned for Clark and his assistant Alan Hill.

FOR LEE, THE immediate future held a delicious moment in store, one which only the intertwining fortunes of popular culture and football could possibly throw up. As Baddiel and Skinner had persisted somewhat ad nauseam with their ridicule of the Forest player and his manager, Lee had taken some comfort from the fact that Skinner was an avid West Bromwich Albion fan. "We always beat them, but they were struggling in Division One at the time, so I didn't get a chance for personal revenge. But then I found out that Baddiel was a bit of a Chelsea nut." With a timing that the *Riverdance* school of prancing would have applauded, Lee was named as a substitute for the league game at Stamford Bridge on 28 September 1996. It was a rare appearance in Lee's fleeting attendance record during his final season at Forest, but the records note that by then his dreadlocks had been shorn and his passion fruit style well and truly peeped.

"Everyone had been telling me to get rid of the hair, but one day my eldest Jasmin came home from school and I let her feel the dreadlocks. She'd only known me with that hair since she was three or four, so I wanted her to see it for one last time. I gave her a pair of scissors and let her cut the first few strands off."

Word that autumnal afternoon in the capital had spread that Baddiel was in the crowd; nothing unusual at Stamford Bridge where an Equity Card and all round Smart Alec badge have always been essential for entry into the enclosures that separate the luvvies from the hoi polloi and the Shed heads since Dickie Attenborough first took a stroll down the King's Road in the late 1940s.

In the days of chairman Ken Bates, Chelsea still harboured pretensions of winning the Premiership without relying on Russian oligarchs, but, with the Blues leading 1-0, Lee alighted from the bench and scored what was to be his first goal of the season and his last for Nottingham Forest to earn a 1-1 draw and damage the west London club's title aspiration. How good could that have been?

"My only thought was to run as fast as I could the length of the pitch to the Forest fans there. They knew how much it meant to me and I think they felt it too. To me it was always the only way you can answer back to people like that. They don't understand the game, they don't play it, all they seem to do is ridicule those of us who are part of it. It was a great feeling and I think I deserved that day. I reckon the Forest fans felt my joy that day." Enough said.

Only seeing the smirk disappearing off the face of Baddiel, sat among the Chelsea glitterati, could have added to the pleasure. Suffice it to say, the moment was not chosen by the comedians for another regular section of *Fantasy Football League*, Phoenix From The Flames, where great goals were re-enacted on bare, park pitches.

In the press box, local Nottingham journalists certainly empathised with the player who had diligently and unflinchingly talked to the press despite *Fantasy Football*, understanding, unlike so many of his peers before and after, that this was not a universal hate campaign or opinion.

The finale could not have been more fitting for Lee. He had loan spells with Charlton Athletic, his first club, and Grimsby Town during the latter stages of the season, but it was to Watford that he moved in the summer because Forest had tumbled out of the Premiership. Soon Dave Bassett and Pierre van Hooijdonk began a relationship that would ultimately end in the latter downing tools in Holland and being rewarded with a lucrative transfer, while the former was dismissed because of it. Margaret Thatcher and Tony Blair would be appalled at the undermining of their policies in seeing the worker not only prevailing in strike action against management, but then getting the manager sacked into the bargain for being accountable. Only in football.

"It wasn't the best of times for me," recalls Lee. "But I don't hold myself responsible for the relegation. I was being farmed out here and there which was fair enough and Stuart [Pearce] took over from Frank and tried to do things his way. For a while it worked, but I wasn't part of anybody's plans."

LEE'S CHOICE TO join Watford in the summer of 1997, becoming Graham Taylor's first signing as he moulded his second renaissance of the Hertfordshire club, was inspirational: Turnip Head of Stockholm 1992 meets Pineapple Head of Stapleford 1995. At least the pair could empathise about the intensity of media coverage. "It was a period of rehabilitation for me and Graham Taylor was brilliant for me," Lee says with conviction.

Sold for the same £200,000 that Forest paid Southend three years earlier, he later shifted to Chesterfield for £250,000. As his wife Ashling and young family became increasingly settled in Nottingham, his career path sailed much closer to home or arterial routes that would expedite his journey home after games or training. Lee's later sojourns would take him to Peterborough United, to be reunited with

Barry Fry, and Falkirk, where he was recommended by Brian Rice, himself something of a ginger-ninja City Ground enigma. There Lee met manager John Hughes, nicknamed Yogi, 'a half crazy character' north of the border, then ran into Steve Evans, another Caledonian with a reputation for being two sporrans short of a full kilt at Boston United in 2004. "It was an eventful time of my life, let's say. There was craziness all around at Boston. We had three former Premiership strikers in myself, Julian Joachim [Leicester City and Aston Villa] and Noel Whelan [Leeds United, Coventry City and Middlesbrough]. I'd thought I'd seen it all in the game, but Noel was a bit crazy and Julian wouldn't hardly say a word. Throw in Andy Kirk who was scoring goals for fun, the manager Steve Evans and then along came Gazza [Paul Gascoigne, the ex-alcoholic, wife-beating, former tear-stained England midfield star]."

By one of those recurring quirks of fate, Evans, whose programme notes, press conferences and general gibberish musings ironically enough would have fitted nicely in the context of *Fantasy Football League*, talked about persuading Stan Collymore out of retirement to play at York Street. The cocktail of Paul Gascoigne and Collymore in Boston adjacent to the Gliderdrome bingo club may have sent locals over the top. A mad scramble to hurl themselves off Boston Stump, the towering glory of England's largest parish church, St Botolph's, infamous as a suicidal maniac's last resort, may have ensued, with Gascoigne fractionally leading the race.

"Gazza just wasn't allowed to do what he thought he'd been brought in to do and that was coaching," Lee says. "I got the impression that he was not fit enough to play and my heart went out to him."

Lee does not patronise or judge, but he acknowledges that Gascoigne's talent, as well as that of Collymore, was largely wasted. "Not everyone is mentally equipped to cope with what life has to throw at them. In football, it's a relentless thing and I've played at clubs with some of the most supremely gifted players, Gazza and Stan being two of them, who just can't handle day-to-day life. It's not a case of whether you can trap a medicine ball or not, someone will have a go at you eventually. Someone will want to see you down. You have to be strong. There are always negative people or the just plain jealous waiting for you to fall.

"They will have a pop, but as I say you have to be mentally strong. I'm not one to play the racial card all the time. There is no point. This is a privileged profession we are in and it should be a great life, but sometimes it just isn't."

LEE TURNED 36 in May 2007. His physique is impeccable, as are his manners and courtesy, befitting a seasoned professional and family man. A virtual teetotaller, he doesn't preach to others, but his children, Jasmin, twins Blaise and Jerome and youngest Candice have benefited from some of his pearls of wisdom.

"My lads have seen the photos of me when I had the long hair and the dreadlocks and they have a laugh about it at school with their mates. They've seen some old video footage and they think it's hilarious. My only point to them is that the world does not owe you a living no matter how talented or special you might think you are. You have to work at it and then, work at it some more.

"I had temptations when I was growing up and could have fallen into the wrong sort of crowd. But you have to be prepared to cut yourself off from that if you want to succeed."

An itinerant traveller during his career, Lee is as much a part of the Nottingham landscape as the old Bell Inn in the Market Square; a tad jaded on the outside, perhaps, displaying a few signs of wear and tear, but sturdy enough of body and mind to entertain passing trade for a few more years yet. Remarkably perhaps, his new-found allegiance with Notts County has not diminished the affection in which he is held by Forest fans, many of whom still stop him in Clumber Street or Bridlesmith Gate and ask the eternal question: "What's the bloody matter at Forest then, Jason?" As if he might know.

At least he can hazard a guess.

"Our dressing room was not full of big time Charlies. We were mostly hungry for success and we wanted to win for one another as well as the fans. Some of us were brash, naïve and some were vastly experienced like Pearcey. But there was an excellent work ethic and I can only imagine that has been lost along the way." He stops short of mentioning the Van Hooijdonks or other potential bad apples that might have dropped into the barrel since his departure. Lee does not seek an antidote to the decline, however. Why should he when he has such a vivid, verdant past to recall?

"There I was as someone who had supported Arsenal as a kid and I was playing at these grounds and holding my own," he says of his Forest years. "They were great times, exhilarating, call them what you want, but the Baddiel–Skinner thing couldn't possibly taint them or take them away. If anything it made me more resilient."

If anything, it also made him more popular: the last true hero of the people in Forest's rich history. Jason Lee deserves that accolade as much as he deserved that goal at Chelsea.